SOVIET MILITARY OPERATIONAL ART

CASS SERIES ON SOVIET MILITARY THEORY AND PRACTICE

Series Editor – David M. Glantz
Ft. Leavenworth, Kansas

This series examines in detail the evolution of Soviet military science and the way the Soviets have translated theoretical concepts for the conduct of war into concrete military practice. Separate volumes focus on how the Soviets have applied and refined theory in combat and on how they have structured their forces to suit the requirement of changing times.

SOVIET MILITARY OPERATIONAL ART

IN PURSUIT OF DEEP BATTLE

Colonel David M. Glantz

Acting Director, Soviet Army Studies Office,
Combined Arms Center, Fort Leavenworth, Kansas

With a Foreword by
General Carl E. Vuono
Chief of Staff, United States Army

FRANK CASS

First published 1991 in Great Britain by
FRANK CASS AND COMPANY LIMITED
Gainsborough House, 11 Gainsborough Road,
London E11 1RS, England

and in the United States of America by
FRANK CASS
c/o International Specialized Book Services, Inc.
5602 N.E. Hassalo Street, Portland, Oregon 97213

The views expressed here are those of the author. They should not necessarily be
construed as those of the U.S. Department of Defense or the United States Army.

British Library Cataloguing in Publication Data

Glantz, David M.
    Soviet military operational art: in pursuit of deep
    battle. – (Soviet military theory and practice)
    1. Soviet Union. Military forces, 1917–1979
    I. Title   II. Series
    355'.00947

    ISBN 0-7146-3362-3 (cased)
    ISBN 0-7146-4077-8 (pbk)

Library of Congress Cataloging-in-Publication Data

Glantz, David M.
    Soviet military operational art : in pursuit of deep battle/
David M. Glantz.
        p.   cm. — (Soviet military theory and practice)
    Includes index.
    ISBN 0-7146-3362-3 (cased)
    ISBN 0-7146-4077-8 (pbk)

    1. Military art and science—Soviet Union—History—20th century.
I. Title.   II. Series: Glantz, David M. Soviet military theory and
practice.
U43.S65G57   1990
355'.00947—dc20   89-31675
                                                    CIP

Printed and bound in Great Britain by
BPCC Wheatons Ltd, Exeter

To Colonel John Stewart (Ret)
for his unwavering support in
most difficult circumstances

CONTENTS

TABLES

NOTES ON SOURCES
FOR FORCE STRUCTURE TABLES

TABLE NO.

6. *Direktivy komandovaniia frontov Krasnoi Armii 1917–1922 gg* [Directives of the Red Army's front commands 1917–1922] (Moskva: Voenizdat, 1978).

8. S. M. Kliatskin, *Na zashchite oktiabria* [In defense of October] (Moskva: "Nauka," 1965).

10. *Ordena lenina moskovskii voennyi okrug* [The Order of Lenin Moscow Military District] (Moskva: Voenizdat, 1971), hereafter cited as *Ordena lenina moskovskii*; N. F. Kuz'min, *Na strazhe mirnogo truda* (1921–1940gg) [On guard for peaceful work] (Moskva: Voenizdat, 1959); S. S. Lototsky, *The Soviet Army* (Moscow: Progress, 1971); S. Sokolov, *Sukhoputnye voiska* [Ground forces], *VIZh* No. 12 (Dec. 1967). Confirmed by "Organization of the Red Army" *G-2 Report* No. 7250 dated 25 March 1925 (Washington, D.C.: Military Intelligence Division, USA General Staff, 1925); *Dislocation of the Red Army and Personnel according to Military Districts* (Washington, D.C.: War Department, Office of the Chief of Staff, 1928).

11. *Ordena lenina moskovskii* ; Lototsky; *50 let vooruzhennykh sil SSSR* [50 years of the armed forces of the USSR] (Moskva: Voenizdat, 1968), hereafter cited as *50 let*, J. Erickson, *The Soviet High Command* (London: St Martins, 1962); "Organization of the Red Army" *G-2 Report*; *Dislocation of the Red Army.*

12. G. K. Zhukov, *Reminiscences and Reflections* Vol. 1 (Moscow: Progress, 1985); *50 let*; "Organization of the Red Army" *G-2 Report; Dislocation of the Red Army.*

22. *Istoriia Velikoi Otechestvennoi voiny Sovetskogo Soiuza 1941–1945 Tom pervyi* [History of the Great Patriotic War of the Soviet Union, Vol.1] (Moskva: Voenizdat, 1961), hereafter cited as *IVOVSS.*

23. *50 let*; P. Malevsky-Malevich, ed, *Russia U.S.S.R.* (New York: William Farquhar Payson, 1933); "Strength of Tactical Units" *G-2 Report* No. 7836 from M. A. Riga dated 23 Nov. 1931 (Washington, D. C.: War Department, Military Intelligence Division, 1931).

24. *Ordena lenina moskovskii*; *50 let*; Zhukov; "Strength of Tactical Units" *G-2 Report*; "Organization of the Russian Army" *G-2 Report* No. 2598 dated June 1936 (Washington, D.C.: War Department, Military Intelligence Division, USA General Staff, 1936).

25. Malevsky-Malevich; Zhukov; "Strength of Tactical Units" *G-2 Report.*

26. A. Ryzhakov,"K voprosy o stroitel'stve bronetankovykh voisk Krasnoi Armii v 30-e gody" [Concerning the formation of Red Army armored forces in the 1930s] *VIZh*, No. 8 (Aug. 1968); Erickson; *50 let*; *Intelligence Summary* (Washington DC.: War Department, Military Intelligence Division, 24 Dec. 1937); *"Organization and Strength of Motor-Mechanized Units" G-2 Report,* No. 19216 from M. A. Riga dated 20 Sept. 1938 (Washington, D.C.: War Department, Military Intelligence Division, 1938). This is representative of many similar reports documenting Soviet armored and mechanized developments.

27. I. I. Lisov, *Desantniki – vozduzhnye desanty* [Airlanding troops – airlandings] (Moskva: Voenizdat, 1968).

28. P. A. Kurochkin ed., *Obshchevoiskovaia armiia v nastuplenii* [The combined arms army in the offensive] (Moskva: Voenizdat, 1966); I. G. Pavlovsky, *Sukhoputnye voiska SSSR* [Ground forces of the USSR] (Moskva: Voenizdat, 1985).

29. *50 let*; *Ordena lenina moskovskii*; Pavlovsky; Kurochkin; A. I. Radzievsky, *Taktika v boevykh primerakh (diviziia)* [Tactics by combat example (division)] (Moskva: Voenizdat, 1976). "Distribution of Major Units of the Red Army" *G-2 Report* No. 9900 from M. A. Riga dated 12 Nov. 1937 (Washington, D.C.: War Department, Military Intelligence Division, 1937); "Distribution of Major Units

and Names of Commanders" *G-2 Report* No. 10261 from M. A. Riga dated 25 Nov. 1938 (Washington, D. C.: War Department, Military Intelligence Division, 1938); "Organization of Infantry Division" *G-2 Report* No. 281 from M. A. Helsinki dated 26 Feb. 1941 (Washington, D.C.: War Department, Military Intelligence Division, 1941).

30. "Kavaleriiskii korpus" [Cavalry corps], *SVE*; "Kavaleriiskaia diviziia "[Cavalry division], *SVE*; *50 let.*
31. Ryzhakov.; same U.S. intelligence reports as cited in Note 29.
32. Ryzhakov; see Note 29.
33. Ryzhakov.
34. *IVOVSS*; V. A. Anfilov, *Proval Blitzkrieg* [The failure of Blitzkrieg] (Moskva: Voenizdat, 1974); K. Kazakov, "Razvitie sovetskoi artillerii v gody Velikoi Otechestvennoi voiny" [The development of Soviet artillery in the years of the Great Patriotic War] *VIZh*, No. 11 (Nov. 1975).
35. Lisov.
36. Kurochkin; *IVOVSS*; Radzievsky, *Taktika*; K. Malanin, "Razvitie organizatsionnykh form Sukhoputnykh voisk v Velikoi Otechestvennoi voine" [The development of organizational forms of ground forces in the Great Patriotic War], *VIZh*, No. 8 (Aug. 1967); Anfilov; *Die Kriegswehrmacht der Union der Sozialistischen Sowjetrepubliken (UdSSR) Stand Dezember 1941* (The Army of the USSR, Dec. 1941) OKH GenStdh OQuIV-Abt Fremde Heere Ost II Nr. 4700/41geh' NAM T-78/550.
37. Kurochkin; Radzievsky, *Taktika*; Malanin.
38. O. A. Losik, "Stroitel'stvo i boevoe primenenie sovetskykh tankovykh voisk v gody velikoi otechestvennoi voiny" [The formation and combat use of Soviet tank forces in the years of the Great Patriotic War] (Moskva: Voenizdat, 1979); "Kriegsgliederungen der Sowjetunion" [Order of Battle of the Soviet Union] 1941–1942, OKH, FHO Reports variously dated NAM T-78/550.
39. "Kavaleriiskii korpus," *SVE*; Malanin; *50 let.*; *Die Kriegswehrmacht*; "Kriegsgliederungen der Sowjetunion" 1942.
40. Losik; A. I. Radzievsky, *Tankovyi udar* [Tank strike] (Moskva: Voenizdat, 1977).
41. Losik; Radzievsky, *Tankovyi udar*; I. M. Anan'ev, B. B. Bashchenko, N. T. Konashenko, "Tankovye armii" [Tank armies] *SVE*; I. M. Anan'ev, *Tankovye armii v nastuplenii* [Tank armies in the offensive] (Moskva: Voenizdat, 1988).
42. Losik; Radzievsky, *Tankovyi udar*.
55. Kurochkin; *50 let;* Radzievsky, *Taktika*.
56. Malanin; R. B. Rigg, *The Red Army Cavalry, Organization and Armament, World War II Summary*, Attaché report prepared for the US Army Cavalry School, September 1945. Rigg served with Soviet cavalry corps (XV and Maj. Gen. Olinsky's Guards Cavalry Corps) during 1944–1945.
57. Losik; Radzievsky, *Tankovyi udar*; Kurochkin; Anan'ev, *Tankovye armii*.
68. Kurochkin; Lototsky; Radzievsky, *Taktika;* Malanin.
69. Malanin; Rigg.
70. Kurochkin; Radzievsky, *Tankovye udar*.
77. A. Dunin, "Razvitie sukhoputnykh voisk v poslevoennyi period" [The development of the ground forces in the post-war period] *VIZh*, No. 5 (May 1978); "New Soviet Wartime Divisional TOE," *Intelligence Research Project*, No. 9250 (Washington, D.C.: OACSI, 15 Feb. 1956); *Soviet Army Organization, The Tank Division and The Mechanized Division* (Washington, D.C.: OACSI, Jan. 1954); "Recent Changes in Soviet Divisional Organization," *Intelligence Review*, No. 222 (Aug.–Sept. 1955); *The Soviet Army: Tactics and Organization, 1949* (London: The War Office, April 1949).
85. "Organizational Employment of Soviet Line Divisions," *Intelligence Review*, No. 254 (July 1962); "Soviet Field Armies: Organizational and Operational Concepts," *Intelligence Research Project, No. P3–10* (Washington, D.C.: OACSI,

1962); "Estimated Wartime TOE Soviet Tank and Motorized Rifle Divisions," *Intelligence Research Project NR:A–1729* (Washington, D.C.: HQS Dept of the Army, OACSI, 1958); "The Soviet Army," *Department of the Army Pamphlet No. 30–50–1* (Washington, D.C.: HQ Dept of the Army, 1958).

86. "Soviet Field Armies"; "Soviet Tactics," *Department of the Army Pamphlet No. 30–73* (Washington, D.C.: Headquarters, Department of the Army, 1961).

87. *Soviet Armed Forces Motorized Rifle Division, AP–220–3–9–68–INT* (Washington, D.C.: Defense Intelligence Agency, Feb. 1968); *Combat Support Systems and Equipment of the Soviet Motorized Rifle Division*, FSTC–381–3034 (Washington D.C.: US Army Foreign Science and Technology Center, 1964); *Soviet Tactics: Tank Division*, PC 220/3–1–64 (Washington, D.C.: Defense Intelligence Agency, 1964); *Soviet Armed Forces Motorized Rifle Division*, AP–220–3–9–68 INT (Washington D.C.: Defense Intelligence Agency, 1968); *Handbook on the Soviet Armed Forces*, AP–220–3–19–69 INT (Washington, D.C.: Defense Intelligence Agency, 1969).

100. Headquarters, Department of the Army, *FM 100–2–3*, "Soviet Army Troop Organization and Equipment," July 1984.

Comment: Soviet order of battle and unit composition during the Second World War are confirmed by virtually hundreds of German studies and reports prepared periodically by Fremde Heere Ost [Foreign Armies East] of OKH.

ABBREVIATIONS

A	Army	IBN	Infantry battalion
AAG	Army artillery group	MC	Mechanized corps
ABN	Airborne	MD	Mechanized division
AC	Army Corps	MECH	Mechanized
AD	Armored division	MOD	Mobile obstacle detachment
ARTY	Artillery		
AT	Antitank	MR	Mechanized regiment
ATR	Antitank region	MRB	Motorized rifle battalion
B	Brigade	MRD	Motorized rifle division
Bn	Battalion	MRCO	Motorized rifle company
CAA	Combined arms army		
CAG	Corps artillery group	MRR	Motorized rifle regiment
CAV		PA	Panzer army
MECH	Cavalry mechanized group	PD	Panzer division
		PR	Panzer regiment
CB	Cavalry brigade	RAG	Regimental artillery group
CC	Cavalry corps		
CD	Cavalry division	RB	Rifle brigade
CR	Cavalry regiment	RBN	Rifle battalion
D	Division	RC	Rifle corps
DAG	Division artillery group	RD	Rifle division
DTCHT	Detachment	RES	Reserve
FROG	Free rocket over ground	RR	Rifle regiment
GA	Guards army	SA	Shock army
GCC	Guards cavalry corps	SPR	Self-propelled artillery regiment
GCD	Guards cavalry division		
GMC	Guards mechanized corps	SR	Shock regiment
		TA	Tank army
GP	Group	TB	Tank brigade (Tank battalion after 1945)
GRD	Guards rifle division		
GTA	Guards tank army	TBN	Tank battalion
GTC	Guards tank corps	TC	Tank corps
HT/SPR	Heavy tank self-	TCO	Tank company
(HTSR)	propelled artillery regiment	TDB	Tank destroyer brigade
		TDR	Tank destroyer regiment
ID	Infantry division	TD	Tank division
IR	Infantry regiment	TR	Tank regiment

FOREWORD

This volume is the first in a series of in-depth studies on the Soviet military sponsored by the U.S. Army Soviet Army Studies Office (SASO) at Ft. Leavenworth, Kansas. Founded in 1986, SASO conducts research and prepares studies on all aspects of Soviet military affairs, with the objective of broadening the Army's understanding of Soviet military experiences and its legacy for the Soviet Army. Together with its sister unit, the United Kingdom's Soviet Studies Research Centre at Sandhurst, SASO has in a scant few years made an important contribution to our understanding of the Soviet military and its national security decision-making process.

For over ten years, the author of this volume, Colonel David M. Glantz, has engaged in research on Soviet military operational experience, extending from the creation of the Red Army in 1918, through the intensive combat of the Second World War, and into the postwar years. As a result of his research, he has published detailed studies of several Soviet operations, most notably a two-volume study of the USSR's 1945 campaign in Manchuria. He has also written special studies on Soviet military deception, wartime intelligence, operational and tactical maneuver, and airborne operations. He has lectured extensively on Soviet military topics in the United States and abroad.

This book represents a distillation of Colonel Glantz's research — a study of the evolution of Soviet operational techniques and force structure within the context of Soviet military art and science. Rather than presenting a simple narrative, Colonel Glantz synthesizes Soviet experience into a unique review of the functional areas of operational art. What results is a panorama of Soviet operational art, which provides perspective from which to judge how the Soviet Army has evolved, why that evolution has occurred, and, most importantly, how that evolution is likely to proceed in the future. In essence, this book is a basic text on operational art, a text which captures and reflects the process of change within the Soviet military. It is as timely as it is profound.

Carl E. Vuono
General, U.S. Army Chief of Staff

PREFACE

There could scarcely be a more opportune time for such a work as this to appear. The rapprochement between East and West, with its promise of a scaling down of the military confrontation between the two blocs, has kindled more public and professional interest in the details of Soviet military deployment and operational concepts than ever before. Unfortunately, outside the confines of the intelligence services there are very few people in the West capable of analysing the development of Soviet military thinking. As a result there is a great danger that Soviet policies and actions, especially in the military sphere, might be misinterpreted.

In producing his current work, Col. Glantz has done us a great service, fully justifying his reputation as the West's most competent analyst of developments in Soviet operational art. His description of the background to, principles of, and development of Soviet operational thinking provides us with an understanding essential for the interpretation of current events in Eastern European and Soviet military policies.

The problem that faces most Western political analysts is that the USSR has a very individual approach to the study and practice of war. It is not perhaps unique, but it is very different from the approaches taken in Western countries. A failure to understand the real essence of the Soviet system and the nature of these differences will result in serious errors of analysis. As reform sweeps through the political systems of Eastern Europe and the USSR, and the dissatisfaction of the populations of these countries with the ruling Communist parties becomes all too evident, many Western observers are hastening to discount the influence of motivating ideology today as a spent force. This seems to me to be unwise. It is undeniable that the Communist parties have lost all credibility and, along with revolutionary fervour, they may well be consigned to the dustbin of history. Whether this judgment is accurate or premature is not our concern here. But the fact is that, whatever its future, Marxist thought leaves a most important legacy. It may no longer be the naive faith of Lenin's day but it has given to the population of the USSR a framework of thought and a code of behaviour that is likely to persist for a long time. Mingled inextricably with Russian values and attitudes, it has shaped the Soviet mind and given the Soviet military system distinct institutions, values and ways of thinking which we in the West simply do not have, or have in very different measure.

All this would be of mere academic interest were it not for the fact that, firstly: these differences translate directly into differences in ways of fighting war, ways of designing equipment, of organizing forces and of training officers and men and, secondly: the West must now confront these differences on the arms control bargaining table and negotiate force reductions and redeployment with a military system which thinks and acts in a totally different way from ours.

For a start, the West lacks the formal framework of doctrine which is such a feature of the Soviet system. Even the word "doctrine" has a very different meaning for a Western politician or military man than it does for his Soviet counterpart. Terminological definitions have been the first stumbling block of our arms control negotiations. The Soviet side uses terms which are strictly defined and imposed on military and civilians alike. This leads to great precision of thought. On the Western side, the lack of agreed definitions coupled with the failure to understand both the precision inherent in Soviet definitions, and the actual meanings of the words used, might put the Western negotiator at a distinct disadvantage. Col. Glantz's explanation of the nature of this doctrinal framework and the impact it continues to have on Soviet thinking is an essential starting point for anyone seeking to understand the Soviet approach to East–West military agreement.

The second most significant difference between East and West military practices is the difference in concepts of scale and the resulting impact on military thinking and organization. Where until recently Western military thinking recognized only "tactics" and "strategy", Soviet military thought has long concentrated on the importance of the intermediate "operational" level as of crucial importance to success in battle.

The development of "operational art" as a scale of warfare has had the most profound impact on Soviet military practices. It gives very different values to tactics, equipment and training when compared to Western armies. The failure to appreciate the impact of thinking and planning on this larger scale was one of the main reasons for the German defeat at the hands of the Red Army in the Second World War. Even today, there is a tendency for former German officers and those who have learned uniquely from the experiences of those men to mis-assess Soviet military capability, applying perceptions which are valid at the tactical level to the operational level, when they are no longer valid. More than one Wehrmacht unit commander has been heard to declare his conviction in the superiority of his troops over his Soviet opponents, pointing to the fact that he had defeated a Soviet force three or four times larger. At the same time, a review of the history of the campaign in which he was fighting shows that, whilst he was winning his tactical victory, the entire field army of which he was part was being engulfed in a catastrophic operational encirclement on a scale which the German commanders could not grasp.

Two further things are essential to an understanding of the development of operational art in the Soviet Armed Forces, and both are well explained by Col. Glantz. The first is the nature and function of the Soviet General Staff as guardians and proponents of Soviet military art and science. The second is the means the General Staff use to do their operational analysis and force development: a scientific exploitation of military historical experience; a sophisticated use of mathematical analysis and prognosis, and a military educational structure. This last not only performs operational analysis but it also stimulates intense debate at all levels in the Armed Forces and applies the results of its analysis and experience most thoroughly in the form of military training, operational concepts, force structure developments and weapons procurement. It is the General Staff that orchestrates the co-ordination of all elements of the military system and ties them in with political requirements to achieve the impressive synergy we see in Soviet preparation for war.

By tracing the development of operational concepts and the force structures and weapons that were tailored to implement these concepts (and themselves contributed to the development of the concepts), Col. Glantz allows us to understand the principles upon which Soviet military thinking today is firmly based. Armed with this knowledge, he then invites the reader to apply this newly learned Soviet mentality to planning future operations and force structures in the light of current political and economic restraints. The result throws a great deal of light on current Soviet force developments in Eastern Europe and the USSR, and allows us to speculate on possible future structures.

This will not of itself answer the question posed – constantly, nowadays – about Soviet intentions, capabilities and motives. But it does give us confidence that we are aware of all the issues and it puts us in an excellent position to determine how best to judge and interpret what we see happen and what we are promised by Soviet spokesmen, to distinguish between fact and fancy, and to avoid that most dangerous of political diseases, wishful thinking.

Christopher Donnelly
Royal Military Academy, Sandhurst

AUTHOR'S PREFACE

This volume had its genesis five years ago while I served in the Center of Land Warfare at the U.S. Army War College, Carlisle Barracks, Pennsylvania. The commandant, Major General Richard D. Lawrence, assembled a team of specialists and tasked them with writing thorough studies on Soviet, U.S., and NATO concepts for warfighting at the operational level. With the full support of the Center's director, Colonel John Stewart, I was given time and encouragement to prepare such a study on the Soviet Army. Although the initial comprehensive effort faltered when its proponents left the War College, this study came to fruition over the ensuing two years.

By design, this volume addresses Soviet operational art in the natural context within which it evolved, as the Soviets themselves have approached the subject. The models for the study are the imposing works of A. A. Strokov and M. M. Kir'ian entitled *Istoriia voennogo iskusstva* [A history of military art], published in 1966 and 1984, respectively, and that edited by I. Kh. Bagramian, published in 1970 and entitled *Istoriia voin i voennogo iskusstva* [A history of war and military art]. These works provide the backbone for the study of military experience at the Soviet Frunze Academy and Voroshilov General Staff Academy and have no Western counterparts. Although these works are, in general, factually sound, I have verified their contents by extensive study of German and other archival materials.

Also by design, this work takes the form of a text on operational art, and it addresses the subject both topically and chronologically. For continuity's sake, I have stressed the evolution of operational art within the context of strategy and tactics, which have provided it with direction, form, and meaning. To round out the study, I have included a detailed survey of the Soviet force structure created to wage war at the operational and tactical level.

My intent is to equip the U.S. soldier, his Western counterpart, and the civilian community in general, with tools for better understanding the traditions and institutions of the Soviet Army, in peace and in war. It is written so that the West can better cope with the

Soviet military in times of crisis, but with the hope that the future will provide the opportunity for Soviets and Americans alike to study Soviet war experiences as a historical subject of natural interest to both sides, in a condition of peace.

My deepest thanks to General Lawrence and Colonel Stewart for their inspiration and encouragement when I undertook this project and to my indefatigable typist, editor, and major domo, Pat Bonneau, whose selfless work made this volume possible. My thanks also to Alice Mink, who typed and corrected the final text. For all errors in form, fact, or interpretation, of course, I alone am responsible.

David M. Glantz

CHAPTER ONE

THE SOVIET STUDY OF WAR

HISTORY AND WAR

The Soviets view history as a process of development in nature and society. As a discipline, history is a science which:

> studies the development of human society in all of its concreteness and diversity; it is studied with the goal of understanding the present and the prospects for the future. Marxist-Leninist historical science studies the development of human society as 'a single natural process, regular in all its great variety and contradictions'.[1]

The process often produces war. War, in its turn, is a socio-political phenomenon, characterized as a continuation of politics by violent means. Thus, "armed forces are used as the chief and decisive means for the achievement of political aims, as well as economic, diplomatic, ideological, and other means of struggle."[2]

Although a natural phenomenon, war can either accelerate or retard the march toward world socialism. Given the importance of war and its potentially damaging effects in the light of recent technological changes, the Soviets approach the study of war scientifically. They strive to understand war's operating laws and through this understanding develop operational and tactical techniques to assure Soviet victory. The Soviets study war within the framework of "military science," one of many sciences which helps explain the historical process. By examining war within an overall scientific framework, the Soviets treat armed conflict as a violent and crucial part of their total concept of war. In brief, the Soviets study war within the context of the entire range of human activity.

From their scientific approach to military science and war the Soviets have been able to articulate and assert the validity of such theoretical precepts as "inevitable victory," "moral superiority," and the classification of "just and unjust wars." These theoretical precepts offer unifying themes to the Soviet political apparatus as well as to the Soviet military and Soviet allies. More important, beneath theory and surface rhetoric there exists a toughminded, practical, and comprehensive analytical process for understanding and exploiting the dynamics of war.

By its very nature Soviet military science differs significantly from what the U.S. construes as military science. The U.S. has neither a well developed and focused body of military knowledge nor an analytical process that compares with Soviet military science. The U.S. does not systematically study and critique its past military experiences and the past military experiences of other nations. U.S. military theorists and doctrine developers tend to consider war outside the context of all other human activities. An understanding of the Soviet approach to the study of war can provide a vehicle for comparison and for analysis and critique of our own study of war.

System informs the development of Soviet military thought as well as military practice. The Soviets have created a hierarchy of terms associated with the complex range of issues extending from overall military doctrine to precise battlefield tactics (see table 1). The entire hierarchy, beginning with military doctrine, originates from, reflects, and receives official sanction from Communist Party dogma and decisions. Military science must accord with politically correct doctrine. Each term in the hierarchy has a distinct meaning, unlike in the U.S., where such terms are often used interchangeably. In addition, these meanings differ significantly from U.S. definitions. Hence, what the Soviets call doctrine is at a far higher level than what U.S. military theorists consider doctrine to be. What U.S. observers consider as doctrine the Soviets call strategy, operational art, and tactics.

MILITARY DOCTRINE

The Soviets define military doctrine as "a nation's officially accepted system of scientifically founded views on the nature of modern wars and the use of the armed forces in them, and also on the requirements arising from these views regarding the country and its armed forces being made ready for war."[3] Military doctrine has two aspects: social-political and military-technical. Consequently, the scope of military doctrine is consistent with the broad Soviet treatment of war in general. Doctrine, so defined, incorporates the "scientifically founded views" of military science with official party sanction, in so doing uniting the objective findings of military analysis with the objective political truths of socialism.

TABLE 1
HIERARCHY OF TERMS

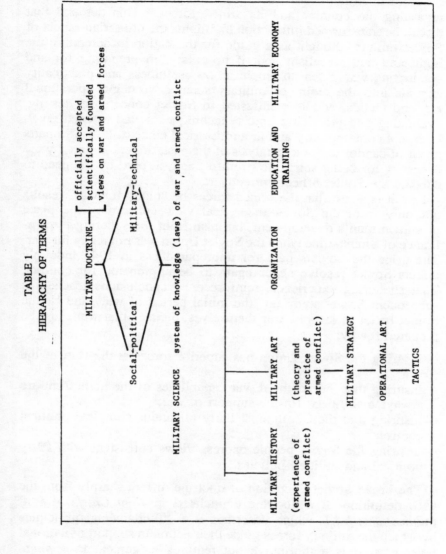

MILITARY DOCTRINE — [officially accepted scientifically founded views on war and armed forces

Military-technical

Social-political

MILITARY SCIENCE   system of knowledge (laws) of war and armed conflict

MILITARY HISTORY (experience of armed conflict)

MILITARY ART (theory and practice of armed conflict)

ORGANIZATION

EDUCATION AND TRAINING

MILITARY ECONOMY

MILITARY STRATEGY

OPERATIONAL ART

TACTICS

At the same time that the definition articulates a sound theoretical basis for doctrine, it also focuses on the practical "requirements – regarding the country and its armed forces." This demand that theory be transformed into action highlights the utilitarian aspect of Soviet military thought as a guide for the nation in defending the homeland and socialism and, if necessary, in preparing for and conducting war. Such an emphasis on usefulness and practicality extends into the realm of military science, strategy, operational art, and tactics, and is manifested in Soviet concern for testing, evaluating and practicing precise techniques suited to each level, both in a contemporary and in an historical context. It also imparts an air of candor to Soviet analysis of the past, driven, in part, by the necessity for being scientific (truthful) and, in part, by the need to educate the Soviet officer correctly.

Soviet concern that the armed forces be "ready for war" results not only from the Soviet theoretical view concerning the place of war in man's development, but also from the sobering remembrance of a harsh time when the Soviet Union was not ready for war. The price the Soviets paid for unpreparedness in 1941 indelibly affects Soviet resolve never again to be unprepared for conflict. That shattering experience, reinforced by conclusions reached in subsequent Soviet study on "the initial period of war" and by the Soviet belief in laws of war themselves, dictates that war must be prepared for by:

– insuring the Soviet Union has superior forces at the start of the war;
– insuring that the potential war capabilities of the homefront are always maximized for the support of war;
– insuring that the Communist Party maintains complete political control;
– insuring the Soviet people express views consistent with Party political and military policies.

The broad Soviet definition of doctrine differs sharply from the U.S. definition of a doctrine enunciated in *Joint Chiefs of Staff Publications, No.1*, which describes it as "fundamental principles by which the military forces guide their action in support of national objectives. It is authoritative but requires judgement in application." A U.S. Army Training and Doctrine Command definition comes closer to actual U.S. usage of the term by stating that doctrine is:

what is written, approved by appropriate authority, and published concerning the conduct of military affairs. Doctrine generally describes how the army fights tactically, thus, what we call doctrine falls into the Soviet categories of operational art and tactics.

MILITARY SCIENCE

Within the context of military doctrine, the Soviets define military science as "a system of knowledge concerning the nature and laws of war; the preparation of the armed forces and nation for war, and the means of conducting war." Specifically,

> military science investigates the laws of war, which reflect the dependence of the course and outcome of war on the politics, economics, and the correlation of morale-political, scientific-technical, and military capabilities of the warring sides, as well as the main processes of preparing and conducting war, depending on its scale, the composition of the participants and the means of armed conflict ... The basic subject of the investigation is armed conflict in war.[4]

Thus, military science is a comprehensive field embracing, in addition to the preparation and conduct of war, such peace-time activities as: organization; military education and training; development of a military economy; and the study of military experience (history). This definition clearly distinguishes between war (*voina*), which includes economic, diplomatic, ideological, scientific-technical and other forms of struggle, and armed conflict (*vooruzhennaia bor'ba*), which is struggle on the battlefield. The political leadership of the state manages war while the military leadership plays a more significant role in the conduct of armed conflict.

Just as certain scientifically derived laws apply to the conduct of war, so also do laws govern the course and outcome of armed conflict. These laws derive from objective analysis of experience (military history) and, although they tend to transcend time, they evolve in consonance with changing political, morale, economic and technological conditions. While the general laws of war have changed only slightly in the past twenty years, technological changes have made the laws of armed conflict more volatile and less certain. Earlier Soviet works cite among the laws of armed conflict such dictums as:

– methods and forms of armed conflict depend on the material basis of the battle and operations;
– any battle or operation at a given moment of its development takes shape in favor of that opposing side whose troops possess the greater combat power in comparison with the enemy.[5]

Although these laws probably remain valid, more recent authoritative Soviet works hesitate to articulate distinct laws of armed conflict and instead refer to the more general laws of war, which they cite as follows:

– the dependence of war on its political aims;
– the dependence of the course and outcome of war on the correlation of economic forces of the struggling states (coalitions);
– the dependence of the course and outcome of war on the correlation of the scientific potential of opposing sides;
– the dependence of the course and outcome of war on the correlation of moral-political forces and capabilities of the struggling states (coalitions);
– the dependence of the course and outcome of war on the correlation of military forces (potentials) of the contending sides.[6]

These laws serve several important purposes. As laws, they must be foremost in the commander's mind when he formulates plans and evaluates operational alternatives. In addition, they provide general guidance throughout the strategic, operational and tactical levels of war, thus providing a focus and unity of thought and practice absent in western military thought. Finally, adherence to objective laws of war produces concrete requirements for force structuring and armament development. These requirements, justified by the materialist aspect of Marxist philosophy and by objective analysis, are absolute and must be met, lest the scientific basis of the system itself be challenged. This imperative manifests itself in the size and complexity of the Soviet force structure and in the seemingly endless process of weapons procurement and fielding.

MILITARY ART

Military art as the main component of military science is concerned with "the theory and practice of preparing and conducting military operations on the land, at sea, and in the air."[7] The growing complexity of war in the twentieth century has dictated the necessity for further refinement of terminology describing the levels and scope of military art. Thus, the Soviets maintain that military art includes the closely interrelated fields of strategy, operational art, and tactics. Each field describes a distinct level of warfare measured against such standards as mission, scale, scope, and duration.

The basic initial tenets of military art:

> are expressed in its principles which apply in common to strategic-, operational-, and tactical-scale military operations, inasmuch as within them is found an expression of the practical use of the objective laws of war.

Moreover, "the state of military art depends on the levels of the development of production and the means of armed conflict, as well as the nature of the social structure." Finally, "the historical and national characteristics of a country, its geographical conditions and other factors influence the development of military art."[8] Military historical experience provides a context for military art by generalizing past military experience and by serving as another source for the development of military science.

A central feature of Soviet military art embraces basic principles which the Soviets define as "the basic tenets, reflecting the objective existing normality of armed conflict. The preparation and conduct of wars, operations, and battles conform to them." Soviet military science, assisted by the dialectic, discovers the nature of these principles, confirms their scientific basis, and shows how they relate to the laws of war. Confirming the evolutionary nature of the principles, the Soviets maintain they "have a historical nature; some of them lose their importance, others operate over a long period and take on new meanings, while still other new principles of military art appear."[9]

The principles of military art as defined by Soviet military theorists have changed over time and will continue to change. Currently, the Soviets list the following as the most important principles:[10]

- high combat readiness to fulfill missions under any conditions at the beginning and during the conduct of war;
- surprise, decisiveness, activeness of combat operations and constant striving to secure and maintain the initiative;
- full use of various means and methods of struggle to achieve victory;
- coordinated use and close interaction of large units (formations)

of all types of armed forces and branches of forces;
— decisive concentration of the main strength at the necessary moment on the most important directions to achieve the main mission;
— simultaneous attack on the enemy to the entire depth of his formation, a timely strengthening of forces and bold maneuver of troops and weapons to develop combat operation at high tempos and defeat the enemy in a short time;
— calculated and full use of the morale-political factor;
— firm and continuous command and control;
— inexorability and decisiveness in fulfilling assigned missions;
— all-round security of combat operations;
— timely restoration of reserves and troop combat readiness.

Since Soviet principles of military art have changed over the years, careful analysis of those changes and of the currently recognized Soviet list of principles can provide a better picture of the contemporary Soviet outlook toward war in general and military operations in particular. The principles are a mere reflection of the practical problems of war which the Soviets address.

MILITARY STRATEGY

The Soviets consider military strategy to be the highest level of military art,

> embracing the theory and practice of preparing the nation and armed forces for war, planning and conducting strategic operations and war as a whole. The theory of military strategy studies the laws and nature of war and the methods for conducting it; and works out the theoretical basis of planning, preparing and conducting strategic operations and war as a whole.[11]

Strategy is derived from military doctrine, past military experience, and a careful analysis of contemporary social-political, economic, and military conditions. Conversely, military strategy has a significant impact on politics.

In a practical vein,

> military strategy concerns itself with definite strategic missions of the armed forces and the forces and equipment necessary to fulfill them; with working out and implementing measures to prepare the armed forces, the theater of military operations,

the economy and the population of the country for war; with planning strategic operations; with organizing deployments of the armed forces and their command during wartime; and also with study of the probable enemy's capabilities to conduct war and strategic operations.

Because it is the highest level of military art, military strategy dominates the other components in the art of war – operational art and tactics. It defines their tasks and the methods of operations of the troops on an operational and tactical scale. The most important principles in the theory and practice of operational art and tactics are developed on the basis of military strategy's requirements. At the same time, military strategy relies on operational art and tactics, takes into account their capabilities, and uses their achievements in the performance of strategic tasks.

Like military doctrine, to which it is closely related, military strategy encompasses far more than the strict military realm. Harking back to Frunze's Unified Military Doctrine of the 1920s, it recognizes the essential interdependence of front and rear and the necessity for preparing a country for war. Hence, the economic and industrial substructure of the Soviet Union, originally designed to ensure the development of a strong military state, remains harnessed to the Soviet military establishment. Therefore, the broad Soviet definition of military strategy contrasts sharply with the U.S. definition found in *JCS Pub 1*.

The Soviets have written much about their military strategy. Although couched in terms of repulsing aggression, the Soviets have openly discussed virtually all of those areas associated with the preparation and conduct of war and strategic operations.[12] The most notable examples are the works of Svechin, Frunze, Tukhachevsky, and Triandafillov in the twenties and thirties; Semenov, Strokov and Sokolovsky in the sixties; and Bagramian, Ogarkov, and Kir'ian in the seventies and eighties. A whole series of works on the "initial period of war," written since 1958, address what remains a very sensitive strategic question. Supplementing these and other books are a host of articles published primarily in *Voennaia mysl'* (Military Thought) and *Voenno-istoricheskii zhurnal* (Military History Journal) that focus on virtually every question of war, including strategic operations.

OPERATIONAL ART

The second level of Soviet military art is the operational level, a level of war the Soviets identified in the 1920s and have used for the analysis of armed conflict ever since. The operational level evolved as a direct by-product of the growing sophistication and scale of war in the nineteenth and twentieth centuries. It slowly became a distinct category of analysis because the older terms, strategy and tactics, were too limited to be able to describe the intricacies of preparing for and conducting large scale modern war. The scope and scale of Russian and Soviet military experiences, in particular during the First World War and the Civil War, when operations spanned thousands of kilometers and involved millions of men, compelled the Soviets to look at operations as a distinct intermediate level of war between military strategy, governing war in general, and tactics, involving individual battles. Strategic success in war depended in large measure upon how well the Soviets could perform at the operational level.

Operational art encompasses the theory and practice of preparing for and conducting combined and independent operations by large units (*fronts*, armies) of the armed forces. It occupies an intermediate position between strategy and tactics. "Stemming from strategic requirements, operational art determines methods of preparing for and conducting operations to achieve strategic goals." Operational art in its turn "establishes the tasks and direction for the development of tactics."[13] Soviet operational art provides a framework for studying, understanding, preparing for, and conducting war. Within the context of strategy and tactics, it makes the study of operations an academic discipline requiring intensive research and scholarship on the part of those who study, write about, plan, and conduct war.

Operational art performs such distinct functional tasks associated with the preparation and conduct of war as:

- investigating the rules, nature, and character of contemporary operations;
- working out the means for preparing and conducting combat operations;
- determining the function of large units (*fronts*, armies) and formations (corps, divisions) of the armed forces;
- establishing means and methods for organizing and supporting

continuous cooperation, security, and command and control of forces in combat;
- delineating the organizational and equipment requirements of large units of the armed forces;
- working out the nature and methods of operational training for officers, and command and control organs;
- developing recommendations for the operational preparation of a theater of military operations (*Teatr voennykh deistviia* – TVD);
- investigating enemy views on the conduct of operational level military operations.

After fulfilling these tasks, operational art analyzes and generalizes the results and articulates:

- basic theoretical positions;
- the subject and structure of operational art;
- the contents, classification, and characteristic features of contemporary operations;
- the principles for preparing and conducting operations;
- the role, position, and missions of large units (formations) of the armed forces;
- the means for coordinating the combat use of large units in combined operations.

While operational art examines the armed forces as a whole, it also looks at each of its parts, including the operational art of combined armed forces, strategic rocket forces, air defense forces, air forces, naval forces, rear services, and civil defense. Highly refined, systematic study of operational techniques results, are designed to successfully exploit the principles of military art in order to produce victory at the operational level.

The Soviets gain an understanding of the current nature of operational art and, more importantly, insights into how operational art has evolved into its current state by studying a wide range of factors which have affected its development. These factors include:

- leadership of the Communist Part in constructing the armed forces;
- the condition and requirements of Soviet military science and military doctrine;
- scientific technical progress;

- technical equipping and organization of the armed forces and their ability to use that equipment;
- the state and direction of development of enemy armed forces capabilities;
- experience of past wars;
- operational and operational-strategic exercises;
- military cooperation with the armed forces of other Socialist states;
- military-political and geographical conditions.

Thus, Soviet study of operational art, like that of war in general, is done within the broad context of human political, economic and technological development. The tasks of operational art are practical and focused directly on mastering those techniques which will produce success in military and combat operations, techniques associated with force structuring, unit missions, command and control, cooperation, security, training, equipment, intelligence on the enemy, and the conduct of operations. These techniques produce victory or defeat on the battlefield. Analysis of these precise tasks produces more generalized objective views in the form of theoretical positions, principles, roles, missions, and statements governing the state of operational art, as a whole, and specific aspects of contemporary operations. Soviet analysis of the broader factors influencing operations, including politics, geography, technology, and the state of weaponry, makes operational art a comprehensive and credible field of study.

This systematic approach clearly defines the scope and limits of the operational realm and provides direction for research and a comprehensive methodology for achieving a better understanding of preparing for and conducting war at the operational level. It produces in the minds of each Soviet officer an understanding of the distinct differences between warfare at the strategic, operational, and tactical levels.

Operational art has been a major area of study since the mid-1920s, and a host of important military theoreticians have studied and written on the subject. Its evolution has been marked by the creation and evolution of numerous general operational theories, many of which provide a basis for current Soviet operational theory. The most significant of these theories have been: the theory of successive operations (1920s); the theory of deep battle and deep operations (1930s); the artillery offensive (1943); and the air offensive (1943). Because of their sound scientific basis, they have become an important element of contemporary Soviet operations. Operational art in general, dormant during the period of the "Revolution in Military Affairs," of the 1960s, when Soviet attention was transfixed by strategic nuclear matters, has, since the late 1960s, again become a critical topic in the Soviet study of war.

TACTICS

Tactics, as the lowest level of military art, studies problems relating to battle and combat, the basic building blocks of operations. Successful conduct of operations depends upon successful tactics in battles and separate combats. Traditionally, and in the U.S. to the present day, tactics has governed the actual employment of a nation's armed forces on the battlefield in the presence of the enemy, while strategy has involved the movement of a nation's army against an opposing army. Thus, war, a series of battles, was the object of study for strategy; and battle has been the object of study for tactics. As the scope of war grew in the past two centuries, and nations began employing multiple armies to achieve strategic goals, operations by those armies became too broad and complex to be adequately analysed by tactics. The Soviet solution was to create the level of operational art to investigate operations primarily by armies and groups of armies (*fronts*) to achieve intermediate operational goals. The Soviets maintained the tactical category to describe that which occurs within the army to contribute to attainment of intermediate operational goals.

Specifically, the Soviets define tactics as:

> a component part of military science, embracing the theory and practice of preparing and conducting battle by subunits (battalions), units (regiments) and formations (divisions, corps) of various types of forces, branches of forces or specialized forces. The theory of tactics investigates the rules, nature and contents of battle and works out the means of preparing for and conducting battle.[14]

Tactics is dialectically interrelated with operational art and military strategy. Strategy determines the nature and methods of conducting future war and the place of combat in that warfare, while operational art determines the specific tasks tactics must address. Conversely, tactics influences operational art and strategy. Combat capabilities of tactical forces, in large part, determine the goals, scale, and methods of operations.

The practice of tactics involves the work of commands, staffs and forces in preparing and conducting battle and includes:

— constant specification of present conditions;
— making a decision and posing missions to subordinates;
— planning and preparing for battle;
— conducting combat operations, and commanding and controlling subunits and units;
— securing combat operations.

Over time, the definition of tactics has expanded. Originally it applied only to ground and naval forces, but by the mid-twentieth century new branches and types of forces had evolved with their own fields of tactics. Today, the Soviets subdivide tactics into general tactics, tactics of the branches of forces, and tactics of the types of forces (ground, air, air defense, naval and border troops).

Ground force tactics, which provides a basis for general tactics, focuses on the preparation and conduct of combined arms battle and involves study of the tactics of combined armed formations (divisions, corps), units (regiments) and subunits (battalions), as well as the tactics of the branches of forces and specialized forces within the ground forces. Specifically, ground force tactics fulfills the following functions:

— investigates the nature of the various types of military operations;
— investigates the role of nuclear, artillery and air strikes, and other means of attack;
— works out forms of maneuver and march, pre-combat and combat formation;
— determines the place and role of formations, units and sub-units of each branch of forces and specialized forces in combined arms battle;
— determines the missions which they perform during combat operations, the methods of their contemporary combat use, and the order of cooperation between them.

On a functional basis, ground force tactics investigates the primary types of combat operations, the offense and defense. In its study of offensive battle, Soviet tactics focuses on such critical issues as: organizing offensive combat; conducting penetration of a defense; pursuing a withdrawing enemy; conducting offensive river crossings; preparing and conducting meeting battles; and mastering the peculiarities of battle at night, in cities, on coastal directions, and in special terrain conditions (mountains, deserts, the far north).

Defensive tactics focuses on the organization and conduct of the defense in the tactical arena, under special conditions, and defense when encircled or when conducting a withdrawal. Ground force tactics also embraces the movement and redeployment of forces on the battlefield in both offensive and defensive situations.

The theoretical aspects of tactics are covered in Soviet field regulations, manuals, textbooks and a huge volume of books and articles which discuss the fine points of tactics. Often these articles present and debate opposing tactical views, thus illustrating the dynamic nature of Soviet tactical thought. The Soviets believe such dynamism is essential because the "determining influence of improving weaponry and military technology and the changing quality of personnel in the armed forces" require it. Of all of the levels of military art, conditions are most volatile and subject to change at the tactical level. This, combined with the complexity of the tactical level, requires constant, probing, and detailed study and debate.

CHAPTER TWO

THE NATURE OF OPERATIONAL ART

ROOTS OF OPERATIONAL ART

Operational art slowly emerged as a distinct category of military art in the twentieth century. The changing nature of war in the preceding century forced European states to recognize the need for altering the more traditional subdivision of military art into strategy and tactics. Very simply, the growing scope and complexity of war forced a refinement of terminology and a more sophisticated approach to the study and conduct of war. Throughout the nineteenth century, beginning with the Napoleonic Wars, the traditional definitions of strategy and tactics had become less and less relevant. Prior to that time, during war a nation's army engaged the army of an opposing state (or states). Political and economic realities of the time dictated that each nation possess primarily one army. Battle between the two forces resulted in either victory or defeat. Battles were of short duration and they occurred between relatively small armies deployed on limited terrain. Each battle constituted a single large engagement. In these circumstances, strategy primarily involved the movement of a nation's army against an opposing army, while tactics governed the actual employment of the army on the battlefield in the presence of the enemy (see table 2).

Thus, war, a series of battles, was the object of study for strategy, and battle was the object of study for tactics. Successful battle, which resulted in the destruction or incapacitation of the enemy force, permitted successful achievement of the strategic goals of the war.

Forces unleashed by the political, social, and economic turmoil of the French Revolution altered the face of war. The use of multiple mass armies, the economic mobilization of the state for war, the unlimited nature of wartime objectives, which, to an increasing extent, involved the outright destruction of opposing political, economic, and social systems, complicated the traditional framework and methods for analysing and understanding war.

Nineteenth-century military theorists recognized and wrestled with those changes. Thus, Clausewitz pondered aspects of war hitherto subject to little concern (absolute war, moral elements of war, etc.), while Jomini addressed the complexity of war by describing a new realm of "grand tactics." Technological innovations of the nineteenth and early twentieth centuries facilitated the mobilization and employment of even larger armies and the application of increased firepower on the battlefield. The development of railroads, new communications means, (telegraph and telephone), and new weaponry (long-range, rapid fire artillery, machine guns, magazine rifles and new classes of warships) combined with a "democratization of war" to produce larger and more destructive wars, waged by multiple mass armies representing the mobilized manpower of the nation as a whole. The carnage of the Austro-Prussian War, the American Civil War, the Franco-Prussian

TABLE 2

DEFINITIONS OF STRATEGY AND TACTICS

Source	Strategy	Tactics
Greeks	Strategos, "generalship, the art of generalship"	Taktos, "ordered or regulated"
1801 French	Stratagème, "the method of defeating or overcoming the enemy"	La tactique, "the science of military movement"
1838 Jomini	"the art of making war upon the map"	"the art of posting troops upon the battlefield
1830s Clausewitz	"the use of engagements for the objects of war"	"the use of armed forces in the engagement"
1861 British	"the art of concerting a plan of campaign"	"the art of handling troops"
1870 British	"moving troops in a theater of war"	"the art of handling troops in the presence of the enemy"
1894 Mahan	"movement of troops not in contact"	"movement of troops in contact"
1908 French	"the art of conceiving"	"the art of executing"

War, the Russo-Japanese War, and finally the First World War demonstrated this increased scale, complexity, and destructiveness of war. Military operations matured to a grander scale and took the form of a series of consecutive and mutually related battles conducted over a protracted period of time. No longer could nations attain strategic victory in a single battle of annihilation, for the destruction of but one army would not ensure an end to a war. Strategic goals could now be attained only by achieving success in operations as a whole.

Soviet theorists maintain that no nation prior to the end of the First World War understood the changing nature of war. Thus, "bourgeois military science could not evaluate correctly the new phenomenon in the conduct of armed struggle, and the armies of almost all governments entered the First World War with old views on the methods of its conduct."[1] Moreover,

> the practice of preparing and conducting combat operations throughout the First World War created the objective prerequisites for the creation in military art of independent sections investigating questions of theory and practice of conducting operations. However, at that time, no army officially recognized the necessity.[2]

A practical manifestation of this growing dilemma in military art was the inability of modern armies in the First World War to achieve more than tactical or temporary operational successes on the battlefield. Given the course of the First World War, according to Soviet theorists,

> objective reality advanced the requirement for the creation of a new branch of military art which would encompass questions of the theory and practice of operations, i.e., operational art. Thus operational art was a logical consequence of the change in the character of armed struggle, reflecting the appearance of its new phenomenon – operations.[3]

DEVELOPMENT OF OPERATIONAL ART

The Soviets claim credit for being the first nation to recognize the changing nature of war and the first to adjust its military art to those changes. Thus:

> to its credit, Soviet military-theoretical thought, having first succeeded in seeing these tendencies in the development of

military affairs, correctly perceived and revealed the new
component part of military art – operational art.[4]

That perception did not emerge immediately after the Russian
Revolution. Rather, it evolved throughout the 1920s and 1930s as
Soviet military theorists pondered the nature of modern war and
specific dilemmas of the First World War, the most important of
which was how to restore mobility and maneuver to the relatively
stagnant battlefield. Soviet military theorists were assisted in this
task by the experiences of the Russian Civil War and allied intervention in Russia, a conflict which was, in many ways and for many
reasons, different from the First World War. However, the Soviets
were not unique either in the questions they studied or in the
conclusions they reached. Western theorists addressed the same
dilemmas. While many reached different conclusions, some
articulated views similar to, if not in advance of, Soviet views.
French, British and American Field Regulations recognized the
nature of modern operations as series of battles, though they did
not treat the operational level of war as a distinct entity. They
recognized that operational results emerged as the sum of the results
of tactical combat. Outside the realm of official military thought,
British theorists Liddell Hart, J.F.C. Fuller and other continental
theorists developed new concepts of warfare at the operational
level. Certainly, the German Army in the 1930s adopted combat
methods suited to the achievement of operational and hence
strategic success in battle. German theorists however, tended to go
no higher than the operational level.

Soviet writers date Soviet concern for operational art as a distinct
field of study to the Civil War years. They claim:

> Soviet operational art began to develop during the Civil
> War and military intervention in Russia (1918–1920). It was
> based on the theoretical theses and instructions of V.I.
> Lenin concerning military questions, and on the generalized
> experiences of the Soviet armed forces in preparing and
> conducting important operations during the Civil War.[5]

It is apparent, however, that the existence of such a distinctive
field as operational art was not readily apparent to Soviet commanders during the Civil War. In that war the Soviets created and
employed *fronts* and armies, units which later came to be known as
operational. Yet direct reference to an operational level of war was
absent. Moreover, during the First World War, Russian forces and

the forces of other nations had employed similar units (*fronts*, army groups, and armies) to control their massive forces. It is more correct to say that conditions which Soviet commanders experienced in the Civil War prompted intense reflection on matters which in the future would be encompassed by the operational level of war. Soviet employment of limited forces over vast areas of Russia and the relatively unsophisticated weaponry of the combatants gave the war more of a maneuver character. The use of cavalry corps and cavalry armies and the creation of shock groups permitted rapid penetration of shallow enemy tactical defenses and exploitation into the operational depth of a defense. Southern Front operations against Denikin in the fall of 1919, and the see-saw offensives of the Russian–Polish War (1920) differed markedly from the positional warfare and limited offensive gains of the First World War. In these circumstances it was natural that in the postwar period Soviet theorists would turn their attention to applying the lessons of the Civil War to solution of the dilemmas of high intensity positional war.

During the immediate postwar years military academies, commanders and staffs, under party guidance, formed associations to discuss military science issues. The most prominent of these associations was the Military Science Society of the RKKA (Workers' and Peasants' Red Army) Staff Academy, a group formed in October 1920, under whose aegis periodic meetings were held to discuss key military science issues.[6] Of particular concern to the society were questions concerning military doctrine, forms of combat action, and reconstruction of the armed forces to match changing military thought. In 1925 an administration for the investigation and use of war experience was formed within the RKKA Staff to reinforce the work of these associations.[7] The resulting analysis of doctrine, the nature of combat, and war experiences, supplemented by study of the results of military exercises, provided a basis for a series of Soviet military theoretical works which appeared throughout the twenties. These works redefined the nature of war, created new definitions for use in army regulations and military school curricula, and argued for a restructuring of the armed forces in consonance with the new definitions. Among the earliest works were articles by S. S. Kamenev and M. N. Tukhachevsky which challenged the importance of one climactic battle and instead emphasized the importance of conducting successive military operations. Kamenev, Commander of the

Red Army from 1919 to 1924, pondered Civil War experiences and concluded that:

> in spite of all victorious fights before the battle, the fate of the campaign will be decided in the very last battle – Interim defeats in a campaign, however serious they may be, subsequently will be viewed as 'individual episodes' – In the warfare of modern large armies, defeat of the enemy results from the sum of continuous and planned victories on all fronts, successfully completed one after another and interconnected in time – the uninterrupted conduct of operations is the main condition for victory.[8]

Tukhachevsky, drawing upon his experiences along the Vistula in 1920, concluded that "the impossibility on a modern wide front of destroying the enemy army by one blow forces the achievement of that aim by a series of successive operations."[9] By the mid-1920s most Soviet theorists accepted the view that army operations would flow continuously from the plans and concepts of the wartime *front* commander. More importantly, "the study of successive operations, to a great extent, created the prerequisites for subsequent development of deep operations."[10]

Rejection of the concept of a single battle of annihilation and acceptance of the necessity for successive operations focused the attention of military theorists on the realm between traditional strategy and tactics – the realm that would become operational art. Terminology evolved slowly as the limits of the operational level of war were defined. In May 1924 a work appeared entitled "Higher Commands – official guidance for commanders and field commands of the army and fleet." This document, produced in part by War Commissar M.I. Frunze, focused on operations by stating:

> (1) The aim of each operation and battle is the destruction of enemy forces and his technical means of combat. (2) That aim can be achieved only by skillful and decisive action, based on simple, but artful maneuver, conducted violently and persistently. In addition, to complete a maneuver operation successfully it is necessary to assess correctly the forces and possible actions of the enemy, to supply material means for the operation and to organize firm and continuous command and control.[11]

In the same year the Military Academy of the RKKA Staff

responded to growing concern for operations by creating a separate faculty to study and teach the conduct of operations, a field hitherto viewed as part of the strategy curriculum. The principal focus of the new faculty was on the nature and future evolution of the concept of successive operations.[12]

By 1926 the limits of the operational realm had become better defined. In several works published in 1926 Tukhachevsky built upon his earlier investigation of successive operations to ponder operations as a whole. He wrote:

> Modern tactics are characterized primarily by organization of battle, presuming coordination of various branches of troops. Modern strategy embraces its former meaning; that is the 'tactics of a theater of military operations.' However, this definition is complicated by the fact that strategy prepares for battle, but it also participates in and influences the course of battle. Modern operations involve the concentration of forces necessary to strike a blow, and the infliction of continual and uninterrupted blows of these forces against the enemy throughout an extremely deep area. The nature of modern weapons and modern battle is such that it is an impossible matter to destroy the enemy's manpower by one blow in a one day battle. Battle in a modern operation stretches out into a series of battles not only along the front but also in depth until that time when either the enemy has been struck by a final annihilating blow or when the offensive forces are exhausted. In that regard, modern tactics of a theater of military operations are tremendously more complex than those of Napoleon, and they are made even more complex by the inescapable condition mentioned above that the strategic commander cannot personally organize combat.[13]

Tukhachevsky's remarks clearly enunciated the need for further refinement of terminology and set the stage for practical work along these lines. Other papers delivered by military theorists at the 1926 Military Science Society session echoed Tukhachevsky's view.

The following year a new work entitled *Strategy* [Strategiia] gave clearer definition to operational art. Its author, A. A. Svechin, a former Russian army general staff officer and in 1926 a member of the Faculty of the Frunze Academy and RKKA Staff Academy, placed operations in a strategic context. Svechin described strategy as "the art of combining preparations for war and the grouping of operations to achieve aims, put forth in war for the armed forces."

Consequently, "strategy decides questions concerning both the use of the armed forces and all resources of the state for the achievement of final military aims."[14] In essence, strategy dictated the basic lines of conduct of operational art.

Svechin built upon the earlier concept of successive operations to develop a definition of operational art stating:

> combat actions are not self sufficient but rather are the basic materials from which operations are composed. Only on a very few occasions can one depend on one engagement to secure the final objectives of military actions. Normally, the path to final aims is broken up into a series of operations, – subdivided in time, by more or less sizeable pauses, comprising differing territorial sectors of a theater of war and differing sharply as a consequence of different intermediate aims –.

This led Svechin to the judgment that:

> we call the operation that act of war, during which struggling forces without interruption are directed into a distinct region of the theater of military operations to achieve distinct intermediate aims. The operation represents an aggregate of very diverse actions: the compilation of operational plans; material preparations; concentration of forces in jumping off positions; the erection of defensive structures; completion of marches; the conduct of battle by either immediate envelopment or by a preliminary penetration to encircle and destroy enemy units, to force back other forces, and to gain or hold for us designated boundaries or geographical regions.

If strategy dictated the aims of operational art, then operational art similarly affected tactics. Svechin declared that

> the material of operational art is tactics and administration: success in the development of an operation depends both on the successful resolution by forces of distinct tactical questions and on the provision to those forces of material supplies – Operational art, arising from the aim of the operation, generates a series of tactical missions and establishes a series of tasks for the activity of rear area organs.

Thus, all branches of military art were interrelated. In Svechin's words, "tactics makes the steps from which operational leaps are assembled; strategy points out the path." Svechin's work and the theoretical work of others in the 1920s created the realm of operational art as a new category of military theory.

THE EMERGENCE OF DEEP OPERATIONS

In the 1920s the tendency to consider successive operations as a centerpiece and foundation for the analysis of the operational level of war resulted largely from the undeveloped state of technology within the Soviet Union in general and the Red Army in particular. Industrial backwardness and the lack of a well developed armaments and automobile industry forced the Soviets to rely on infantry, artillery and horse cavalry to conduct major operations. Hence, an optimistic view of prospects for successful successive operations postulated that an offensive would develop slowly with armies advancing 75–90 kilometers and the *front* as a whole up to 200 kilometers in a six or seven day period.[15] Even if this optimism were borne out by events, these operations would be costly, especially if conducted against a better equipped foe. Consequently, by the late 1920s theorists began pondering the impact of impending industrial development on future military operations. The 1929 Field Regulation (*Ustav*) expanded the theory of successive operations by contemplating the impact of future mechanization and motorization on Soviet forces conducting offensive warfare. The *Ustav* established as a goal the conduct of deep battle (*glubokii boi*) to achieve success throughout the tactical depth of enemy defenses by the simultaneous use of infantry support tanks and long-range action tanks, and infantry, with artillery and aviation support.[16] The 1929 Regulation was a statement of intent which could only be implemented once industrialization had taken place. The ensuing forced collectivization and industrialization of the Soviet Union soon created conditions necessary to translate that intent into reality.

Spurred on by a barrage of written works, the promise of 1929 was quickly realized in both regulations and in the Soviet force structure. In February 1933 the Red Army officially sanctioned the concept of deep battle in its *Provisional Instructions on the Organization of Deep Battle*. New and more explicit instructions appeared in March 1935, and the *Field Regulation* (*Ustav*) of 1936 made deep battle and its operational variant deep operations, established tenets of Soviet military art. The concept of deep operations (*glubokaia operatsiia*), like its predecessor successive operations, provided a focal point for Soviet understanding of the operational level of war. The 1936 *Ustav*, prepared under the supervision of Tukhachevsky and A.I. Yegorov, defined deep operations as:

> Simultaneous assault on enemy defenses by aviation and artillery to the depths of the defense, penetration of the tactical zone of the defense by attacking units with widespread use of tank forces and violent development of tactical success into operational success with the aim of the complete encirclement and destruction of the enemy. The main role is performed by the infantry, and the mutual support of all types of forces are organized in its interests.[17]

With the complete articulation of deep battle and deep operations, Soviet operational art became fully defined, at least in theory, and the operational level of war emerged as a distinct component of Soviet military science. After 1936, although the definition of operational art underwent few changes, the dynamism with which Soviet theorists investigated operational theory suffered severe reverses.

Stalin's purge of the Soviet military in 1937–1938 liquidated the generation of officers who had given definition to operational art and who had formulated the theories of deep battle and deep operations. Tukhachevsky, Egorov, Kamenev, Uborovich, Svechin and a host of others, the cream of the crop of innovative military theorists, were purged and killed. Inevitably their ideas and theories fell under a shadow, and those officers who survived the purges were generally conservative and reluctant to embrace the ideas of their fallen predecessors. M. Zakharov, Chief of the Soviet General Staff in the 1960s said of the purges:

> the repression of 1937 and successive years brought to the army, as well as the rest of the country, tremendous harm. It deprived the Red Army and Navy of the most experienced and knowledgeable cadre and the most talented and highly qualified military leaders. It had a negative impact on the further development of military-theoretical thought. The deep study of military science problems ... became narrow ... Strategy in military academies ceased to be studied as a science and academic discipline. All that resulted from not only unfounded repression but also from an impasse in science, in particular military science. Military theory, in essence, amounted to a mosaic of Stalin's military expressions.

The theory of deep operations was subject to doubt because Stalin said nothing about it and its creator was an 'enemy of the people.' Some of the elements like, for example, the independent action of motor-mechanized and cavalry formations in advance of the front and in the depth of the enemy defense were even called sabotage and for that foolish reason were rejected –. Such measures attested to the about-face in military theory – back to the linear form of combat on an operational scale.[18]

As the shadows of the Second World War spread over Europe, the price the Soviet Union and the army paid for the purges slowly became apparent. While Soviet military analysts still used the term "operational" as a framework for analysis, that analysis was thin, and the results of the analysis were acted upon slowly. An article published in March 1941 analysing the May 1940 attack on France testified to continued analysis. It concluded by stating:

> to achieve a decisive victory and destroy the enemy army, operations of the modern army require, as the regulation (German) points out, cooperation and massive use in new forms of tank formations, motorized infantry, parachutists and aviation. The cooperation of these forces together with infantry carried out to the entire depth of the operation and the basic forms of operational art – surprise attack on the enemy, penetration, envelopment and encirclement – as before are recognized as the most valued means for achieving victory.

The article then qualified its commitment to deep mobile operations by stating:

> The powerful equipment of modern armies requires for successful defeat of the enemy not less than 2 to 1 superiority and large reserves in the shock group, which could, in the continuation of the operation, feed it with fresh forces while supporting the tempo of the offensive.
>
> In spite of the considerable specific weight (importance) in modern armies of aviation, artillery and tanks, the experience of war in the West affirms that infantry remains the main and basic type of force. All the strength of remaining types of forces are directed to secure infantry's unimpeded movement, to consolidate occupied territory, and to ease its fulfillment of the mission of destroying enemy forces.[19]

During the years of crisis immediately preceding the war, the Soviets attempted to repair damage done to operational art by the purges. Military council meetings, the reshuffling of General Staff personnel, and the wholesale reconstruction of mobile forces, however, could not compensate for the negative effects of inexperience and conservatism within the officer corps. By Soviet admission, military theorists were unable to generalize and use the experience of battle at Lake Khasan (1938), Khalkin-Gol (1939) or even the experiences of the Soviet–Finnish War (1939–40). Later, the Soviets bitterly claimed that "Fascist Germany used the methods of deep operations which we developed earlier. The Germans borrowed the achievements of Soviet military-theoretical thought and with great success used them in the war with Poland and the West."[20]

Soviet neglect of operational art cost the USSR dearly after June 1941. While claiming that the course of war confirmed the correctness of earlier Soviet theories on the preparation and conduct of *front* and army operations, in a masterful example of understatement the Soviets admit that

> commanders and staffs were not fully familiar with all the theories of conducting deep battle and there were shortcomings in the materiel base that hindered its realization. Thus, during the war it was necessary to reassess and clarify some aspects of preparing and conducting offensive operations and decide anew many questions on the conduct of defensive operations on a strategic and operational scale.[21]

THE TEST OF WAR

Those questions were addressed anew under the immense pressure of combat conditions and as a part of a quest for survival. The German attack in June 1941 yielded strategic, operational and tactical surprise and encountered only a partially prepared Soviet defense. To make matters worse, Soviet high level commanders performed with an ineptness which was only partially compensated for by the fervor of junior officers and the stoicism of the hard pressed troops. *Front* and army commanders often were unable to construct coherent defenses against the Germans' armored thrusts and displayed an alarming propensity for launching costly uncoordinated counterattacks almost predestined to fail. Looming disaster drove the Soviet High Command to action. Slowly it purged the command structure of inept commanders and the Soviet Army began to reeducate itself in the conduct of war, in particular concerning defense at the operational and tactical levels. *Front* commanders and the *STAVKA* itself played a major role in the re-forming of the Armed Forces by issuing new regulations and directives pertaining to the proper use of all types of forces. *STAVKA* Directive No. 3, issued on 10 January 1942, echoed an earlier Western Front Directive and ordered commanders to concentrate their forces and use shock groups to achieve success in offensive operations. *STAVKA* Order No. 306, issued in October 1942, required commanders to use single-echelon formations whenever possible to bring maximum force to bear on the German defenses, and *STAVKA* Order No. 325 of 16 October 1942 established parameters for the use of the fledgling tank forces, including the operational use of new tank and mechanized corps.[22] A *STAVKA* directive issued on 6 November 1942, entitled *Instructions Concerning the Study and Application of War Experience in Front and Army Staffs*, evidenced growing *STAVKA* concern for constructive (and necessary) study of all aspects of war, in particular operational aspects. Declaring that "the timely study, generalization and application of war experience is an important task of all commanders and staffs," the instructions ordered elements of *front* and army operational sections to collect systematically war experience. It stated:

> The basic task of these working groups is, under the orders of the chief of staff and under the direct supervision of the chief of operations section, to carry out on a daily basis for the entire command, the collection, study and generalization of war experience, and to make timely distribution by various media of the generalizations and conclusions of the study.[23]

The instructions specifically required war experience reports to address such operational concerns as: organization and conduct of *front* and army operations; control and direction of *front* and army operations and of combined arms combat; organization of coordination between the arms and services in operations and in combined-arms actions; the basic characteristics of infantry combat and of the actions of the arms and services under varying conditions; and a variety of the combined arms tasks.

The General Staff ultimately collected and published more than sixty massive volumes of war experiences. These provided the basis for innumerable orders issued to field headquarters concerning the conduct of operations and for the *Field Regulations* of 1942, 1943, and 1944. The 1942 Regulation incorporated the requirement to collect war experiences into the duties of the operations staff section at each level of Command.[24] The *Field Regulation of 1944*, without specifically resurrecting the early term deep battle, nevertheless stated: "this regulation views tank actions as a group of direct support for infantry and cavalry and as an echelon for exploiting successes in the operational depths with the support of powerful aviation."[25] The 1944 Regulation's concept of battle and its assignment of specific tasks to units marked the full realization of the aims of the 1936 Regulation. A central theme of the 1944 Regulation was the necessity to achieve tactical penetrations and the exploitation of those penetrations by mobile groups into the operational depths of the enemy defenses.

Other regulations underscored renewed Soviet interest in and refinement of basic operational techniques. The *Instructions on the Penetration of a Positional Defense* described the process of converting tactical into operational success stating:

> mobile formations, which are earmarked for the exploitation of success in the operational depth, can be used for the purpose of effecting an independent breakthrough or concluding the breakthrough of the second defence zone only if the resources of combined arms formations have been exhausted –. Once the combined arms formations have succeeded in breaking through the second defence zone, the mobile formations are immediately thrown into the breach in accordance with a prearranged plan.[26]

The regulation for the use of cavalry forces assigned those forces operational missions stating, "large cavalry forces – having high operational and tactical mobility – are operational formations of the Front and High Commands and are used in mass in the direction of the main effort."[27] Cavalry was specifically required to form part of the exploitation echelon and to conduct operational pursuit.

Thus, the refinement of Soviet operational practices, developed and used during the war years, found full theoretical expression in the orders, directives and instructions of the *STAVKA* and General Staff and in regulations and military writings. While those practices reflected the spirit of the deep battle theory of the 1930s, the Soviets avoided specific references both to deep battle and the creators of deep battle. The renaissance in Soviet military thought which occurred during the war years was driven by the reality of war and accomplished only because the specter of military and political collapse permitted it to occur. The major question in 1945 was whether Stalin would permit that renaissance to continue.

OPERATIONS AND THE REVOLUTION IN MILITARY AFFAIRS

In the immediate postwar years Soviet concern for the operational level of war continued. Stalinist controls over open and detailed discussion of operational matters in written works produced the outward appearance of extreme atrophy in Soviet military science. Most general texts and shorter articles paid deference to Stalin's role in military science and stressed the universal application of Stalin's permanent operating factors to matters of war. Whether the retrenchment in military art was real or a product of native Stalinist suspicion and censorship is debatable. What is clear is that Soviet military theory developed on the basis of the Second World War experiences; postwar operational art evolved in logical consequence to that experience, and the armed forces were restructured and reequipped in consonance with the evolving operational art and the wholesale postwar technological changes.

Although specific reference in Soviet postwar military literature to deep battle theory as the embodiment of operational art was absent, overall Soviet offensive concepts still mirrored the theory and practice of earlier deep operations concepts. A 1947 article on offensive combat parroted the 1936 and 1944 regulations by stating: "offensive combat consists in suppressing the enemy by the powerful fire of all weapons and a blow in his entire depth of defense and is conducted by a decisive offensive by the entire combat order."[28] A Frunze Academy lesson on rifle corps offensive operations declared that modern offensive operations were characterized "by the decisive nature of the actions, fast pace, great depth and wide and impetuous maneuver." Moreover:

> the rapid seizure of the tactical zone of the enemy defense by the large rifle units makes it possible to commit in the penetration the mobile groups (tanks, mechanized and large cavalry units) which carry out, in cooperation with the large rifle units and aviation, the decisive maneuver for the destruction of main enemy groupings —.[29]

The same lesson then sketched out the relationship between battles and operations stating:

> A number of battles broken up on the front and in the depth

tied in with each other by a single goal and aimed at the carrying out of an operational-tactical mission of the given stage of the operation is called a "large battle"–

Operations and large battles are carried out by armies, which are operational combinations, both independently and in cooperation with other armies; the rifle corps, as a large tactical unit, conducts combat operations which constitute a large battle.[30]

A 1945 article by Lt Gen Z. Zlobin described the *front* as the premier operational level organization created to perform both operational and strategic tasks. He described *front* operations as "a series of army operations executed either simultaneously or successively" and emphasized the deep aspect of operations stating:

the operational capabilities of these new weapons increase the depth and range of operations and make it possible to split the operational structure of the enemy along the front and in the depth into separate isolated pockets and destroy them one by one –. The ultimate objective of this maneuver is to encircle and defeat the resisting enemy forces in a given direction with the envelopment of the whole depth of his operational organization.[31]

In the postwar period the vertical dimension of operational level warfare emerged as a product of wartime experiences. An article on airlanding operations stated that airlanding operational missions would be conducted in support of a *front* "at a point when the operation has developed to the point where the enemy's system of defense in depth has been broken, his reserves have been committed or the possibility has already arisen of disrupting the combat formation of his main body."[32] These and a host of other articles, lectures, and theoretical works attested to the fact that operational art remained a major concern in the postwar Soviet Army. Moreover, specific operational techniques still sought to attain the goals of deep battle, although the terminology itself was avoided for obvious political reasons.

While the Soviets refined their theories for the conduct of operations within the overall context of Stalin's permanent operating factors, the precise definition of operational art remained consistent with those objectives set forth by Svechin in 1927. A 1953 survey of Soviet military art described operational art as a component of military art, interconnected and interrelated with the other components, strategy and tactics. Operational art had the function of "working out the principles of organizing and conducting army and *front* operations – in a theater of military operations which most closely correspond to the given stage of war, while governed by the dictates of strategy and the aims of strategy." As such the

> theory of operational art arms the cadre of our army with a creative approach in matters of the use of forces and means, designated for the conduct of operations of *front* and army significance, and teaches them that the achievement of overall strategic results can be secured only by an unswerving increase in the combat success of forces.[33]

The death of Stalin in 1953 and the growing prospect that future war would be nuclear had an enormous impact on Soviet military thought and the structure of Soviet military forces. Stalin's death permitted Soviet military theorists slowly to strip off the veneer of Stalinist principles which had insulated that theory from outside examination and which had prevented more active open discussion of operational questions. It also allowed those theorists to ponder more fully the likelihood and nature of nuclear war. Theoretical debates grew in intensity and culminated in 1960 with full Soviet recognition of the existence of a "Revolution in Military Affairs," a revolution created by prospects that future war would be nuclear. Stalin's death also presaged G. K. Zhukov's wholesale reorganization of the Soviet Armed Forces and the subsequent reorganization of 1960–62 aimed at creating a force capable of fighting and surviving in a nuclear environment.

In general terms, the revolution in military affairs did not alter appreciably the definition of operational art. It did, however, signal a de-emphasis of operational art with regard to questions of strategy and, in particular, it evidenced lessened concern for conventional operational techniques and greater concern for strategic nuclear concepts. This shift in emphasis was apparent in the works of V. A. Semenov, V. D. Sokolovsky, and A. A. Strokov and in the relative decrease in the number of articles in Soviet military journals analyzing the operational techniques of the Second World War. The operational literature published during this period began making direct reference to the older concept of deep battle but implied that deep operational concepts of the 1930s had been stillborn.

V. A. Semenov's survey of operational art stated:

> In the 30s the theories of Soviet operational art were deepened

and firmed up in conformity with the actions of large units – armies and *fronts*. This found expression in the working out of instruction on the preparation and conduct of deep offensive operations (*glubokaia nastupatel' naia operatsiia*), in regulations and instructions of the Red Army and also in a series of military-theoretical works on operational questions ...[34]

Semenov acknowledged that these theoretical works recognized that "future offensive operations – will be more active, will pursue decisive aims, and will develop in the manner of powerful successive blows to the entire operational depth of the enemy defense." Semenov noted, however, that, despite these theorists' efforts, "expedient means and forms of penetrating and developing success in the operational depths were not found nor were methods of using existing forces and means in an operation and battle." Semenov left to later authors the task of explaining just why that theoretical development had not been realized in practice. He argued, however, that during the Second World War Soviet operational art overcame prewar weaknesses and solved a myriad of offensive and defensive problems including that of "developing the offensive to great depth."

Having dealt with the origins and evolution of operational art, Semenov offered a current definition which echoed earlier definitions. Operational art, as a component of military art subordinate to strategy, concerned itself with working out the following questions:

– the study of the nature of operations on the basis of military-historical experience;
– the perception of the laws governing operations;
– the development of basic means and forms for preparing and conducting operations.

Finally, Semenov declared that "operational art at the present has been transformed into a large scientific field of military affairs, possessing its own theory, its own specific rules, its own problems, and its own scientifically grounded methodology."[35]

In his analysis of operational art Semenov recognized the existence of atomic weaponry but played down its effect. Thus, "under contemporary conditions the use of weapons of mass destruction in operations can achieve greatest success only in combination with artillery fire and aviation strikes." Moreover, "the use of atomic weapons considerably lessens the requirements for artillery in the conduct of an offensive operation, but that new weapon cannot entirely abolish or replace artillery and aviation, which will play a large role in the course of an operation."[36] Semenov warned that the appearance of new weapons always required careful reassessment of operational art and the development of powerful nuclear weapons made such study essential.

By 1962 that reassessment was complete and Soviet theoreticians articulated new, more extreme views regarding the "revolution in military affairs." The new view of the "revolution," prompted in part by Premier N. S. Khrushchev, recognized the preeminence of nuclear weapons in war, elevated the relative importance of strategy (signified by the establishment of and emphasis on strategic rocket forces) and diminished the importance of operational art. The work best illustrating this changing emphasis was V. D. Sokolovsky's *Military Strategy (Strategiia Voennaia)*. In it he maintained that "both gigantic military coalitions will deploy massive armies in a future decisive world war; all modern, powerful and long range means of combat, including multimegaton nuclear-rocket weapons, will be used in it on a huge scale; and the most decisive methods of military operations will be used."[37] Strategic nuclear forces may decide the outcome of war in themselves without resort to extended ground operations. If ground operations were required, they would be conducted in close concert with nuclear strikes. Thus, according to Sokolovsky:

> Mass nuclear-rocket strikes will be of decisive importance for the attainment of goals in a future world war. The infliction of these assaults will be the main, decisive method of waging war — armed conflict in ground theaters of military operations will also take place differently. The defeat of the enemy's groupings of ground troops, the destruction of his rockets, aircraft and nuclear weapons — will be achieved mainly by nuclear-rocket strikes. — Great possibilities are created for waging extensive mobile offensive operations with the aid of highly mobile mechanized troops.[38]

The ground forces would exploit the effects of nuclear strikes, defeat enemy forces, and conquer and occupy territory. In this nuclear environment, ground forces would play a distinctly secondary role to strategic rocket forces. Thus strategy became dominant over operational art.

All this shows that the relationship between the role and importance of armed combat waged by forces in direct contact with the enemy in the zone of combat actions, employing simultaneously tactical, operational and strategic means of destruction on the one hand and the role and importance of armed combat waged beyond the confines of this zone by strategic means alone on the other hand has shifted abruptly towards an increase in role and importance of the latter.[39]

A. A. Strokov, writing in 1966, noted the increased stature of strategy, stating, "Nuclear-rocket weapons have emerged as strategic means. The arming of large units and formations with them has produced a change in operational art and tactics." Specifically, the use of such weapons could achieve strategic results "independently from the conduct of operations and battles (operational art and tactics)."[40] In general war, operational art was only an adjunct to the use of nuclear weapons, although it did regain its importance in "local" wars.

REEMERGENCE OF THE OPERATIONAL LEVEL AND THE REBIRTH OF DEEP OPERATIONS

Soviet preoccupation with nuclear war and the importance of strategy, and the resulting eclipse of operational art began to erode after the mid-1960s. Although theorists couched their investigation of military art in a clear nuclear context, the amount of attention devoted to operational art and operational techniques mushroomed. Such theoretical works as V. G. Reznichenko's *Tactics*, A. Kh. Babadzanian's *Tanks and Tank Forces* and A. A. Sidorenko's *The Offensive*, while retaining a strong nuclear context, devoted considerably more attention to operational techniques. Simultaneously, a wave of comprehensive studies began appearing on virtually every aspect of the Red Army's operational experience in the Second World War (in particular its later stages). As if to keynote these new concerns, the Soviets published an anthology of works written by preeminent pre-Second World War military theorists. This work entitled *Questions of Strategy and Operational Art in Soviet Military Works (1917–1940)* signaled the rehabilitation of the purged generation of Tukhachevsky and renewed interest in deep operations and the techniques necessary to achieve them. The preface to the volume, written by Chief of the General Staff M. V. Zakharov, completed the story of prewar failure which Semenov in 1960 had begun to relate. The works of P. A. Kurochkin and A. I. Radzievsky (the combined arms army); I. E. Krupchenko, R. A. Rotmistrov, A. I. Radzievsky and O. A. Losik (tank forces); I. I.

Lisov and later D. Sukhorukov (airborne forces) and a host of other writers intensely analysed Second World War combat experiences. I. Kh. Bagramian's general history of war and military art added operational detail to the general descriptions of nuclear war presented earlier by Strokov, and V. E. Savkin cast light on the nature of contemporary operational art and tactics.[41]

The intense and ongoing concern for operational art, paralleled by Soviet restructuring of the armed forces to improve its operational capabilities, has elevated the importance of that field from its relative position of neglect in the early 1960s to a major area of contemporary concern. The nearly total subservience of operational art to the overall strategic considerations of nuclear war has lessened. Even the seemingly mandatory nuclear context for the discussion of operational art is often absent. Thus, "successful operations by formations and units of the armed forces, or branches of the armed forces, and of specialized forces, especially during combat using conventional weapons, retain their importance."[42]

Since the late 1960s and early 1970s the growing importance of operational art has been underscored by the increased degree of importance attached to operations in theoretical writings and by the intensified Soviet focus on theater, *front*, and army operations, often in a conventional context. Even Sokolovsky's view has evolved. In 1962, he wrote,

> Armed combat in ground theaters of military operations will also take place differently. A defeat of the enemy's groupings of ground troops, the destruction of his rockets, aircraft, and nuclear weapons in carrying out any operation, will be achieved mainly by nuclear-rocket strikes.[43]

The 1968 version of Sokolovsky's *Strategy* transformed this blunt statement into a question:

> But in essence, the argument is about the basic method of conducting future war: will it be land war with the use of the nuclear weapons as a means of supporting the operations of ground troops, or a war that is essentially new, where the main means of solving strategic tasks will be the nuclear rocket weapon? The theory of military art must give an answer to such important questions as: what types of strategic actions will be used in a nuclear war, and what form military operations must take.[44]

His tentative answer was that theater operations would occur, but on the battlefield "the decisive role will be played by fires of nuclear weapons; the other means of armed combat will utilize the results of nuclear strikes for the final defeat of the enemy."[45]

From the late 1970s and on into the 1980s a definite shift in emphasis away from Sokolovsky's fixation on the dominance of nuclear weapons had occurred and is still occurring. The Soviets agree that the introduction of nuclear weapons has altered the development of operational art and changed the nature of operations. Thus, "along with battles and engagements one could now include nuclear strikes, which play a main role in achieving assigned objectives."[46] The addition of nuclear weapons and other technological means (radio-electronic, advanced high precision weaponry) have increased the combat capabilities of large units to participate in combined and joint operations and have improved command and control of those units, while, at the same time, they have complicated the task of coordinating, securing, and supporting those operations. Recent technological changes have altered traditional Soviet concepts of mass and concentration and have necessitated future Soviet reliance on operational and tactical maneuver and smaller combined arms entities operating in concert.

Changes in technology and methods of warfare have made the initial period of war vastly more important:

> First operations have acquired decisive importance. They will be distinguished by surprise, decisive aims and operations from the very beginning, over large areas, with high dynamism, by massive use of forces and weapons to destroy important objectives, by participation of large quantities of various types of armed forces, by keen radio-electronic combat, and by complicated command and control and rear area security.[47]

Moreover, the operational tasks of the ground forces will be extensive, including: the conduct of offensive and defensive operations of various scale and composition under varying conditions and situations; the conduct of hasty and extensive operational regrouping for combat; and participation in air assault and amphibious assault operations. The ground forces will perform all of these tasks on a greater scale and with greater dynamism and speed than in the Great Patriotic War.

However, in carefully chosen words the Soviets now qualify Sokolovsky's words on the nature of war stating:

> In nuclear war, if it is unleashed by aggressive countries,

simultaneous nuclear strikes on the enemy and skillful exploitation of the results of those strikes is most important. During combat with only conventional weaponry skillful concentration of superior forces and weaponry is required to deliver blows on selected axes and also rapid dispersal of those forces after fulfillment of the combat missions.[48]

By adding the statement, "further development of army aviation and other mobile means attach to the operation a more dynamic and maneuverable character," Soviet theorists again raise the issue of deep operations. Specifically:

the possibilities of defeating the enemy in the entire depth of his operation combat formations have increased. Motorized rifle and tank forces, in coordination with other types of armed forces and branches of forces, can perform very complicated combat tasks with decisive aims, at great depths and at a high tempo.[49]

This modern reaffirmation of earlier principles of deep operations is symptomatic of renewed Soviet interest in that subject. The current Soviet theory of the theater strategic offensive incorporates both the concept of deep operations and that of successive operations. Future successive operations will unfold without pause into the enemy's operational and strategic depths, propelled in part by new concepts of air and ground force echelonment.[50] The burgeoning amount of research and writing on modernized theories of deep battle and deep operations and the mechanics of their implementation testify to the dominant position those older, battle tested theories occupy in current Soviet operational art. In this regard Soviet theorists have heeded the words of former Chief of the General Staff Zakharov, who wrote in 1970, "the theory of deep operations has not lost its significance today. It can serve as a basis for the creative work of command cadres when resolving the many-sided and complex problems of today."[51]

CHAPTER THREE

THE FRAMEWORK OF OPERATIONS

Operational art by definition directly concerns itself with the preparation and conduct of operations within distinct geographical limits to achieve aims and objectives commensurate with the political goals of the nation. National political goals dictate the strategic nature and form of an operation and, hence, establish the context for operational and tactical measures necessary to achieve the strategic goals. To define the relationship between the distinct levels of war, the Soviets have developed an elaborate set of terms related to war aims, the geographical arena of operations, and the size and nature of forces engaged. These terms provide a framework essential for understanding the nature of past, contemporary, and future operations (see table 3).

MISSIONS

The strategic aim (*strategicheskaia tsel'*) of any conflict dictates the nature, scope and form of military operations.[1] Established by the political leadership of a nation, strategic aims represent the desired end of strategic-scale military actions. Achievement of strategic aims generally leads to significant, and sometimes fundamental, changes in military-political and strategic conditions, which, in turn, can contribute to the victorious conclusion of a war. The Soviets subdivided strategic aims into overall (*obshchie*) strategic aims which represent the "fundamental results of the war" and particular (*chastnye*) strategic aims, which result from successful campaigns or strategic operations. The strategic war aims determine the size and nature of strategic groupings of forces within a theater of military operations or on a strategic direction and determine the form of military actions undertaken. These aims transcend all other considerations.

TABLE 3

RELATIONSHIP OF TERMINOLOGY WITH MISSION, TERRITORY, ACTION, AND FORCE

MISSIONS	TERRITORY	ACTIONS	FORCE*	
Strategic Aim	Theater of military Operations (TVD)	Strategic operation		High Command of forces in a TVD (group of fronts)
Strategic Mission	Strategic direction	Front operation**		Operational-strategic large unit (front)
Operational Mission	Operational direction	Army operation battle (srazhenie)	Operational large unit (army)	Operational formation (airborne division)
			Operational-tactical large unit (corps)	Operational-tactical formation (corps)
Tactical Mission		Battle (boi)	Unit (regiment)	Tactical formation (division)
			Subunit (battalion)	

* Units and formations can help perform missions at a range of levels. Thus an airborne division, although it is an operational formation, can perform a tactical, operational, or strategic mission. Mission transcends all other considerations.

** also includes air, air defense and airborne/naval landing operations, and in some cases, strategic nuclear strikes in the theater.

TERRITORY

Strategic aims are achieved by warfare conducted in theaters of war and theaters of military operations.[2] The theater of war (*teatr voiny*) is that area, usually of continental size with adjacent oceans and airspace, where nations or coalitions of nations, conduct operations on a strategic scale.

A theater of war lacks distinct geographical boundaries but usually encompasses several theaters of military operations (for example, Western Europe from the North Cape of Norway to the Mediterranean Sea). A theater of military operations (*teatr voennykh deistvii*-TVD) is a portion of a continent with associated coastal areas, inland seas, and airspace, within whose limits strategic groupings of forces (air, land or sea) deploy and conduct military operations (for example, Central Europe from the Baltic Sea to the Alps). The size, geographical limits, and composition of a theater of military operations are determined by a nation's political and military leadership and depend on the nature of strategic aims, the location of important strategic objectives, and the possibilities for deploying and employing large strategic groupings of forces in the region.

Within theaters of military operations are strategic directions (*strategicheskie napravleniia*), extensive areas within which large groups of forces can deploy and conduct operations to accomplish strategic missions[3] (for example, the Northern German plain approach to Western Europe on an axis Berlin–Hannover–the Ruhr–Brussels–Antwerp). Strategic missions (*strategicheskie zadachi*) are component parts of a strategic aim. They are large scale and involve fundamentally important tasks whose successful fulfillment can produce sharply changed conditions within a theater of military operations or on a strategic direction. Successful accomplishments of strategic missions contribute to the achievement of particular aims or the overall strategic aim.[4] Strategic groupings of forces consisting of *fronts* (army groups), armies, and divisions of various types of forces operate on strategic directions in order to fulfill strategic missions.

The Soviets further subdivide strategic directions into operational directions (*operativnie napravleniia*), which are territorial sectors with associated coastlines and airspace in which important operational objectives are located.[5] *Fronts*, armies, divisions and units of all types conduct operations on operational directions to accomplish operational missions. Operational missions (*opera-tivnye zadachi*), when successfully accomplished, contribute to successful conduct of the entire strategic operation, and usually require that specific operational objectives be achieved within a specified period of time.[6]

Thus, strategic aims, strategic missions, and operational missions are interdependent. They relate to distinct geographical arenas — the theater of military operations, the strategic direction, and the operational direction — and they are carried out by operations and forces tailored to suit precise goals.

ACTIONS

The Soviets define the operation (*operatsiia*), the basic building block for the conduct of war, as:

> a totality of battles, strikes and maneuvers of various types of forces united by mutual aims, missions, location, and timing, conducted simultaneously or successively according to a single concept or plan aimed at accomplishing missions in a theater of military operations, on a strategic direction or operational directions — in a predetermined period of time.[7]

Within and beneath the operational level, the Soviets categorize and define a range of combat actions that differentiate between operations of various scales and types (e.g. air, air defense, naval, frontal, etc) and distinguish operations from tactical combat (see table 4). The operation is a basic form of combat action, and can be strategic, *front* or army. Based upon its forces it can be combined arms, combined, or independent; or by virtue of its orientation it can be offensive or defensive. According to its timing it can be initial or subsequent.

The basic nature of an operation and its manner of preparation and conduct "is decisively influenced" by a number of factors including:

— war aims and the nature of strategic and operational missions;
— the military-economic capabilities of the nation;
— the combat capabilities of opposing forces;
— the physical-geographical features of the theater of military operations;
— command and control systems;

TABLE 4

FORMS OF COMBAT ACTION (*BOEVYE DEISTVIIA*)

combat (*boi*)	an organized clash of combatant units
blow (*udar*)	a short term attack on the enemy with conventional or nuclear forces or weapons (nuclear, torpedo, main, frontal, flank)
battle (*srzahenie*)	an aggregate of combat and blows aimed at achieving operational aims or particular objectives. The basic form of army combat actions.
operation (*operatsiia*)	actions conducted by large operational units (*front*, army); an aggregate of combat, blows and battles conducted in a theater of military operations or on a strategic (operational) axis, with mutual and interconnected aims, locations, and timing, according to a single concept or plan aimed at achieving strategic, operational-strategic or operational objectives (strategic, *front*, army, flotilla)
systematic combat (*sistematicheskie boevye deistviia*)	actions conducted with limited missions and aims during the intervals between major operations (reconnaissance, air attacks, counterattacks, radio-electronic combat, etc.)

— the morale-political condition of the forces;
— the level of operational, tactical and political training.[8]

The Soviets define the largest-scale operation, the strategic operation (*strategicheskaia operatisiia*), as a "totality of operations, strikes and combat actions united by aims, mission, place and time, of large units [*fronts*, armies] and formations [divisions] of various types of armed forces, conducted according to a single concept or plan in order to achieve strategic aims."[9] In modern war the strategic operation is the basic form of strategic combat action conducted in a continental (oceanic) theater of military operations. It usually involves the participation of several *fronts* (fleets), strategic nuclear forces, aviation formations, and air defense forces. A strategic operation may be either offensive or defensive and may also be used to repel an enemy attack from the air or outer space (cosmos) (the Soviets included the COSMOS (space) in this definition after 1980). Each *front* participating in a strategic operation "can conduct successively two or more *front* operations."[10] Thus a strategic operation within a TVD will consist of successive operations conducted with or without pause.

A strategic operation within a TVD normally consists of air, air defense, naval landing, and several *front* operations conducted simultaneously or successively. In its turn, a *front* operation consists of several army and/or corps operations. The Soviets define operations further by assigning to them certain indices (norms) related to: quantity of forces; width of combat sectors; duration of the operation; and, on the offensive, the depth and tempo of operations. Norms are descriptive rather than rigidly prescriptive; and they permit analysis of past operations, study of present operations, and sound planning for future operations. In essence, they provide a realistic frame of reference for military planners and commanders. Norms are derived from analysis of past experience juxtaposed against changes in technology, analysis of exercises, war games, and simulations, as well as study of real current conditions.

A *front* operation (*frontovaia operatsiia*), a component part of a strategic operation, represents:

> a totality of operations, battles, strikes, and maneuvers united by aims, mission, place, and time, conducted according to a single concept or plan by *front* forces in cooperation with large units [*fronts*, armies] and formations [divisions] of various types of armed forces.[11]

Front operations can be offensive or defensive.

A *front* offensive operation (*frontovaia nastupatel' naia operatsiia*) aims at "defeating enemy army groups and occupying their territory on one strategic or several operational directions within a continental theater of military operations."[12] A *front* defensive operation (*frontovaia oboronitel' naia operatsiia*) seeks to

> frustrate an enemy offensive operation on a distinct strategic direction, strike a blow against his attacking force, hold on to separate regions containing important objectives, win time, economize forces, and create conditions for transition of one's own forces to a counterattack or resumption of offensive operations.[13]

Front operations can occur as a part of a strategic operation in a continental theater of military operations or as an independent operation. *Front* operations normally include the following types:

Type	Posture
— first and successive operations (on separate directions)	offense
— operations of first echelon armies and corps	offense and defense
— operations of second echelon armies and corps	offense and defense
— *front* counterattacks	defense
— combat actions of *front* rocket forces, artillery, air forces, air defense forces, specialized forces and *front* reserves	offense and defense
— air assault and amphibious assault operations	offense
— repulse of amphibious assaults in cooperation with naval forces	defense

Front defensive operations can be prompted by enemy action or can be voluntarily undertaken as a prelude to a subsequent offensive. Offensive and defensive *front* operations are composed of several distinct army operations conducted in cooperation with other *front* forces and naval elements.

An army operation (*armeiskaia operatsiia*), the major component of a *front* operation, is conducted by a combined arms or tank army in cooperation with other armies and *front* forces and, when appropriate, with naval forces. Army operations are either offensive or defensive. An army offensive operation (*armeiskaia nastupatel'naia operatsiia*) seeks to "destroy defending enemy groups and secure regions (objectives) of operational importance," while an army defensive operation (*armeiskaia oboronitel'naia operatsiia*) aims at "disrupting the offensive of a superior enemy, striking blows at his forces, holding important boundaries (regions), winning time, and creating conditions for resumption of the offensive."[14] Although most armies operate as a part of a *front*, an army can conduct independent offensive or defensive operations in separate operational directions. Army operations include combat by army first and second echelon forces, rocket forces, and artillery, aviation, air defense, specialized and army reserve forces.

Beneath the hierarchy of operations, which are given shape, substance and a degree of coherence by strategy and operational art, exist the individual combats, attacks, and battles that complete the spectrum of combat. These lower level actions, with their associated tactical missions, are the subject of the tactical level at war.

FORCES

Parallel to and reflecting this framework for operations are organized elements within the armed forces which prepare for and conduct operations at the various levels of war. While there is a general correlation between the size of units, the area within which they operate, and the scope of mission they perform, that correlation is not absolute. In fact, it is ultimately the mission that a unit performs that determines the level of war within which it operates.

The Soviets use generic terms to describe elements of their armed forces force structure. Specific types of units in the force structure fall into one of several generic categories called *ob' edinenie, soedinenie, chast'*, and *podrazdelenie* – in order of decreasing size. Each category is further defined by the type of mission the force performs and the level of war at which it operates.

The largest generic category with respect to size is the *ob' edinenie* (literally a unification or union) which the Soviets define as a "troop formation (*formirovanie*), including several *soedineniia* (divisions) or *ob' edineniia* of smaller composition (armies) as well as units (*chast'*, regiments) and establishments."[15] Based upon the composition of each and the mission which it is assigned, the *ob' edinenie* can be labeled operational-strategic, operational, or operational-tactical.

Operational-Strategic Ob' edineniia: Fronts

The first type of *ob' edinenie* is operational-strategic in nature and consists of several *ob' edineniia* of smaller composition (armies), separate *soedineniia* (divisions), and *chasti* (regiments) of various types of forces. The most common units in this category are *fronts*, fleets, and, in Western armies, army groups. Although fleets exist in peacetime, *fronts* are formed only in wartime (usually from forces of a military district (*voennyi okrug*)), each labeled a territorial combined arms *ob' edinenie* (*territorial' noe obshchevoiskovoe ob' edinenie*) and bearing responsibility for preparation for wartime operations. In wartime, operational-strategic *ob' edineniia* are normally controlled by the High Command or the theater of military operations (TVD) commander (a TVD may be controlled by a commander with a full staff, by an operational group, or by a High Command Representative).

Operational Ob' edineniia: Armies

The second type of *ob' edinenie* is operational and consists of several *soedineniia* (divisions) and *chasti* (regiments) from several branches of one service of the armed forces. Existing in peacetime as well as wartime, operational *ob' edineniia* fulfill the basic operational tasks of conducting combined arms, independent, or combined operations. This category includes armies, flotillas, squadrons and other more specialized commands. In wartime, operational large units can be part of an operational-strategic large unit (*front*) or they can be independent.

Operational-Tactical Ob' edineniia: Corps

The third and last category is the operational-tactical *ob' edinenie*, which consists of *soedineniia* (divisions) and *chasti* (regiments) of various types from one branch of the armed forces. Operating usually as part of an operational-strategic *ob' edinenie* (*front*), although sometimes as part of an operational *ob' edinenie* (army), this *ob' edinenie* performs operational-tactical and tactical missions. In wartime the operational-tactical *ob' edinenie* is usually part of a combined arms army or *front*, and in peacetime it is subordinate to a military district. Various types of corps can be operational-tactical large units.

Beneath the *ob' edinenie* in size and role is the *soedinenie* (literally a combination). This the Soviets define as a "troop formation [*formirovanie*] consisting of several units [*chasti*-regiments] or formations of lesser size, usually various types of forces, specialized forces, as well as security and support units (subunits)."[16] Most *soedineniia* are permanent with a fixed TOE (establishment) organization. Depending on their mission, their composition, and the nature of the theater of military operations, *soedineniia* can be called operational, operational-tactical or tactical.

Operational Soedineniia

Operational *soedineniia* are usually temporary ones assigned limited-scale operational or operational-strategic missions either as part of an operational-strategic *ob' edinenie* (*front*) or as an independent force (for example, an operational group or an airborne division used in an operational air landing mission subordinate to *front* control).

Operational-Tactical Soedineniia

Operational-tactical *soedineniia* of either permanent or temporary makeup fulfill operational-tactical or operational missions as part of an operational-strategic *ob'edinenie (front)* or as part of an independent force fulfilling a limited mission on a separate operational direction.

Tactical Soedineniia

Tactical *soedineniia* having permanent TOEs perform tactical missions as part of an operational *ob'edinenie* (army) or of an operational-tactical *soedinenie* (corps). The basic units in this category are the various types of TOE divisions.

Within the *ob'edinenie* and *soedinenie* are *chasti* (regiments) and *podrazdelania* (battalions) that engage in combat at the tactical level of war.

CONCLUSION

The Soviet framework for operations is both comprehensive and useful. It integrates the factor of geography with the decisive requirements of aim and mission, and it categorizes forces and units based on the combat functions they are called upon to perform. In addition, the functional framework subdividing warfare into strategic, operational and tactical levels embraces a host of other military considerations, including such diverse areas as planning, deception, the grouping and regrouping of forces, the conduct of maneuver, and the role of reserves. The Soviets use precise terms to distinguish between the fielding and deployment of military forces to engage in combat actions within each level of war. Thus, at the strategic level, as the Soviets carry out strategic deployment of forces (*strategicheskoe razvertyvanie*), at the operational level they array their forces in operational formation (*operativnoe postroenie*), and at the tactical level they deploy forces in combat formation (*boevoi poriadok*). Likewise, the Soviets describe maneuver as strategic, operational, and tactical; and they form strategic, operational, and tactical reserves. Each of these terms is unique to the level of war it describes and involves specific actions and techniques geared to that level of war.

No single term in this framework can be understood without

understanding the relationship of all the terms and the broader relationship of the strategic, operational, and tactical levels of war. Such an understanding provides a necessary context for studying Soviet operations and operational art, and the Soviet approach to the conduct of war in general.

This Soviet framework for operations, with its seemingly complex array of levels and terms, is the result of long-term study and reflection on the nature of war. It is a true distillate of vast military experience, and it is that experience which undergirds its validity. Because of that study and reflection, the terminology automatically has meaning to those who have properly studied war. The logic of the structure will be apparent to all those who wish to understand how and why the Soviet Army operates the way it does.

CHAPTER FOUR

THE FORMATIVE YEARS OF SOVIET OPERATIONAL ART – 1917–1941

INTRODUCTION

Few nations have suffered more from the effects of war and armed struggle than has the Soviet Union and its historical ancestor, the great Russian state. The realities of geographical location and the existence of neighbors whose strength or weakness made them either potential threats to Russia's existence or potential victims of Russian expansionism contributed to that long history of armed struggle. The immense size of Russia's population and land area produced conflicts of vast scope and often epic proportions. Frustrations born of long and bitter wars produced on the part of the would-be invaders and the Russians alike a combat ferocity seldom matched in other wars. The impact of these ferocious struggles reinforced a natural Russian penchant for the study of war.

In the twentieth century ideology has provided further impetus for Soviet study of the nature of war and has shaped the form of that study. The revolutionary mission inherent in Soviet Marxism-Leninism provides a basic element of continuity throughout all areas of military doctrine and imparts to Soviet strategy, operational art, and tactics a distinctly offensive character. That offensive character has been tempered by reality and by a Soviet belief in the inevitable victory of Socialism, a belief which conditions the Soviets to approach war cautiously – as a means to an end but by no means the only one. It has also conditioned the Soviets periodically to emphasize the defensive nature of their doctrine to meet practical political necessities. In this sense, Soviet ideology displays a patience not apparent in other militant twentieth century ideologies (most notably Fascism). To the Soviets, war has been and is a phenomenon requiring careful study and cautious application. Moreover, its use must correspond with the conditions of the times. This and subsequent chapters will reflect on these conditions and address

how the Soviets have approached the science of war throughout the
twentieth century.

Largely due to ideological considerations, the broader aspects of
Soviet military doctrine have remained remarkably consistent since
1917. The ideological tenets of Soviet military doctrine and the
scope and requirements of military science and military art have
changed little. Nor have the parameters of strategy, operational art,
and tactics significantly changed. What has changed are the conditions confronting Soviet military science and the conclusions
the Soviets have reached regarding the role of war and methods
required for its conduct.

Of principal concern to the Soviets has been the necessity for
preserving the Socialist revolution though maintaining the security
of the Soviet homeland. Tangentially, the Soviets have also sought
to protect the homeland by seeking to create adjacent buffer
regions, regions under Soviet control or neutralized areas. Concurrently, the Soviets have waged war (under war's broadest definition)
to assist in the expansion of Socialism – in essence to hasten the
inevitable. Characteristically, this warfare has been primarily
political, diplomatic, economic, and social, and only seldom has it
involved armed conflict. The manner in which the Soviets have
waged war and the attitude they have assumed towards all aspects of
military science usually have been affected by changing world
conditions (the correlation of forces) and by realities (usually
political and economic) within the Soviet Union itself. Militarily,
the central issue the Soviets have addressed is how best to structure
Soviet society and institutions to achieve maximum military
potential and meet security requirements while not overly inhibiting the economic growth potential of the nation as a whole.

Soviet military development forms several distinct periods, each
marked by a series of unique challenges the Soviets have had to
address. Principal among these have been political, military and
technological challenges. In the post-revolutionary years of the
1920s, world conditions forced the Soviet Union to retrench and
adopt a defensive military posture, a posture consistent with her
economic weakness and domestic political uncertainty at home and
her political isolation from the world community. Reinforcing this
posture was Soviet inability to compete technologically with more
advanced Western nations. Stalin's consolidation of power,
collectivization of agriculture, and forced industrialization of the
Soviet economy through institution of the Five Year Plans drastically
altered Soviet military potential. The resulting Soviet rearmament

of the 1930s was paralleled by a renaissance in Soviet military thought and wholesale changes in Soviet military art which made the Soviet military one of the world's most progressive, in theory and, to an increasing extent, in practice. This renaissance abruptly ended in 1937 with the purge of most of the Soviet military leadership, a purge that ripped the dynamism out of Soviet military thought and practice when it was most needed, and left the Soviets drifting towards the next challenge, that of surviving war against a foe bent on destroying the Soviet state.

The second period of challenge (and the most difficult) opened in 1941 with the German invasion of the Soviet Union. The ensuing disasters of 1941 and 1942 left the Soviets with the herculean task of revitalizing Soviet military art at all levels, reconstructing the Soviet armed forces, and creating the economic strength and weaponry necessary to win the war. This the Soviets did, while fighting a war for their very survival. The regeneration of a highly refined force structure, the development of a competent officers corps to command that force structure, and the articulation of an advanced military theory to govern all levels of war occurred in a short period of three years, but at a tremendous cost to the Soviet nation. These experiences of 1943–45 represented the most creative period in Soviet military art, and it is to that period that contemporary theorists most often turn for inspiration and concrete guidance on contemporary strategic, operational and tactical matters.

The immediate post-Second World War period saw some retrenchment in Soviet military thought as Stalin reasserted his full control over the state. In this period, however, the third and most recent challenge was already emerging. That new challenge had two facets. The first facet was the emerging dominance of nuclear weapons over military affairs. The second facet, one which complicated the first, was the changing world political order characterized by the emergence of the U.S. (ultimately with its allies) as the Soviet's primary foe and the creation of power vacuums in the Third World as colonial relationships weakened.

A new renaissance has occurred in Soviet military thought to master the new challenge. Intense Soviet analysis of all aspects of military science has accelerated since the death of Stalin and the period of de-Stalinization. Early in this new renaissance Soviet theorists accepted the fact that a "revolution" had occurred in military affairs, and they adjusted their thought to the needs of that revolution. However, the revolution resulted in nuclear stalemate. Thus, in the early 1970s the Soviets began seeking ways out of the nuclear dilemma. Since that time Soviet writings and actions have reflected an attempt to escape from the paralysis that strategic nuclear weapons has imposed on military affairs by developing new options for the use of military force. This process in many ways has resembled the period of intellectual ferment of the 1920s–30s when Soviet theorists sought solutions for the dilemmas posed by the positional warfare of the First World War – warfare also paralyzed by the crushing weight of firepower and technology. Simultaneously, the Soviets have embraced new, less direct, and less risky forms of armed conflict, variously labeled wars of national liberation, local wars and war by proxy. As the nineties approach military theorists ponder the new challenge of a technological revolution in conventional weaponry which threatens to make those weapons as lethal on the battlefield as their nuclear counterparts.

These recurring challenges are an inherent ingredient in the Marxist dialectic and the Soviets accept them as such. Characteristically, the Soviets approach each challenge with gusto and intellectual vigor. Experience indicates their success in meeting challenges. It has also been characteristic for Soviet military art to stagnate when challenges fade. Whether this is inherent in the system or historical irony is simply conjecture.

THE CIVIL WAR AND LENINIST BASE OF MILITARY DOCTRINE (1917–1921)

Context

In the chaotic, uncertain days following the Bolshevik Revolution of November 1917, the Red Army was born, and with it a Marxist-Leninist military doctrine. That doctrine matured during the Civil War years, when internal struggle and foreign intervention threatened the fledgling Bolshevik regime's existence. The Bolshevik (Communist) Party maintained close control over political power and, understanding the realities of politics, also seized a commanding position in the formulation of official military doctrine. Lenin was the chief interpreter of Marxism, and the new Marxist-Leninist theory encompassed all aspects of man's existence, especially the relationship of statecraft and military power.

Lenin's voluminous theoretical work found partial expression in the concepts he formulated in *Imperialism, the Highest Stage of Capitalism (1916)*. In it he described the economic and political essence of imperialism, the highest and final stage of capitalism. This stage, unforeseen by Marx, explained why workers joyfully marched to war in 1914 in support of their capitalist masters. Bought off by the minimal social reforms of capitalist governments, workers would require longer to reach the point of full alienation. Thus, revolution would be delayed. Lenin, in describing the imperialist stage, broadened his definition of exploitation by including within it the exploitation of underdeveloped countries by capitalist powers. The inevitable revolution would now include both workers and the peoples of colonial nations joined together in revolution against capitalist oppression. From this time, Soviet military and political strategy sought to encourage revolution and ferment in lesser-developed lands.

Doctrine

Lenin gave shape to Soviet military doctrine. The Soviets credit him with developing the most important Marxist views on war, the army, and military science, and with "developing the entire doctrine concerning the defense of socialism."[1] While confirming that war was a continuation of politics by other armed means, Lenin developed further the ideas of Marx and Engels that war and politics were related by underscoring the class nature of politics and its socio-economic roots. He recognized war as "a continuation of the policies of given interested powers – and various classes within them – at the present time"; as a concentrated expression of economics. Lenin classified the types of war found in the imperialist stage (national liberation, revolutionary, civil, imperialistic, in defense of socialism) and pointed out the role of economics and the morale-political factor in war, stating "war will now be conducted by the people" and "the connection between the military organization of the nation and its entire economic and cultural structure was never as close as at the present."[2]

Lenin worked out and put into practice during the Civil War the principles of military construction for a Socialist government, the most important of which were:[3]

– rule of the armed forces by the Communist Party;
– a class approach to construction of the armed forces;
– the unity of the army and the people;
– the truth of proletarian internationalism;
– centralized command and control and single command;
– cadre organization;

– creation of soldierly discipline;
– constant readiness to repel aggression.

Lenin's work created the basis of Soviet military science and the military art of the armies of other Socialist governments.

> He formulated the views on the factors and the decisive course and outcome of struggle. ... In his works he emphasized the most important principles for conducting armed combat: determining the main danger and the direction of the main attack; concentration of forces and weapons in the decisive place at the decisive moment; securing by all methods and means of struggle their use in accordance with existing conditions; the decisive role of the offensive; the objective evaluation of opposing forces; initiative and surprise; firmness and decisiveness; securing success; maneuver of forces; and pursuit of the enemy to his full destruction.[4]

The legacy of Lenin, also encompassing the exploits of his discredited and forgotten comrades (for example, Trotsky) and personifying the exploits of the new Red Army, became the foundation of future Soviet military doctrine.

Strategy

As an armed conflict the Russian Civil War and military intervention contrasted sharply with the nature of the First World War at all levels of war. The Civil War was a war for the political survival of the Bolsheviks; thus, Soviet strategy incorporated the major recommendations of Lenin. Lenin's program of "War Communism" resulted in the militarization of the entire nation (strategic rear) and a mobilization of the limited economic power of the nation for war. Under the firm control of Lenin and the Party Central Committee, the relatively small Soviet armed force was massed and switched from one decisive strategic direction to another to meet the most critical threats.

> An important feature of the Soviet military strategy was its flexibility and its ability to select types of strategic operations appropriate to the situation and to employ them in various combinations. 'We must never in any way tie our hands in a single strategic maneuver,' said Lenin, illustrating his pragmatism when faced by reality.[5]

The most striking feature of military operations during the Civil

War was the vastness of the regions in which they took place. This vastness placed a high premium on rapid movement and careful concentration of forces and gave rise to what the Soviets called *"eshelonaia voina"* (echelon – or railroad-war). The chief type of Red Army strategic operation was the strategic offensive, which, in light of the scale of the war, was carried out by the conduct of a series of successive offensive operations using the forces of one or two *fronts* without significant pauses.* The Soviets then launched main offensives against enemy groupings whose defeat would decisively alter the military-political situation. The relatively small size of forces, poor communications, and inadequate logistics limited the Soviets' ability to sustain these strategic offensives and forced Soviet commanders to rely primarily on the use of successive operations.

Often an offensive began as a counteroffensive after a defensive period of combat by Soviet troops. The Soviets employed the counteroffensive to destroy attacking enemy shock groups and to regain the strategic initiative. Usually the Soviets regrouped their forces and launched counteroffensives from a defensive posture, against the enemy's flank. Strategic reserves under High Command control played a key role in these counteroffensives. Thus, unlike the positional warfare of the First World War, Civil War military operations were characterized by relatively high maneuverability and expanded scope and scale. In the theater of military operations Soviet *fronts* usually deployed in sectors of 700 to 1,800 kilometers wide and concentrated their offensive operations in sectors of 400–1,000 kilometers against objectives at a depth of 600–3,000 kilometers.** Ensuring operations involved a tempo of advance of 6–10 kilometers per day.[6]

The Soviets resorted to the strategic defensive only when forced to do so because of limited forces and marked enemy superiority. In 1918 such defensive operations bought time for the Soviets to conduct mobilization, but by 1919 the Soviets used defensive operations deliberately to economize on forces necessary to conduct offensive operations in other sectors. Partisan operations, a military manifestation of mobilizing the people and the rear for war, developed extensively on both sides and became an effective means of disrupting the enemy's strategic rear area.

---

* A *front* is equivalent to a western army group.
** The Soviets first formed *fronts* in June 1918.

Operations

Soviet operational art began to evolve as a distinct level of war during the Civil War years, although the Soviets did not coin the term "operational art" until the 1920s. The broad expanse of the theater of war, Soviet inability to conduct successfully a massive single strategic offensive with the bulk of their forces, the consequent necessity of relying on the cumulative effect of *front* and army operations, and the limited applicability of contemporary tactics to highly maneuverable *front* and army operations forced Soviet theorists to focus their attention on an essentially new level of war – the operational level. *Fronts* (considered strategic units) of three to five combined arms armies, and combined arms armies (considered tactical units) of two to five rifle divisions, reinforced by mobile cavalry divisions, cavalry corps and later cavalry armies, evolved slowly and participated in operations under increasingly centralized control (see tables 5–6).[7]

At first, *fronts* and armies deployed in single echelon formation with only small reserves, but by 1920 the depth of *front* and army combat formations increased as larger reserves were formed (one division per army) (see table 7). By war's end second echelons existed, as well as large cavalry groups formed to conduct exploitation operations. The relative paucity of forces compelled Soviet commanders to mass forces and create shock groups for operations in more critical combat sectors. Often cavalry forces supplemented these shock groups and exploited their success. Offensive maneuvers, in the form of wide and shallow envelopments, deep slashing attacks, and penetrations, were effective in light of the shallow depth of enemy defenses. As operations matured throughout 1919 and 1920 offensive sectors narrowed as a result of more thorough mobilization and better concentration of forces.[8] The following indices resulted.

Width of sector	Depth of attack	Duration of attack	Tempo of attack (Per Day)
Front			
300 to 1,000 km	200–300 km	30–50 days	10–12 km – attack
Army			
125 to 200 km	50–150 km	10 days	20 km – pursuit

The Soviets conducted army defensive operations to economize forces and win time necessary to renew the offensive. Armies

TABLE 5

FRONT COMPOSITION: 1918–1921

Theory:

1918	1920
2-6 field armies	2-6 field armies, separate
separate groups of forces	groups of forces, cavalry,
reserve formations	corps, or army, reserve
specialized forces	formations, specialized
river or lake flotillas	forces, river or lake
	flotillas

- - - - - - - - - -

Practice:

Eastern Front: October 1918	Southern Front: June 1919
5 field armies	6 field armies
2 garrisons	
2 groups	
strength: 132,000 men	strength: 44,631 combat
113,000 combat	
Western Front: November 1919	Southern Front: June 1919
3 field armies	4 field armies
Petrograd garrison	1 cavalry corp
1 separate rifle division	
	strength: 99,361 combat
strength: 93,050 combat	
Western Front: July 1920	Southwestern Front: July 1920
4 field armies	3 field armies
1 group	1 cavalry army
	detachments
	reserve
strength: 240,189 men	strength: 251,583 men
139,132 combat	102,414 combat

Source: *Direktivy komandovaniia frontov Krasnoi Armii 1917–1922 gg* [Directives of the Red Army's front commands 1917–1922] (Moskva: Voenizdat, 1978).

defended in wide sectors (300–500 km and more), covered only the most important directions, and maneuvered to prevent enemy penetrations into their rear area. The Soviets emphasized the defense of regions and cities (Tsaritsyn, Petrograd, Orenburg, Ural'sk) important for their political, economic, and military value. Positional defenses were organized on the approaches to cities and

TABLE 6
ARMY COMPOSITION: 1918–1921

Theory:

1918	1919-1920
infantry divisions	3-7 rifle divisions
separate regiments	1-2 cavalry divisions
separate battalions	strength: 30,000-100,000
detachments	men 12,000- 50,000 rifle-
	men/cavalrymen

Practice:

1st Army: Sep 1918	4th Army: Sep 1918	1st Ukrainian Army: Jun 1919
4 infantry divisions	3 infantry divisions	3 rifle divisions
	1 group -	1 rifle brigade
		1 cavalry
		brigade
		1 armored train
strength: 9,000 men	strength: 22,500 men	strength: 23,000
combat	combat	combat

7th Army: Jun 1919	14th Army: Nov 1919	14th Army: May 1920
2 regions	5 rifle divisions	4 rifle divisions
1 sector	1 rifle brigade	1 cavalry brigade
3 infantry	1 cavalry division	1 separate
divisions		brigade
1 group	1 separate cavalry	armored units
	brigade	
	combat	combat
strength: 43,780	strength: 27,000	strength: 27,000 men

15th Army: Jun 1920
  6 rifle divisions
  1 cavalry division

strength: 135,000 men
             38,000 combat

the bulk of defending forces were committed to a linear all-round defense.

Soviet Civil War operational experiences had a major impact on future Soviet operational theory. They provided the analytical basis for future operational art, they imparted to Soviet commanders a fixation on the offensive and maneuver war, and they provided embryonic justification for future Soviet combat techniques such as the use of shock groups and echelonment to achieve tactical success, and mobile groups to develop tactical success into operational success.

TABLE 7
FRONT AND ARMY OPERATIONAL FORMATION: 1919–1920

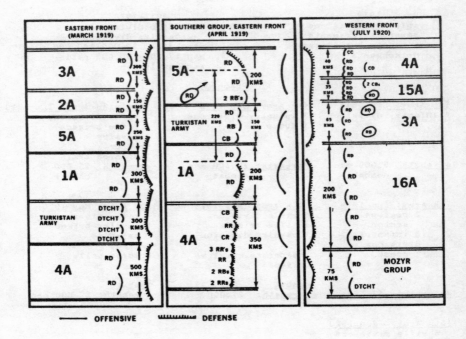

Tactics

Soviet Civil War tactics resembled in many ways those of the First World War (and, in fact, Soviet forces used Russian First World War tactical manuals). The major differences that existed resulted from the irregular nature of Soviet tactical units and the vast expanse over which they operated. At first the Red Army consisted of various-sized volunteer detachments which operated according to Frunze's dictum:

> the Red Army tactics have been and will be imbued with activity (*activnost'*) in the spirit of bold and energetically conducted offensive operations. This results from the class nature of the workers' and peasants' army and at the same time corresponds with the demands of military art.

Irregular detachments attacked under the personal control of commanders. As regularly conscripted TOE units evolved (infantry and later rifle divisions and cavalry divisions) to supplement existing detachments, more systematic tactics evolved. The large infantry (rifle) divisions, consisting of up to 58,000 men, organized into three brigades in order to operate over wide expanses, remained at only 10 to 20 percent strength, thus requiring considerable improvisation by commanders (see table 8).[9] Faced with covering large sectors, commanders could no longer directly control their entire divisions, and individual brigades operated along their own axes against precise points (objectives) or lines. In such combat, initiative was an important quality. As the war progressed and the Soviets fielded additional forces, offensive sectors narrowed and tactical concentration improved, thus producing the following norms.

Tactical
Densities/1 km[10]

Year	Width of Division Main Attack Sector	Bayonets*	Machine Guns	Guns	Depth of Close Mission
Early 1919	50km	100	2–3	.5	–
Late 1919	25–30 km	130	4	1	–
1920	7–15 km	750	19	4	7–10 to 2 km

* Bayonets is a Soviet term denoting combat strength

The combat formation (*boevoi poriadok*) of tactical units consisted of combat sectors and reserves, and batteries and individual guns integrated into the combat formation provided artillery support (see table 9). Extensive use of maneuver and integration of machine guns into the combat formation resulted in abandonment of linear formations and the subsequent use of small groups of infantry attacking under cover of machine gun fire. Around-the-clock pursuit followed successful attacks but pursuit was limited by the lack of reserves and by poor logistical support. Deeper echelonment of rifle formations by 1920 and the use of larger operational cavalry formations provided for more sustained deep pursuit. Tactical cavalry units and armored vehicle units conducted reconnaissance, provided security, repelled counterattacks, and initiated the pursuit. The limited number of aircraft available conducted reconnaissance, dropped propaganda leaflets, and provided some air support, which was particularly effective against enemy cavalry.

Tactical defenses erected on a broad front were shallowly

TABLE 8

RIFLE (INFANTRY) DIVISION COMPOSITION: 1918–1921

Theory:

April 1918 Infantry Division
3 rifle brigades
  2 rifle regiments
1 artillery brigade
  3 light artillery battalions
  1 mortar battalion
  1 heavy artillery battalion
  1 antiaircraft artillery
    battalion
  1 lightened artillery battalion
1 cavalry regiment
1 signal battalion

1 engineer battalion
1 air observation detachment
1 aviation detachment
  rear service units

strength: 26,972 men
           14,222 combat
           68 guns
           288 machine guns
           10,048 horses

November 1918 Rifle Division
3 rifle brigades
  2 rifle regiments
  1 sapper company
  1 signal company
1 cavalry squadron
9 artillery battalions
  3 light artillery
    battalions

  2 howitzer battalions
  2 heavy artillery
    battalions
  1 antiaircraft artillery
    battalion
  1 cavalry artillery
    battery
1 armored car detachment
1 aviation group
strength: 56,654 men
           17,503 combat
           116 guns
           470 machine guns
           21,642 horses

December 1920 Rifle Division

3 rifle brigades
  3 rifle regiments
1 cavalry battalion
1 howitzer artillery battalion
1 heavy artillery battalion
1 signal battalion
2 sapper companies
2 road, bridge companies
strength: 40,686 men (wartime)
           28,828 men (peacetime)

Practice:

28th Rifle Division
4 rifle regiments
1 rifle battalion
1 artillery brigade
1 cavalry regiment

24th Rifle Division
3 rifle brigades
1 rifle regiment

30th Rifle Division
4 rifle brigades
2-4 rifle regiments

echeloned and non-contiguous. Divisions defended in sectors of more than 50 kilometers with brigades and regiments deployed in a single line, defending only the most important directions. Soviet forces relied on the use of strong points, maneuver of forces and

TABLE 9
COMBAT FORMATION, 51ST RIFLE DIVISION AT PEREKOP, 1920

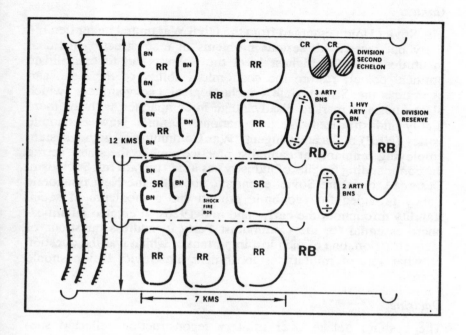

reserves, and artillery fire to repulse enemy attacks. The inevitable overextension of attacking enemy units and their resulting vulnerability to concentrated counterattack assisted Soviet defenders in repelling enemy offensives.

Soviet Civil War tactical experiences became an intense arena for scrutiny by postwar military theoreticians. The achievement of tactical penetrations of a defense and the envelopment of a defense by mobile forces were major subjects of study, and ultimately that study resulted in the development of the tactical theory of deep battle, the critical basis for the future operational concept of deep operations. Soviet Civil War failures to construct tactical formations of requisite size to conduct modern combat operations forced postwar military leaders to undertake wholesale reconstruction of the Soviet tactical force structure.

THE EVOLUTION OF A SOCIALIST
MILITARY DOCTRINE (1921–1929)

Context

The Soviet Union emerged from the Civil War united under Lenin's Party but faced with serious problems of reconstructing national institutions. At the highest level the Soviets had to consolidate political power, restore the economic viability of the state, and overcome the Soviet state's technological backwardness, which placed her at a marked disadvantage in comparison with the more highly industrialized Western nations. Lenin's New Economic Policy (NEP) replaced stringent "War Communism" with a system employing remnants of capitalist practices, while the state "seized the commanding heights of industry" as a step toward full Socialism. Designed to restore Soviet economic strength, the New Economic Policy provided for economic growth and a modicum of social stability throughout the early- and mid-1920s. It created an atmosphere essential for the Communist Party to address questions of reconstruction, one of the most important of which was the question of what sort of military establishment the Soviet Union should possess.

Doctrine

The ensuing debate over military reconstruction reflected sub-surface political struggles of the twenties and hinged on several issues. Paramount was the issue of ideology – what role would the armed forces play in a Socialist state committed to extending world revolution? A corollary of this ideological question related to army composition: should the army be socially pure (a workers' army) or should it contain "experts," remnants of the former bourgeois class? A third more practical question related to the size and nature of the army. What size was feasible in light of the need for labor to revitalize industry and agriculture, and should the army be a large, well-trained permanent cadre force or a small, less tactically proficient militia force? All of these questions had ideological ramifications.

Debate over these issues began in 1919 and, although basically resolved by 1922, it continued through 1924. Even though the main protagonists were Commissar of War L. D. Trotsky and one of the preeminent Civil War Commanders, M. V. Frunze, the debate reflected more deep-seated political struggles which occurred during Lenin's later years and which intensified after his death in 1924. Trotsky advocated a small, permanent, professional army supported by a large militia, incorporating within it the expertise of ex-Tsarist officers and NCOs. He also argued against the existence of a unique Socialist military doctrine. Frunze, on the other hand, in a series of articles written from 1921 to 1924, articulated an opposing view. His article "The Unified Military Doctrine of the Red Army" advanced the concept of the necessity for a new Marxian doctrine of war which he defined as:

> that concept accepted in the army of a given state which established the nature of the creation of the armed forces of the country, the method of combat training of the troops and their leadership on the basis of the views held by those ruling the state regarding the nature of the problems facing them and the methods of solving them, such methods arising from the class character of the state and determined by the level of productive forces of the country.[11]

Frunze concluded that:

> the character of the military doctrine of a given state is determined by the political line of the social class that stands at the head of it ... one of the fundamental theoretical tasks of those concerned with military affairs is the study of the peculiar nature of the building of the Red Army and its combat methods.[12]

The Unified Military Doctrine resolved itself into four general statements. The first two were ideological in character and the latter two had far-reaching implications for the future development and tone of Soviet military doctrine. Theoretically Frunze asserted:

- there is a proletarian method of war, and
- the method of war must reflect the society and the means of production.

Practically he asserted:

- certain fundamentals, notably maneuver, offensive and *aktivnost'* (dynamism or activity) are essential in military operations;
- the Soviet military is a vehicle for spreading the revolution in the interests of the world proletariat.

A second article by Frunze, entitled "The Front and Rear in

Future Warfare," demonstrated the necessity of mobilizing the full power of the state in future military conflicts. Frunze predicted that future war would be a "long and cruel conflict" which would draw upon the full economic and political forces of the belligerents. The immense importance of the rear, together with the impossibility of maintaining a large standing army in peacetime, created an:

> urgent, burning and immediate task: to strengthen the general work of preparing the country for defense ... the adoption, while still at peace, of a firm course in the militarization of the work of all civil apparatus ... There must be established the same kind of definite plan for converting the national economy in time of war as we have worked out for the army.[13]

Frunze's general view prevailed and Trotsky, undermined by the political machinations of Stalin and the death of Lenin, began fading from the political scene. The Unified Military Doctrine has since remained a cardinal tenet of Soviet military doctrine, as have Frunze's concepts of the offensive and maneuver. In addition, the regular/cadre system, Frunze's officer training system, and his principles of one-man command (*edinonachal'stvo*) persist today. Above all, Frunze provided an ideological justification for the current position of the armed forces in Soviet society.

Force structure

While ideological questions were being debated, Frunze and others reorganized the structure of the Red Army to suit the realities of the 1920s and the results of the ideological debates. Demobilization reduced Red Army strength from 5.5 million to 562,000 men, and the cumbersome army force structure of the Civil War years was streamlined (see tables 10–12). The Soviets abolished field armies, leaving rifle and cavalry corps as the largest peacetime formations, and created new smaller rifle and cavalry divisions, subdivided first into brigades and later into regiments. In 1924–25 Frunze completed implementation of the territorial cadre system for the Red Army. He established common TOEs for cadre and territorial rifle divisions, which were manned at several distinct levels of peacetime strength but mobilizable into full divisions in the event of war. Symbolizing Frunze's concern for readiness and maneuver, the bulk of cavalry divisions were kept at full strength.[14]

Frunze became Red Army Chief of Staff in 1924, with B. M. Shaposhnikov and M. N. Tukhachevsky as his deputies. The RKKA Staff, an embryonic version of what Shaposhnikov would refer to as

TABLE 10
RIFLE CORPS TOEs: 1920s

January 1923 Rifle Corps	September 1925 Rifle Corps
2-3 rifle divisions	3 rifle divisions
artillery administration with	2 artillery battalions
1 heavy artillery battalion	(107 mm guns,
engineer administration with	152 mm howitzers)
1 sapper battalion	1 sapper company
1 signal company	1 engineer park
	rear service units

strength: 50,000 men
           516 guns
           450 mortars

TABLE 11
RIFLE DIVISION TOEs: 1920s

1922 Rifle Division	1924 Rifle Division
3 rifle regiments	3 rifle regiments
1 cavalry squadron	1 artillery battery (6 x 76mm)
1 light artillery battalion	1 light artillery regiment
1 howitzer battery	1 light artillery battalion
1 sapper company	(24 x 76 mm)
1 signal company	1 howitzer artillery battalion
1 air detachment	(12 x 122 mm)
	1 cavalry squadron
	1 sapper company
	1 signal company
	rear service units

strength: 15,300 men   strength: 1st line cadre:
          24 guns   6,300 men (peacetime)
          156 machine guns   18,600 men (wartime)
                                      2nd line cadre:
                                         604 (peacetime)
                                      12,300 (wartime)
                                      territorial:
                                      190-2,400 (peacetime)
                                      12,000-13,000 (wartime)
                                         54 guns
                                         270 machine guns

the "Brain of the Army," concerned itself with all aspects of planning national defense, including preparation of the entire country for war, thus fulfilling Frunze's concern for uniting the front and rear. Also in 1924, Frunze established the air force as a semi-independent service capable of developing operational concepts free of ground force biases. Secret military contacts with Germany, first on production of military materiel and then involving training,

TABLE 12
CAVALRY DIVISION TOEs: 1920s

<u>1923 Cavalry Division (Territorial)</u>
6 cavalry regiments
    4 cavalry squadrons
1 cavalry artillery battalion

1 engineer squadron
1 signal squadron
<u>strength</u>:   3,900 men (peacetime)
               6,500 men (wartime)

<u>1924 Cavalry Division (Cadre)</u>
4 cavalry regiments
    2 cavalry battalions
1 cavalry artillery
    battalion
1 signal battalion
1 engineer battalion
<u>strength</u>:   4,700 men (peacetime)
               7,800 men (wartime)

<u>1925 Cavalry Division (Cadre)</u>
3 cavalry regiments
    4 sabre squadrons
    1 machine gun squadron
1 weapons regiment
1 cavalry artillery battalion
1 signal squadron
1 engineer squadron
<u>strength</u>:   7,000 men

<u>1928 Cavalry Division (Territorial)</u>
6 cavalry regiments
    4 sabre squadrons
    1 machine gun squadron
1 cavalry artillery battalion
1 engineer squadron
1 signal squadron

<u>strength</u>:   6,303 (peacetime)
               8,507 (wartime)

in particular air training, tank training, and chemical warfare, began under Frunze's aegis and persisted until the rise of Hitler terminated them. These contacts benefited both sides, but in particular Germany, whose military efforts were restricted by the Treaty of Versailles. The Germans shared technological information and staff procedures with the Soviets, while German officers benefited from some of the more advanced offensive concepts being developed by Soviet theorists (successive operations, deep battle).

Strategy

While Frunze and his successors worked out their reforms, Soviet military art developed out of assessments of Civil War experiences and the growing necessity to harness technological changes to the development of new offensive concepts. Soviet military strategy in the 1920s, derived from the experiences of the First World War and the Civil War, concluded that future war would begin with extensive maneuver operations, would occur over vast regions, and would consume huge economic and human resources. S. S. Kamenev, Red Army commander from 1919 to 1924, wrote:

in spite of all victorious fights before the battle, the fate of the campaign will be decided in the very last battle – interim defeats will be individual episodes ... In the warfare of modern large armies, defeat of the enemy results from the sum of continuous and planned victories on all fronts, successfully completed one after another and interconnected in time.[15]

Kamenev rejected the possibility of using a grand strategic stroke to win quick victory in war (like the Schlieffen Plan). Instead, he argued, "the uninterrupted conduct of operations is the main condition for victory." Tukhachevsky, drawing upon his experiences along the Vistula in 1920, concluded that "the impossibility, on a modern wide front, of destroying the enemy army by one blow forces the achievement of that end by a series of successive operations."[16] V. K. Triandafillov, in his 1929 work, *The Character of Operations of Modern Armies*, echoed and further developed Tukhachevsky's view of future war and concluded that only successive operations over a month's time to a depth of 150–200 kilometers could produce victory. Triandafillov introduced the idea of using tanks supported by air forces to effect penetration of the tactical enemy defense and extend the offensive into the operational depth.[17]

By 1929 the theory (but not yet the practice) of successive operations was fully developed. The *front*, as a strategic entity, would accomplish missions assigned by the High Command. It would unite all forces in a theater of military operations and would attack along several operational directions to achieve overall strategic aims.* The width of a *front's* offensive zone was 300–400 kilometers, and its depth of operations was 200 kilometers.[18] This view of strategic operations persisted into the 1930s and forced Soviet military theorists to seek an answer to the question of how to implement Triandafillov's views and escape the specter of attrition warfare. The evolution of a new level of war seemed to provide the tentative theoretical answer – the level of operational art.

Operational art

Soviet rejection of the strategic concept of a single battle of annihilation and acceptance of the necessity for conducting successive military operations focused the attention of theorists on the realm between the traditional concepts of strategy and tactics – the realm that would become operational art. Slowly, new terminology and

* The Soviet term "direction" is almost synonymous with the English term axis.

concepts evolved defining the limits of the operational level of war. In May 1924, a work appeared, written in part by Frunze, entitled *Higher Commands–Official Guidance for Commanders and Field Commands of the Army and Fleet*. It focused on operations, stating:

> the aim of each operation and battle is the destruction of enemy forces and equipment by combat. The aim can be achieved only by skillful and decisive action, based on simple but artful maneuver, conducted violently and persistently.[19]

Kamenev's, Tukhachevsky's and Triandafillov's subsequent work provided a more detailed explanation of Frunze's general comments regarding the emerging important operational level.

In 1927, A. A. Svechin, a former Tsarist officer, in his work *Strategy*, articulated a new framework for the levels of war to meet the obvious needs of the time. Svechin described strategy as "the art of combining preparations for war and the grouping of operations to achieve aims put forth in war for the armed forces ... Strategy decides questions concerning both the use of the armed forces and all resources of the state for the achievement of final military aims." Based on that definition Svechin pondered the concept of successive operations and built a definition for operational art, which has since endured. Demonstrating the relationship of all three levels of military art, Svechin wrote: "tactics makes the steps from which operational leaps are assembled; strategy points out the path."[20]

The tendency in the 1920s to conceive of successive operations as the focal point for the operational level of war resulted from the state of technology within the Soviet state in general, and the equipment possessed by the Red Army in particular. Industrial backwardness and the lack of a well-developed armaments industry dictated that the Soviets rely on infantry, artillery and horse cavalry to conduct operations. Hence, an optimistic view postulated that a *front* could attack in a 300–400–kilometer section to a depth of 200 kilometers, while an army, the basic operational large unit designated to operate as part of a *front* or on a separate operational direction, could attack in a sector 50–80 kilometers wide to a depth of 25–30 kilometers: It could also conduct a series of consecutive operations as part of a *front* offensive (see tables 13–15). Each operation would last for 5–6 days, and would entail a relatively slow rate of advance of 5–6 kilometers per day. Already, by 1929 the Soviets planned to increase that rate of advance to 25–30 kilometers per day by following Triandafillov's recommendation to introduce tanks and mechanized vehicles into the force structure.[21]

TABLE 13
FRONT OPERATIONAL FORMATION – 1930

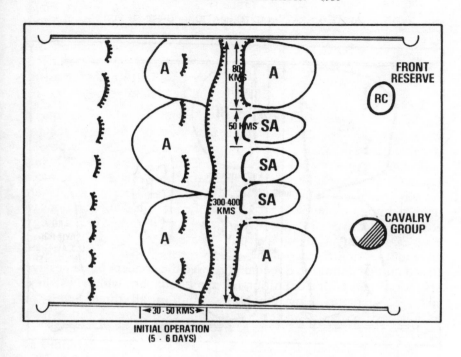

The 1929 *Field Regulation* [*Ustav*] developed the theory of successive operations a step further by injecting the idea of future mechanization and motorization into concepts for future offensive operations.[22] The *Ustav* enunciated the aim of conducting deep battle (*glubokii boi*) to achieve success in penetrating the tactical depth of enemy defenses by the simultaneous use of infantry support tanks and long-range action tanks cooperating with infantry, artillery, and aviation forces. This would also produce a capability to conduct more rapid operations. In 1929 deep battle was but a promise whose realization depended on economic reforms and industrialization. Moreover, deep battle was only a tactical concept.

Tactics

Soviet tactics of the 1920s were governed by a series of new regulations issued between 1925 and 1928, the provisions of which were

TABLE 14
ARMY OPERATIONAL FORMATION – OFFENSE 1930

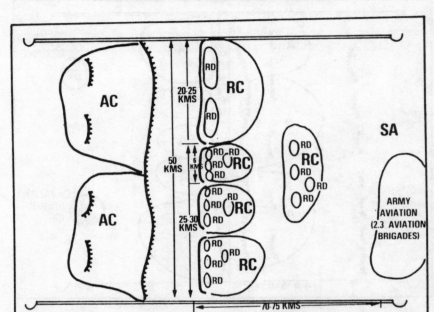

derived from Civil War and the First World War experiences, with
due consideration given to advances in weaponry. The regulations
emphasized maneuver war, the meeting engagement, attack on a
defending enemy, and defense in a war of maneuver. Group tactics
of the later Civil War years persisted whereby combat formations
were organized into groups of subunits echeloned in depth instead
of in skirmish lines. These groups would penetrate the enemy
defense in separate sectors and then merge into a common battle
front.

General tactics emphasized the combined arms nature of battle.
The *Infantry Combat Regulation of 1927* and the *Field Regulation of
1929* prescribed that offensive infantry combat formations consist of
a shock group (two-thirds of the force) operating on the main
direction of attack, and a holding group (one-third of the force)
deployed on a secondary direction (see table 16). A reserve (of up to
one-ninth of the force) was to accomplish unanticipated missions,

TABLE 15
ARMY OPERATIONAL FORMATION – DEFENSE 1930

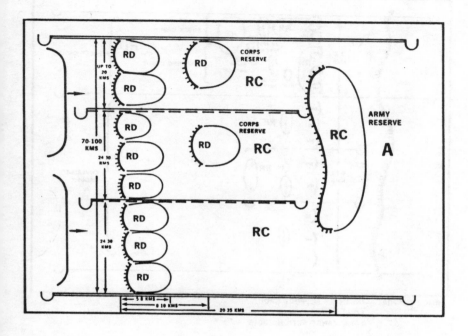

and firing groups of artillery would provide support. On the defense the first echelon consisted of the holding group (two-thirds of the force) and the shock group or groups deployed in the depths (in second echelon) with the task of counterattacking and destroying penetrating enemy units (see table 17).

Rudimentary tactics for the use of the fledgling armored forces first appeared in the 1928 *Provisional Instructions for the Combat Use of Tanks.*[23] Initially tanks would only provide support for infantry. Immediate support tanks (1–3 platoons) would be assigned to rifle battalions. Forward echelon tanks (a freely maneuvering group of 1–2 tank companies) would fight independently in tactical contact with each first echelon rifle regiment (out of fire and visual contact) in order to suppress or destroy enemy artillery, forward enemy reserves, command posts, communications centers, or other objectives. Tank reserves of the division

TABLE 16
RIFLE DIVISION COMBAT FORMATION – OFFENSE 1930

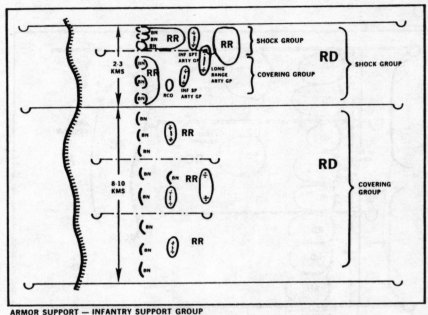

ARMOR SUPPORT — INFANTRY SUPPORT GROUP
              LONG RANGE SUPPORT GROUP
              LONG RANGE ACTION GROUP

commander would be used to develop success into the tactical depths or to replace depleted support units. Tank tactics would improve, and the integration of armor into combined arms formations would accelerate in the 1930s with the virtual industrial revolution that swept the Soviet Union.

THE TECHNICAL RECONSTRUCTION OF THE ARMED FORCES AND THE THEORY OF DEEP OPERATIONS (1929–1937)

Context

By the late 1920s it was apparent to Soviet leaders that unless drastic measures were undertaken to industrialize the Soviet economy the Soviet military establishment would continue to lag behind other

TABLE 17
RIFLE DIVISION COMBAT FORMATION – DEFENSE 1930

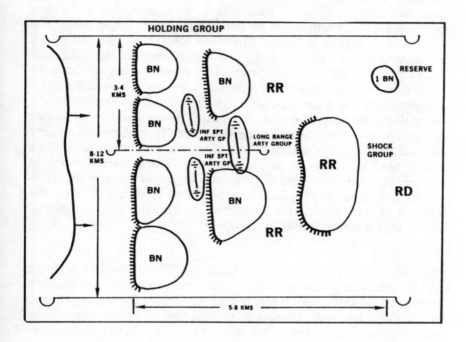

major European nations. The Red Army was still at a strength of
562,000, the cadre-territorial system had not produced a proficient
fighting force, and advanced weaponry was in short supply. It was
clear that a massive transformation of the predominant rural
economy toward industrialization was necessary. Moreover, the
financing of such a program and the manning of new industry would
require measures to extract the resources from the population at
large. In essence, a social revolution was required in tune with
Frunze's recommended militarization of the state, prompted from
above and controlled by centralized state planning. Consequently,
in October 1928 Stalin announced his first Five Year Plan, which
was based on an earlier military five year plan.

Stalin's "New Socialist Offensive" built upon his earlier concept
of "Socialism in One Country," enunciated several years before to

discredit Trotsky's concept of "Permanent Revolution." The "New Socialist Offensive" wrought revolutionary change and massive human deprivation across the face of the Soviet Union. The forced collectivization of agriculture demolished the rural landowning class and drove millions of people from the countryside into cities, labor camps, or death, but in so doing it created a larger proletariat to man new Soviet industry. The Five Year Plan stressed heavy industry, and the technological knowledge required to build that industry, then lacking in the Soviet Union, was imported from the West along with thousands of technical advisers. The industrialization program was a success, although at a huge human cost. Soviet industrial production soared, in particular production of heavy equipment and armaments, some domestically designed but many adopted from foreign designs. This industrial revolution provided a strong base upon which to continue the vigorous renaissance in military thought and, more importantly, to permit the new theory to be implemented in practice. The promises of 1929 became the realities of the 1930s, with a potential for transforming the Soviet Union into a leading military power.

Doctrine

The details and spirit of Frunze's Unified Military Doctrine endured into the 1930s and were actually implemented more fully by Stalin's attempt to mobilize the resources of the nation for industrial and military development. Moreover, the movement in the mid-thirties away from the cadre/territorial system toward a larger and better-equipped army promised to improve the peacetime readiness of the Soviet armed forces. Military doctrine in the 1930s remained an arena of dynamic analysis and debate at a time when Stalin was ruthlessly centralizing his political power and conducting bloodless party purges preliminary to the physical liquidation of all potential competition within party circles. Stalin, for as yet unexplained reasons, allowed the military to preside over the rapid rearmament and to develop, in relative freedom, a military art advanced for its time. Only when that military art was nearing full development and reflection in the Soviet force structure did Stalin strike at the remaining potential threat to his absolute power – the military – in a purge of far-reaching consequences for the Soviet Union.

Strategy

Soviet military strategy in the 1930s built upon the assumptions of the 1920s, although it was increasingly affected by the industrial and technological revolution occurring within the Soviet Union and by looming threats from hostile powers abroad. Soviet strategy maintained that the class character of war would result in implacable and decisive future military combat, and that war would ultimately pit the Soviet Union against a coalition of imperialist nations. Long and bitter war would require the consecutive defeat of the Soviet Union's enemies, the use of large strategic reserves, resort to many means and forms of armed combat, and the conduct of large scale maneuverable combat operations. War would require the achievement of decisive aims, including the full destruction of the enemy on his territory. Quite naturally, the Soviets considered the offensive as the most decisive and fruitful form of strategic operation.

The strategic offensive would take the form of simultaneous or successive *front* operations conducted by closely cooperating combined arms forces.[24] The ground forces would play a decisive role, especially the newly emerging tank and mechanized units. Air forces would support all types of ground force operations and could perform independent air operations as well, while naval forces would cooperate on coastal directions. The theory of deep operations (*glubokie operatsii*) was particularly important to Soviet military strategy in the 1930s, in part because it focused Soviet attention on the offensive to the detriment of defensive concerns. Soviet strategy considered the defense a valid form of military operations and emphasized activity (*aktivnost'*) and the use of counteroffensives. Much attention was devoted to the nature of the initial period of war and the requirements of strategic leadership in wartime. The Soviets recognized that a surprise attack by hostile powers was possible. In this regard they believed that, unlike the practices of earlier wars, forces of the covering echelons (on the borders) could undertake an offensive of their own against the enemy before the completion of main force strategic deployments or undertake defensive measures to cover the main force deployment. By the Soviets' own admission, military strategy:

> did not devote adequate attention to the development of defensive operations on a strategic scale ... questions of repelling an unexpected attack by previously fully-mobilized enemy forces as well as the overall problem of the initial period of war under changing conditions were not properly worked out. Not all of the correct theoretical principles worked out by Soviet military science with respect to military strategy were

promptly taken into account in the practical work or included in regulations.[25]

This was an easy admission, considering what happened in 1941. To provide strategic leadership in armed conflict, a special organ similar to the Civil War period Council of Labor and Defense would be formed as well as a STAVKA (HQ) of the High Command (VGK).

Operational art

Operational art, developed as a level of war in the 1920s, blossomed into the most creative area of Soviet military art in the following decade, largely due to technological and industrial developments and the theoretical work of a host of imaginative military theorists. The impact of new weaponry, first felt in the tactical realm, by the mid-1930s affected the operational level. In essence, the promise of the 1929 *Field Regulation* to achieve deep battle was realized.

The most important aspect of Soviet military science in the 1930s was the full development of the concept of deep battle and the emergence of the concept of deep operations. The deep operation, a form of combat action conducted by operational large units,

> consisted of simultaneous attacks on the enemy defense with all means of attack to the entire depth of the defense; a penetration of the tactical defense zone on selected directions and subsequent decisive development of tactical success into operational success by means of introducing into battle an echelon to develop success (tanks, motorized infantry, cavalry) and the landing of air assaults to achieve rapidly the desired aims.[26]

The theory of deep operations represented a qualitative jump in the development of operational art and a total escape from the impasse of First World War positional warfare.

The theory of deep operations evolved out of the earlier theory of deep battle formulated at the end of the 1920s in theoretical works of Tukhachevsky, Triandafillov, A. I. Egorov and others, who concluded that the appearance of new weapons (long-range artillery, tanks, aircraft) and types of forces (tank, air assault, mechanized) would permit the creation of more maneuverable forms of combat and ease the problem of penetrating a tactical defense. Early experimentation with deep battle techniques occurred in the Volga, Kiev and Belorussian Military Districts and, as a result, in February 1933 the Red Army gave official sanction to deep battle in its *Provisional Instructions on the Organization of Deep Battle*.[27] New and more explicit instructions appeared in March 1935, and the *Field Regulation* [Ustav] of 1936 made deep battle, as well as the larger scope deep operations, an established tenet of Soviet military art. While deep battle focused on the tactical defense and combat by units within an army, deep operations focused on operational level combat involving *fronts* and armies alike.

The theoretical basis of deep operations, field tested in military exercises in the mid-thirties, was established by 1936 and described in the *Regulation* of that year as:

> simultaneous assault on enemy defenses by aviation and artillery to the depths of the defense, penetration of the tactical zone of the defense by attacking units with widespread use of tank forces, and violent development of tactical success into operational success with the aim of the complete encirclement and destruction of the enemy. The main role is performed by the infantry and the mutual support of all types of forces are organized in its interests.[28]

The heart of deep operations involved the use of an operational formation consisting of: an attack echelon; an echelon to develop success; reserves; aviation forces; and air assault forces, all designated to achieve tactical and operational success. Deep operations could be conducted by a single *front* or (according to views of the late 1930s) by several *fronts* supported by large aviation forces. By this time the Soviets considered a *front* to be an operational-strategic large unit (earlier it had been considered only a strategic large unit).

Fronts conducted the largest-scale deep operations by employing successive army operations to penetrate enemy defenses along converging directions in order to encircle and destroy enemy main forces. Successful penetration of an enemy defense required considerable overall superiority in forces and creation of high force densities in penetration sectors. Development of the offensive into the operational depths required use of mechanized and cavalry corps, *front* reserves, and air assault landings in the enemy rear. To conduct deep operations a *front* had to consist of:

3–4 shock armies
1–2 standard armies

1–2 mechanized, tank or cavalry corps
15–30 aviation divisions.[29]

Such a *front* could attack in a sector 250–300 kilometers wide against
objectives at a depth of 150–250 kilometers and deliver the main
attack in a sector of 60–80 kilometers (see table 18). Force densities
of one division per 2–2.5 kilometers, 40–100 guns per 1 kilometer of
front and 50–100 tanks per 1 kilometer of front would result. A *front*
operation would last 15–20 days with an average tempo of advance
of 10–15 kilometers per day for infantry and 40–50 kilometers per
day for mobile forces.[30] Within the *front* the attack echelon would
consist of strong shock and combined arms armies, and the echelon
to develop success would be composed of mobile groups formed
from tank, mechanized and cavalry corps. Aviation groups and
reserves would support the *fronts*.

TABLE 18
FRONT OPERATIONAL FORMATION 1936–1941

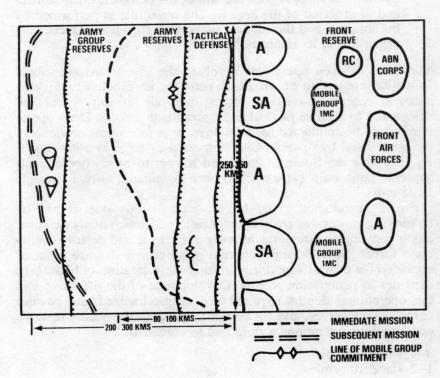

Armies, as operational large units, could operate within a *front* or independently along a separate operational direction. Armies participating in deep operations on *front* main attack directions would consist of:

4–5 rifle corps
1–2 mechanized or cavalry corps
7–9 artillery regiments
7–8 air defense artillery battalions
2–3 aviation divisions (in support).[31]

The army attack echelon, consisting of rifle corps reinforced by tanks and artillery, would advance in a sector 50–80 kilometers wide with its main strength concentrated in a penetration sector 20–30 kilometers wide to penetrate the tactical enemy defenses to a depth of 25–30 kilometers (see table 19). The echelon to develop the

TABLE 19
SHOCK ARMY OPERATIONAL FORMATION 1936–1941

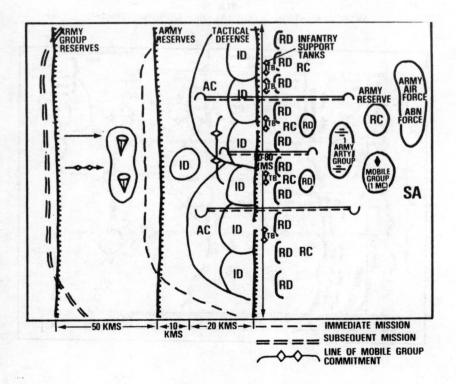

penetration, an army mobile group of several mechanized or cavalry corps, would complete the penetration of the enemy's tactical defense or attack after penetration of the enemy's second defense belt to develop tactical success into operational success to a depth of 70–100 kilometers.[32] In both *front* and army deep operations the Soviets paid particular attention to the organization of air defense using fighter aviation and air defense artillery units. The Soviets exercised deep operation concepts in maneuvers in the Kiev, Belorussian, Moscow and Odessa Military Districts in the mid-thirties.

Theoretical work on operational level defense focused on the preparation and conduct of army defensive operations (see table 20). An army could defend a sector of 80–100 kilometers to a depth of 60 kilometers.[33] However, as was the case with the strategic defense, by the Soviets' own admission, their fixation on the offensive caused too little attention to be paid to *front* defensive operations, a deficiency evident in 1941.

TABLE 20
ARMY OPERATIONAL FORMATION – DEFENSE 1936–1941

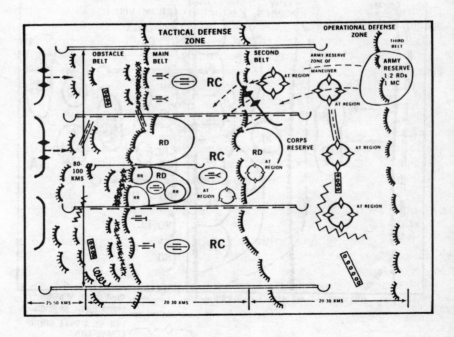

Tactics

The theory of deep battle, which was worked out before the development of the theory of deep operations and which echoed tactical concepts of 1929, was the tactical counterpart of that broader operational theory. By 1936 those tactical concepts were close to realization while deeper operations still existed only in theory. Deep battle as envisioned in the 1936 *Regulation* involved the creation in the combat formation of corps, divisions, and regiments of shock groups, holding groups, reserves, and artillery groups. The shock group, consisting of two-thirds of the force, attacked on the main attack direction. In the case of considerable superiority over the enemy, two shock groups could attack on converging directions. The holding group, consisting of almost one-third of the force, operated on the secondary attack direction to distract the enemy and protect the shock group's flank. A reserve amounting to one-ninth of the force was retained to fulfill unexpected missions. Rifle corps' shock groups sought to penetrate the enemy defense to a depth of 10–12 kilometers, which was the average depth of the enemy's tactical defense. Rifle corps on the main attack direction in the army first echelon advanced in an 18–20–kilometer sector and rifle divisions in a 5–7–kilometer sector (with the divisions' shock group deployed in a 3–3.5–kilometer sector).[34]

Tactical defense in the early 1930s, like that of the late twenties, involved the use of covering groups (two-thirds of the force) and shock groups (one-third of the force) (see table 21). The tactical defense zone consisted of an engineer-chemical obstacle belt 10–15 kilometers deep, a combat security belt 1–3 kilometers from the forward edge of the main defensive belt; a main defensive belt 6 kilometers deep and a rear defensive belt 12–15 kilometers from the forward edge of the main defensive belt. A rifle division defended in a sector 8–12 kilometers wide and a rifle regiment in a 3–5–kilometer sector.

Tanks, subdivided into three groups, played a significant role in the conduct of deep battle. Immediate infantry support tanks (NPP – *neposredstvennoi podderzhki pekhoty*), long-range support tanks (DPP – *dal'nei podderzhki pekhoty*), and long range action tanks (DD – *dal'nego deistviia*) attacked in advance of and with the infantry, fired on enemy artillery and tanks, and accompanied the advance through the tactical depth of the defense, respectively.

TABLE 21
CORPS COMBAT FORMATION – DEFENSE 1936–1941

Artillery groups for infantry support (PP – *podderzhki pekhoty*), formed in each first echelon rifle regiment, long-range artillery groups (DD – *dal'nego deistviia*), established in each first echelon rifle division of corps, and, in some instances, artillery destruction groups (AR – *artillerii razrusheniia*), created in corps, provided continuous fire support for the attack.[35]

Force structure

Rapid industrialization of the Soviet Union, the creation of a burgeoning armaments industry, and the renaissance in military thought, manifested in the development of the offensive theories of deep battle and deep operations, wrought major changes in the size and nature of the Soviet force structure. Throughout the 1930s the Soviet armed forces increased in size from 562,000 men to 1.4

million men.[36] After the mid-thirties the Soviets moved away from the cadre/territorial manning system toward the peacetime maintenance of a large regular army. Although territorial units still existed in 1940, by the late 1930s the bulk of Red Army units were regular ones. Older, established units in the force structure (rifle corps and divisions, and cavalry corps and divisions) increased in personnel strength and weaponry but, more important, the Soviets created new mobile units necessary to conduct deep operations (see tables 22–25).

TABLE 22
THEORETICAL ARMY STRUCTURE: 1936

Shock Army	Combined Arms Army
3-4 rifle corps	2-3 rifle corps (optional)
12-15 rifle divisions	10-12 rifle divisions
1-2 mechanized or cavalry corps	1-2 tank brigades
or	5-6 artillery/mortar regiments
1-3 tank brigades	5-6 engineer battalions
3-4 air divisions	1-2 mixed air divisions
10-12 artillery regiments	
tank regiments (infantry support)	

TABLE 23
RIFLE CORPS TOEs: 1930s

1932 Rifle Corps	1935 Rifle Corps
2-3 rifle divisions	3 rifle divisions
1 artillery regiment (107 mm, 152 mm)	2 artillery regiments
1 sapper battalion	1 antiaircraft artillery battalion
1 signal battalion	1 sapper battalion
	1 signal battalion

TABLE 24
RIFLE DIVISION TOEs: 1930s

1932 Rifle Division	1935 Rifle Division
3 rifle regiments	3 rifle regiments (6 x 76 mm)
3 rifle battalions	2 artillery regiments
1 howitzer battery (6 x 76 mm)	1 reconnaissance battalion
1 artillery regiment	1 antitank battalion
1 cavalry troop	1 antiaircraft battalion
1 antiaircraft battery	1 tank battalion
1 sapper company	1 sapper company
1 signal company	1 signal battalion
strength: 48 guns	strength: 12,800 men
270 machine guns	18,000 wartime
	57 tanks
	96 guns/mortars
	530 machine guns

TABLE 25
CAVALRY FORCES: 1930s

<table>
<tr><td valign="top">

1932 Cavalry Corps
2-3 cavalry divisions
1 cavalry artillery regiment
  (or battalion)
1 signal squadron

1932 Cavalry Division
4-6 cavalry regiments
1 cavalry artillery battalion
1 sapper squadron
1 signal squadron
1 armored car section

</td><td valign="top">

1935 Cavalry Division
4 cavalry regiments
  4 cavalry squadrons
  1 machine gun squadron
  1 artillery battery
  1 antiaircraft squadron
1 sapper squadron
1 signal squadron
1 mechanized regiment (BT-5)
1 artillery regiment
  1 artillery battalion
  (122 mm howitzer)
  1 artillery battalion
  (76 mm guns)
<u>strength</u>:   6,000 (peacetime)
          9,200 (wartime)

</td></tr>
</table>

The Soviets created a wide variety of new tank and mechanized forces to provide the offensive punch necessary to penetrate enemy tactical defenses and thrust deep into the enemy's operational rear area. After experimenting with tank battalions and regiments in the late twenties, in May 1930 the Soviets created their first mechanized brigade, consisting of 60 tanks and 32 tankettes*. The following year they established their first mechanized corps organized with two mechanized tank brigades, a rifle-machine gun brigade, and a total of 490 tanks. By 1936 Soviet mechanized forces numbered 4 mechanized corps and 6 mechanized brigades for use as operational-level mobile groups plus 6 separate tank regiments, 15 mechanized regiments (in cavalry divisions) and 83 tank battalions or companies (in rifle divisions) (see table 26). Thus, by 1936 the Soviets had created mechanized and tank units to support infantry in the tactical penetration battle, to spearhead deep operations, and to cooperate with cavalry. These units were equipped with T-26, BT-5, T-28, T-35 and T-37 tanks which were armed with guns of up to 76 mm but lacked radios necessary for smooth coordination of operations.[37]

The Soviets also developed and tested air assault units. By the mid-thirties they had fielded 3 airborne brigades and 3 airborne regiments to cooperate with exploiting Soviet ground forces (see table 27).

---

* Tankettes were light tanks armed with heavy machine guns.

TABLE 26
MECHANIZED FORCES: 1930s

1930 Mechanized Brigade
1 tank regiment (MS-1)
  2 tank battalions
1 motorized infantry regiment
  2 motorized infantry battalions
1 artillery battalion
1 reconnaissance battalion

strength: 60 tanks
             32 tankettes
             17 armored cars

1931 Mechanized Brigade
Reconnaissance Group (Regiment)
  1 tank battalion
  1 armored car troop
  1 machine gun battalion
  1 artillery battalion
Shock Group (Regiment)
  2 tank battalions
  2 artillery battalions
  1 motorized infantry battalion
Artillery Group (Regiment)
  2 artillery battalions
  1 antiaircraft battalion

strength: 4700 men
             119 tanks

1936 Separate Mechanized Brigade

3 tank battalions
1 motorized rifle battalion
1 security (recon) battalion
1 repair, reconstruction battalion
1 aviation transport battalion
1 signal company
1 reconnaissance company

strength: 2745 men
             145 tanks (T-26)
              45 artillery tanks
              28 armored cars

1931 Mechanized Corps
1 mechanized tank brigade(T26)
  3 tank battalions
  1 rifle/machine gun battalion
  1 artillery battalion
  1 sapper battalion
  1 antiaircraft machine gun
    company
1 mechanized tank brigade (BT)
  3 tank battalions
  1 rifle/machine gun battalion
  1 artillery battalion
  1 sapper battalion
  1 antiaircraft machine gun
    company
1 rifle/machine gun brigade
1 reconnaissance battalion
1 mortar battalion
1 antiaircraft battalion
1 sapper battalion
1 traffic control company
1 supply/maintenance unit
1 aviation unit

strength: 490 tanks

1935 Mechanized Corps
(Renamed Tank Corps in 1938)
  2 mechanized brigades(BT)
    4 tank battalions
    1 motorized rifle battalion
  1 rifle/machine gun brigade
  1 reconnaissance battalion
    (T-37)
  1 signal battalion

strength: 8965 men
             348 tanks (BT)
              63 tankettes (T-37)
              52 flamethrower
                 tanks
              20 guns

Elsewhere in the force structure, artillery, air defense, antitank, and other units were formed and equipped with modern weaponry to permit them to support the new operational concepts. Similar development occurred in the field of aviation as the Soviets fielded a new generation of bombers and fighters.

The vigorous theoretical and practical progress the Red Army made between 1929 and 1936 increased its combat capability and

TABLE 27
AIR ASSAULT FORCES: 1930s

1933 Special Purpose Airborne Brigade

```
     1 parachute battalion
     1 motorized battalion
     1 artillery battalion
     1 mechanized battalion
     1 air group
     2 heavy squadrons (TB-3)
     1 light squadron (R-5)

     strength:    3,000 men
```

contributed to a more offensive posture by the nation in general. This was done during a time of crises both in the West and in the East, where Fascist and Japanese militarism threatened to tear apart the fabric of capitalist society. The renaissance in Soviet military thought and force capability, if left to develop unimpeded, portended a more active offensive stance on the part of the Soviet Union in world affairs, a stance already presaged by Soviet encouragement of "popular fronts" to resist the force of Fascism and assist in the spread of Socialism. Ironically, however, Soviet military progress was hampered by events occurring within the Soviet Union, events which strangled the renaissance in military thought and reduced Soviet military capabilities at a time when she most needed them.

CRISIS IN THE SOVIET MILITARY ESTABLISHMENT (1937–1941)

Context

Abruptly in 1937 Stalin lashed out at the only remaining segment of Soviet society capable of challenging his power – the military. In a fit of paranoia Stalin extended his purges and, without benefit of the show trials and legal niceties characterizing his earlier purges, he summarily arrested, shot or incarcerated the bulk of the Soviet officer corps on the charge of high treason:

> 35,000 victims in all, or about half the total officer corps; three of five marshals; thirteen out of fifteen army commanders; fifty-seven out of eighty-five corps commanders; 110 out of 195

division commanders; 220 out of 406 brigade commanders. All eleven vice-commissars of War; seventy-five out of eighty members of the Supreme Military Council, including all military district commanders as of May 1937. In percentage of ranks: 90 per cent of all generals, and 80 per cent of all colonels.[38]

Recent Soviet sources admit:

In 1937–1938 three of five Marshals of the Soviet Union, all commanders of forces, members of the military councils, and chiefs of the political departments of the military districts, the majority of the chiefs of the central administrations of the People's Commissariat of Defense, all corps commanders, almost all division and brigade commanders, about half of the regimental commanders, about one-third of the regimental commissars, many teachers of higher or middle military and military-political schools were judged and destroyed. Among the innocently perishing commanders and political workers were such distinguished military figures as V. K. Bliukher, Ia B. Gamarnik (who took his own life), I. A. Egorov, P. E. Dybenko, E. I. Kovtiukh, A. I. Kork, M. N. Tukhachevsky, I. P. Uborevich, I. S. Unshlikht, I. F. Fed'ko, R. P. Eideman, I. E. Iakir and others. Generals P. V. Rychagov – commander of the Red Army Air Force, G. M. Shtern – commander of Air Defense Forces, I. V. Smushkevich – chief inspector of the Air Force and twice hero of the Soviet Union fell victim to the unlawful repression. Generals K. A. Meretskov, K. K. Rokossovsky, and A. V. Gorbatov were repressed, but later freed. The repression embraced all military districts.[39]

The purge of the military liquidated the generation of officers who had given definition to Soviet strategy, operational art, and tactics, who had formulated the concepts of deep battle and deep operations, and who had orchestrated the reconstruction of the Soviet armed forces. Tukhachevsky, Yegorov, Kamenev, Uborovich, Svechin and a host of others, the cream of the crop of innovative military theorists, were purged and killed. Inevitably, their ideas and theories fell under a shadow. Those officers who survived the purges were junior, generally orthodox, or reluctant for obvious reasons to vocally embrace the ideas of their fallen predecessors.

M. V. Zakharov, Chief of Staff of the Soviet Army in the 1960s, said of the purges:

The repression of 1937 and successive years brought to the army, as well as the rest of the country, tremendous harm. It deprived the Red Army and Navy of the most experienced and knowledgeable cadre and the most talented and highly qualified military leaders. It had a negative impact on the further development of military-theoretical thought. The deep study of military science problems became narrow ... Strategy in military academies ceased to be studied as a science and academic discipline. All that resulted not only from unfounded repression but also from an impasse in science, in particular military science. Military theory, in essence, amounted to a mosaic of Stalin's military expressions. The theory of deep operations was subject to doubt because Stalin said nothing about it and its creator was an "enemy of the people". Some of its elements, like, for example, the independent action of motor mechanized and cavalry formations in advance of the front and in the depth of the enemy defense, were even called sabotage and for that foolish reason were rejected ... Such measures attested to the about-face in military theory − back to the linear form of combat on an operational scale.[40]

Strategy

As the shadows of the Second World War spread over Europe, the price the Soviet Union and its military had paid for the purges slowly became apparent. While Soviet military analysts still pondered the nature of modern war, the analysis was thin and the results of the analysis were acted upon slowly. Analysis of the experiences of Soviet tank specialists in the Spanish Civil War cast doubt on the feasibility of using large tank units in combat because of the difficulty in controlling them and because of their vulnerability to artillery fire. Soviet occupation of eastern Poland in September 1939 highlighted the command and control and logistical difficulties involved in employing large mechanized forces*. Zhukov's successful use of tank forces against the Japanese on the Khalkhin-Gol River in August 1939 received attention − not for the successful use of tank forces − but rather for the excessive amount of time required to crush the stubborn Japanese resistance. All of these instances led to a November 1939 Soviet decision to disband the tank corps.

To a degree, Soviet confusion in the strategic realm reflected

---

* Two Soviet tank corps participated fumblingly in the operation.

confusion in the political realm. The decision to abandon support of popular fronts and to sign non-aggression pacts with the most threatening of capitalist powers, Germany and Japan, was paralleled by the lack of Soviet study of the nature of the initial period of war, specifically, the likelihood of enduring and repelling a surprise attack. Soviet unpreparedness in June 1941, in the face of a clear and impending threat, resulted from Soviet failure to ponder strategic questions — a failure since 1956 attributed directly to Stalin.

Operational art

Soviet experiences in the Soviet–Finnish War of 1939–40 combined with the earlier experiences to produce some changes in operational art and tactics. Soviet forces performed dismally in the initial offensive operations during that war. Offensive preparations were poor, coordination of forces weak, and command and control ineffective. Consequently, the first offensive failure was a major embarrassment. Only after more extensive mobilization and intensive preparations was the Finnish defense crushed.

This experience further discredited the tank forces, which had played a limited and largely ineffective role in the war. It also led to adjustments in Soviet operational techniques, which were subsequently incorporated into the 1941 *Field Regulation*. The wartime difficulties the Soviets experienced in penetrating deep, well-equipped defenses prompted the Soviets to increase force concentrations and create higher densities of supporting artillery. Consequently, the width of a projected *front* offensive decreased somewhat as did the planned depth of operations. The *front* penetration sector decreased, but the army offensive sector and penetration sectors remained as they had been. Truncation of the *front* offensive sector improved concentration of forces and increased the projected depth of army operations to 100 kilometers.[41] However, the advance was to be achieved by using infantry, artillery, and infantry support tanks rather than large combined arms mechanized units.

Tactics

Tactics also changed in response to the experiences of the late 1930s. Analysis of Soviet–Finnish War offensive experiences indicated that holding (covering) groups tended to become passive and, consequently, did not actively contribute to the success of battle. The effectiveness of long range action tanks was also limited. Therefore the 1941 *Field Regulation* organized rifle corps, divisions, and regiments on the offensive into combat echelons, artillery groups, tank support groups, and reserves (general, tank, anti-tank). The rifle corps formed in single echelon while rifle divisions, regiments, and battalions deployed in two or three echelons. The three existing types of artillery groups (PP, DD and AR) were supplemented by antitank and anti-aircraft groups, and a single infantry support tank group (TPP — *tankovoi podderzhki pekhoty*) was created in the rifle division to replace the existing three tank groups. The offensive frontage of a rifle corps decreased to 8–12 kilometers and that of a rifle division to 3.5–4.5 kilometers. The depth of rifle corps and division missions increased to 20 kilometers, a result of greater concentration of combat force in narrower attack sectors.*[42] These changes, however, did not eradicate the persistent command and control problems.

In 1941 the Soviets abandoned the use of shock and holding groups on the defense and instead constructed tactical defenses on the basis of combat echelons, artillery groups, and reserves. The growth in power of potential enemy offensive forces caused the rifle division defensive sector to decrease to 6–10 kilometers. On the eve of the German invasion the tactical defense zone included a security belt, a combat security position, a basic defense belt, and a second defense belt. In comparison with 1936, the depth of the tactical defense increased to 20 kilometers and the main defense belt to 10 kilometers. Defenses were deep but still fragmentary and the absence of continuous trenches inhibited lateral maneuver and hidden movements and deprived defenders of defensive cover against enemy artillery fire and air strikes.[43]

On the eve of war

Soviet force development after 1937 progressed unevenly, reflecting on the one hand intent to strengthen the armed forces and, on the other hand Soviet ambivalence over the value of using large mechanized formations to solve operational missions. This unevenness was accentuated by the absence of qualified military theorists who could or would speak out against what they perceived to be Stalin's views. Younger officers like Zhukov, Romanenko, Eremenko, Bagramian and others did what they could in relative isolation to develop earlier operational concepts.

While Soviet expansion of the army was still under way, and rifle

---

* Rifle corps and division immediate missions were 8 kilometers and subsequent missions 20 kilometers.

TABLE 28
ARMY STRUCTURE: 1940–1941

Theoretical

Shock Army
4-6 rifle corps
    14-18 rifle divisions
1 mechanized corps (in 1941) or cavalry corps
6-8 tank brigades
2-3 air divisions
10-12 artillery regiments

strength: 200,000-300,000 men
           1,400 tanks
           2,700 guns/mortars

- --

Actual Army Composition 1941

2-3 rifle corps
    6-15 rifle divisions
1 mechanized corps (incomplete)
artillery regiments
air divisions

strength: 60,000-80,000 men
           400-700 tanks
           1,200-1,300 guns/mortars

corps and rifle divisions were being strengthened and rearmed, the
Soviets severely truncated their mechanized forces (see tables
28–31). In November 1939, after several months of study, the Kulik
Commission recommended disbandment of the 4 tank corps
(renamed tank in 1938), and recommended they be replaced by 15
smaller motorized divisions, 8 to be formed in 1940 and the remainder during the first six months of 1941 (see table 32).* On 15
January 1940 the 4 tank corps were abolished and their tanks were
used to create new heavy and light tank brigades designated to work
in close coordination with rifle corps (see table 32).[44]

* Simultaneously, the Soviets created motorized rifle divisions with a lighter armor
complement.

TABLE 29
RIFLE FORCES: 1939–1941

1940-41 Rifle Corps

3 rifle divisions
2 artillery regiments
1 antiaircraft battalion
1 sapper battalion
1 signal battalion

strength: 50,000 men
           966 guns/mortars

1941 Rifle Division

3 rifle regiments
     6 x 76 mm guns
     4 x 120 mm mortars
     6 x 45 mm AT
2 artillery regiments
1 reconnaissance battalion
1 antitank battalion
1 antiaircraft battalion
1 sapper battalion
1 signal battalion
1 tank battalion

strength: 14,483 men
           294 guns
           150 mortars
           16 light tanks
           13 armored cars

1939 Rifle Division

3 rifle regiments
     4 x 76 mm guns
     4 x 120 mm mortars
     6 x 45 mm AT
2 artillery regiments
     1 artillery battalion (16 x 76mm)
     1 artillery battalion (8 x 122mm)
     2 artillery battalions (12x122mm)
     1 artillery battalion (12 x152mm)
1 reconnaissance battalion
1 antitank battalion (12 x 45mm)
1 antiaircraft battalion
     8 x 37 mm
     4 x 76 mm
1 sapper battalion
1 signal battalion
1 tank battalion

strength: 14,483 men
          (18,000 wartime)
          144 guns
          66 mortars
          45 light tanks
       1,762 machine guns
          13 armored cars

TABLE 30
CAVALRY FORCES: 1940–1941

1941 Cavalry Corps

2 cavalry divisions
1 artillery regiment
1 tank brigade (light)
1 signal squadron

strength: 19,000 men
          128 light tanks
          44 armored cars
          264 guns/mortars

1941 Cavalry Division

4 cavalry regiments
4 cavalry squadrons
1 machine gun squadron
1 mechanized regiment (BT-5)
1 cavalry artillery battalion
1 antiaircraft battalion

strength: 9,224 men
          64 light tanks
          18 armored cars
          132 guns/mortars

TABLE 31
TANK FORCES: 1938

1938 Tank Corps

2 tank brigades (BT)
    4 tank battalions
    1 reconnaissance battalion
    1 motorized rifle battalion
1 rifle/machine gun brigade
1 reconnaissance battalion
1 signal battalion

strength: 12,710 men
               560 tanks
               118 guns

1938 Light Tank Brigade

4 tank battalions
    (54-BT, T-26;
      6 x 76 mm arty tanks)
1 motorized rifle battalion
1 reconnaissance battalion

strength: 216 tanks
             24 arty tanks

1938 Heavy Tank Brigade

4 tank battalions
    (31-T-28, T-35;
      6 x 76 mm arty tanks)
1 motorized rifle battalion
1 reconnaissance battalion

strength: 124 tanks
             24 arty tanks

TABLE 32
MECHANIZED AND TANK FORCES: 1939–1940

1940 Motorized Division

2 motorized rifle regiments
1 tank regiment
1 artillery regiment
1 antiaircraft battalion
1 antitank battalion
1 reconnaissance battalion
1 signal battalion
1 light engineer battalion
supply units

strength: 11,650 men
               275 tanks
                98 guns/mortars
                49 armored cars

1939 Motorized Rifle Division

3 motorized rifle regiments
1 tank battalion
1 artillery regiment
1 antiaircraft battalion
1 antitank battalion
1 reconnaissance battalion
support units

strength: 10,000 men
                37 tanks
               209 guns/mortars
                58 armored cars

1940 Light Tank Brigade

4 tank battalions
1 motorized rifle battalion
1 reconnaissance battalion

strength: 258 tanks
              (BT, T-26)

1940 Heavy Tank Brigade

4 tank battalions
1 motorized rifle
    battalion
1 reconnaissance
    battalion

strength: 156 tanks
              (T-28, T-35)

The French Army's débâcle of June 1940, which repeated the lesson in mobile warfare the Germans had taught the world in Poland in September 1939, stunned the Soviet leadership, who subsequently bitterly noted that "Fascist Germany used the methods of deep operations which we developed earlier. The Germans borrowed the achievements of Soviet military-theoretical thought and with great success used them in the war with Poland and the West."[45] The Soviets responded to the defeat of France with a hasty program to rebuild a large mechanized force structure. They began forming large mechanized corps consisting of tank and motorized divisions numbering, on paper, 1031 tanks each (see table 33). Twenty-nine corps were to be created by 1942, equipped in part with modern T-34 and KV tanks, just then entering production. Simultaneously, the Soviets created antitank brigades and heavier artillery units in order to repair the damage done to the force structure since 1939 (see table 34).[46] Ironically, while tank forces were being emasculated, the formation of air assault units continued

TABLE 33
MECHANIZED FORCES: 1940–1941

1940 Mechanized Corps	1941 Mechanized Corps
2 tank divisions	(organization same as 1940)
1 motorized division (1940 TOE)	
1 motorcycle regiment	
1 signal battalion	
1 motorized engineer battalion	
1 aviation troop	
strength: 37,200 men	strength: 36,080 men
1,108 tanks	1,031 tanks
	(420 T-34,
	126 KV)

1940 Tank Division	1941 Tank Division
2 tank regiments	(same organization as 1940)
1 motorized rifle regiment	
1 artillery regiment	
1 antiaircraft battalion	
1 antitank battalion	
1 signal battalion	
1 reconnaissance battalion	
1 pontoon-bridge battalion	
strength: 11,343 men	strength: 10,940 men
413 tanks	375 tanks

unanabated. The number of air assault brigades increased in the late 1930s, and in 1941 the Soviets formed 5 airborne corps of 10,000 men each, designated to conduct the vertical dimension of deep operations (see table 35).

TABLE 34
ARTILLERY UNITS: 1941

1941 Gun Artillery Regiment	1941 Heavy Gun Artillery Regiment
12 batteries (122 mm, 152 mm guns)	6 batteries (152 mm guns)
strength: 48 guns	strength: 24 guns

1941 Howitzer Artillery Regiment	1941 Heavy Howitzer Artillery Regiment
12 batteries (152 mm howitzer)	6 batteries (203 mm howitzer)
strength: 48 guns	strength: 24 guns

1941 Separate Heavy Artillery Battalion	1941 Special Antitank Brigade
3 batteries (210 mm guns, 280 mm mortars, 305 mm howitzers)	2 antitank regiments 1 mine sapper battalion 1 auto transport battalion
strength: 15 guns	strength: 120 guns 28 antiaircraft machine guns 4,800 antitank mines

TABLE 35
AIR, ASSAULT FORCES: 1941

1941 Airborne Corps	1941 Airborne Brigade
3 airborne brigades 1 tank battalion (light) 3 tank companies 1 long range signal platoon 1 control aircraft flight 1 mobile equipment platoon	4 parachute battalions (6 x 76 mm guns, 12 x 45 mm guns, 6 x 82 mm mortars) 1 bicycle recon company 1 antiaircraft machine gun company
strength: 10,419 men 50 tanks (T-37)	strength: 3,000 men

Characteristically, the term deep operations remained entombed with the bodies of its creators, signifying the difficulty Stalin had in returning to the theoretical principles of 1936, at least in name. In time Stalin and a new military leadership would return to, and in large measure perfect, those principles, but it would take the disasters of war to prompt that return. The creators of deep operations themselves would not be rehabilitated until the late 1950s.

While claiming that the ensuing war confirmed the correctness of earlier Soviet theories on the preparation and conduct of *front* and army operations, in a masterpiece of understatement the Soviets admit:

> that commanders and staffs were not fully familiar with all of the theories of conducting deep battle and there were shortfalls in the material base that hindered its realization. Thus, during the war it was necessary to reassess and clarify some aspects of preparing and conducting offensive operations and decide anew many questions, on the conduct of defensive operations on a strategic and operational scale.[47]

A former associate of Tukhachevsky and a survivor of the purges was more direct, stating:

> the old, experienced military leaders, who created Soviet military theory and could with high artfulness put it into practice, were no more and there were insufficient numbers of operationally prepared commanders at the beginning of war. Therefore, a painful drama, played out in the summer of 1941, had a deep political and strategic meaning related to the Stalin cult of personality. The consequences of that were immensely painful. It cost tremendous casualties and evoked huge losses.[48]

CHAPTER FIVE

THE GREAT PATRIOTIC WAR AND THE MATURATION OF OPERATIONAL ART: 1941–1945

TRAGEDY AND REBIRTH OF AN ARMY (1941–1942)

Context

On the morning of 22 June 1941 Nazi Germany unleashed a sudden and massive offensive aimed at destroying the Soviet state. The ambitious German undertaking, based on the premise that the bulk of the Red Army could be annihilated in the immediate border regions by use of large-scale blitzkrieg, caught the Soviets only partially prepared for war. Force reconstruction and reequipment programs were underway but incomplete, and, although the Soviets had ample warning, for as yet inexplicable reasons Stalin forbade the Soviet military from taking prudent defensive precautions, thus granting the Germans the benefits of strategic, operational and tactical surprise. German hammer blows staggered the Soviet armed forces and almost destroyed them. By Soviet admission:

> our pre-war views on the conduct of armed struggle in the initial period of war did not investigate the possibility of concealed timely deployment and simultaneous enemy armed forces operations on the land, in the air and at sea. Mistakes in theory had a negative effect on resolving the practical questions of covering the state borders and deploying the armed forces, which, along with other reasons, caused serious misfortunes in the war.
>
> There were many problems in working out command and control and organizing communications with operational large units. The assertion that the defense found fullest expression only in the realm of army operations was incorrect, as was the view that the struggle for air superiority must be realized on the scale of *front* and army operations. The complicated views at

the beginning of the war concerning the organization of the
army and forces' rear did not fully answer the demands of the
theory of deep offensive operations and battle. Operational
and forces rear services remained cumbersome and immobile.

There were also serious deficiencies in the theoretical
training of commanders and in the combat training of forces
...[1]

These Soviet admissions, as frank as they were, understated the
scale of the problem. In the initial months of the war, Soviet
commanders at higher levels demonstrated an ineptness only
partially compensated for by the fervor of junior officers and the
stoicism and bravery of the hard pressed troops. *Front* and army
commanders were unable to construct coherent defenses against
the German armored thrusts and displayed an alarming propensity
for launching costly uncoordinated counter-attacks predestined to
failure. Only looming disaster drove the Soviet High Command to
action in a war which quickly became one of survival.

Ultimately the Red Army successfully met this second great
challenge and triumphed, but only after years of attrition, frustra-
tion, and an agonizing process of military reeducation conducted
during wartime. Throughout the war a new generation of commanders emerged, new equipment was developed and fielded, and
military theories matured after their late 1930s' hiatus. In essence,
the concept of deep operations, in fact if not in name, became the
focal point of Soviet offensive theory and the means of converting
tactical success into operational and even strategic success. By late
1943 Soviet military theory and the Soviet force structure were wed
into a successful formula for achieving victory. During the ensuing
two years of war the Soviets experimented with operational techniques, refined their force structure, and worked to overcome
resource and logistical constraints. This second great renaissance in
Soviet military thought and practice is ignored in the West today
because it was overshadowed by the Soviet disasters of 1941 and
1942 which were thoroughly covered in the works of victorious
German generals. Today, however, that renaissance is viewed by
the Soviets as the most important period in Soviet military affairs, a
vast laboratory for military analysis and a repository of experience
that can be and is tapped for inspiration and concrete advice when
addressing contemporary and future military problems.

For the sake of analysis the Soviets subdivide their "Great Patriotic
War" into three distinct periods, each characterized by broad

unifying themes reflecting Soviet fortunes in war and the state of military art.* The first period of war (June 1941 – November 1942) found the Soviets on the strategic defense punctuated by several Soviet attempts to undertake offensive operations on several important directions. The second period (December 1942 – December 1943) was one of transition from defensive operations to a general Soviet offensive designed to wrest the strategic initiative from the Germans. The third period (1944–1945) was a period of general Soviet offensives culminating in the achievement of total victory.

The first and most difficult period commenced in June 1941 with the German invasion and the series of border battles during which the Germans swallowed up large segments of deployed Soviet forces amounting to as much as fifty percent of the Soviet peacetime army. The large scale encirclements of Soviet forces at Minsk, Smolensk, Kiev, Briansk, and Viaz'ma culminated in the fall of 1941, when German forces tried to cap their victorious advance with the seizure of Moscow by one last envelopment. The German failure to take Moscow prompted the first major Soviet attempt to regain the strategic initiative. A desperate Soviet winter offensive in the Moscow environs, broadened into an attempt to expand the offensive across the front from Leningrad to Rostov and the Crimea, foundered because of insufficient Soviet forces and materiel, and left the Soviets vulnerable to renewed German strategic thrusts in the summer of 1942. The ill-fated and costly Soviet offensive failures at Khar'kov and Kerch in May 1942 were followed by a general German offensive in south Russia, which, by late fall, had reached the Volga at Stalingrad and the passes of the Caucasus Mountains. Like the 1941 German offensive effort, by late fall the Germans were overextended, even as the Soviets again husbanded their resources for a major counteroffensive. Unlike 1941, in 1942 the Soviets undertook organizational and theoretical measures to better parry the German offensive as it lost momentum on the banks of the Volga. The Soviet November offensive around Stalingrad saw the strategic initiative pass into Soviet hands and marked the end of the first period of war.

Force structure

The German attack in 1941 smashed the large and complex Soviet

* Prior to 1953 they subdivided the war into four periods by treating 1944 and 1945 as separate periods.

force structure and clearly demonstrated that the Soviet officer corps was incapable of efficiently commanding and controlling so elaborate a force. Likewise, Soviet industry had been unable to supply the necessary weaponry to equip so extensive a force. Thus, by late summer 1941 the Soviets were forced to dismantle that portion of their force structure the Germans had not already destroyed. They severely truncated the size of all units to improve span of control, and they concentrated scarce artillery and armor assets under High Command control (see tables 36–39). The Soviets abolished rifle corps and created smaller armies consisting of rifle divisions and rifle brigades. Rifle divisions were reduced in strength, and smaller, more easily controlled rifle brigades, in essence light divisions, were formed to supplement rifle divisions. The Soviets abolished the mechanized corps and their component mechanized and tank divisions and consolidated armor assets in a handful of small tank brigades earmarked to support the smaller armies.* Field, antitank, and antiaircraft artillery, withdrawn from rifle divisions, corps and armies, were also formed into battalions, regiments and brigades under High Command control to reinforce armies operating along specific directions. The Soviets also created numerous small light cavalry divisions, combined into cavalry corps, in order to compensate for shortages in armor and provide some mobile offensive capability for the basically footbound Soviet army.[2]†

These measures, designed to truncate the Soviet force structure and implemented along with improvements in strategic and operational command and control, provided the basis for Soviet offensive successes in the winter of 1941–42. But it was clear that further improvements were necessary if the Soviets hoped to expand their limited offensive capabilities. In particular, larger and more effective mechanized formations were essential for developing tactical success into operational success. Thus, in the spring of 1942, while larger artillery units were evolving and Soviet riflemen were being reequipped with an array of automatic weapons, the Soviets created new tank corps designated to exploit success in army operations (see table 40).** Later, in the summer, tank armies of mixed composition (rifle, cavalry and infantry forces) were formed to conduct larger scale exploitation, and in early fall mechanized

* In December 1941 the Soviets possessed 79 tank brigades.

† The Soviets formed 80 light cavalry divisions in December 1941.

** By December 1942 the Soviets had formed 28 tank corps.

TABLE 36
RIFLE FORCES: DECEMBER 1941

Army

```
5-6 rifle divisions or rifle brigades
1-2 cavalry divisions
1-2 separate tank brigades or battalions
    artillery regiments
    guards mortar battalions (multiple rocket
                        launchers)
  1 sapper battalion

strength: 70,000 men
          20-90 tanks
          30-450 guns/mortars
          8-19 multiple rocket launchers
```

Rifle Division

```
3 rifle regiments (4 x 76 mm gun, 6 x 45 mm AT)
1 artillery regiment (8 x 122 mm, 16 x 76 mm)
1 antiaircraft battalion
1 antitank battalion (12 x 45 mm)
1 sapper battalion
1 signal company

strength: 11,626 men
              36 guns
             162 mortars
```

Rifle Brigade

```
3 rifle battalions
1 artillery battalion
2 mortar battalions (82 mm, 120 mm)
1 antitank battalion

strength:  4,400 men
```

corps were formed which combined heavy armor and large numbers of mechanized infantry (often scarce in tank corps) (see tables 41–42).* Although the new composite tank armies proved unwieldy and difficult to coordinate, the tank and mechanized corps provided the offensive punch necessary for the Soviets to unleash the successful Stalingrad counteroffensive in November 1942. These structural changes combined with increased Soviet production of the weapons of war and revitalized Soviet military theory to produce the turnabout in Soviet battlefield fortunes in the late fall of 1942.

* The Soviets created 6 tank armies and 8 mechanized corps. At the end of December 1942 the Soviet armored force counted 2 tank armies, 24 tank corps, and 8 mechanized corps.

Table 37.   Rifle Forces: 1942

May 1942 Rifle Army
        6-10 rifle divisions or rifle brigades
        2-4 tank brigades, regiments or battalions
        1 antiaircraft regiment
        artillery regiments
        1 guards mortar battalion
        1 sapper battalion
        1-2 tank corps (optional attachment)

    strength: 80,000-100,000 men
                250-450 tanks
              1,000-2,500 guns/mortars
                 24-426 MRLs

1942 Rifle Corps
        2-3 rifle divisions
        (no support)

March 1942 Rifle Division
        3 rifle regiments (4 x 76 mm, 6 x 45 mm)
        1 artillery regiment (20 x 76 mm, 12 x 122 mm)
        1 antiaircraft battalion
        1 antitank battalion (12 x 45 mm)
        1 sapper battalion
        1 signal company

    strength: 12,795 men
                 44 field guns
                170 mortars
                  6 AA guns
                 30 AT guns

July 1942 Rifle Brigade
4 rifle battalions

1 artillery battalion

1 mortar battalion (120 mm)
1 automatic weapons battalion
1 antitank rifle company

strength: 6,000 men

July 1942 Rifle Division
3 rifle regiments (4 x 76 mm, 6
x 45 mm)
1 artillery regiment (20 x
76 mm, 12 x 122 mm)
1 antiaircraft battalion
1 antitank battalion
1 sapper battalion
1 signal company

strength: 10,386 men
              44 guns
             188 mortars
               6 AA guns
              30 AT guns

Doctrine

Soviet military doctrine during the first period of war, and during the war in general, remained consistent with the pre-war focus on defense of the homeland and socialist revolution in the Soviet

TABLE 38
TANK FORCES: DECEMBER 1941

Tank Brigade	Separate Tank Battalion
2 tank battalions	1 heavy tank company
1 heavy tank company (5 KV)	1 medium tank company
1 medium tank company (7 T-34)	2 light tank companies
1 light tank company (10 T-60)	
1 motorized rifle battalion	strength: 202 men
1 reconnaissance company	36 tanks
1 repair, reconstruction company	(5 KV, 11 T-34, 20 T-60)
1 transport company	
1 medical platoon	

strength: 1,471 men
           46 tanks (10 KV, 16 T-34, 20 T-60)

TABLE 39
CAVALRY FORCES: DECEMBER 1941

Cavalry Corps
     2-3 cavalry divisions and/or
     2-3 light cavalry divisions
       1 tank brigade (optional)
     1-2 rifle divisions (optional)
       1 artillery regiment
       1 signal squadron

Cavalry Division	Light Cavalry Division
4 cavalry regiments	3 cavalry regiments
1 cavalry artillery battalion	1 cavalry artillery battalion
1 tank regiment (BT-5)	1 signal squadron
1 antiaircraft battalion	
1 reconnaissance battalion	
1 signal squadron	strength: 3,447 men
1 sapper squadron	

strength: 9,224 TOE
         6,000 actual
           64 light tanks
           18 armored cars
         132 guns/mortars

Union. In the early war years this meant simple survival, but soon it encompassed liberation of all Soviet territory. By mid-war and certainly by war's end the definition of security broadened to include the defense of the nation and socialism by liberation of adjacent lands and the establishment of friendly (socialist) governments in territories adjacent to the Soviet Union. Only in post-war years would the limits of this realm become clear.

TABLE 40
TANK CORPS: 1942

March 1942 Tank Corps
          2 tank brigades (3 in April)
          1 motorized rifle brigade
          (no supply or support units)

          strength: 5,603 men
                       100 tanks (20 KV, 40 T-34, 40 T-60/T-70)
                        98 guns/mortars

July 1942 Tank Corps
          3 tank brigades
          1 motorized rifle brigade
          1 mortar battery
          1 guards mortar battalion (8 x BM-13)
          1 motorcycle battalion
          1 armored car battalion
          1 transport company
          1 engineers-mine company
          2 repair companies
            (tank, artillery)

          strength: 7,800 men
                       168 tanks (70 T-70, 98 T-34)
                        98 guns/mortars

   As war unfolded the Soviets softened the political aspects of
doctrine to draw strength from Russian traditions and nationalism.
Simultaneously the Soviets emphasized practical measures necessary to achieve victory. Under Stalin's leadership, the General Staff
made tremendous efforts to investigate strategic, operational,
and tactical methods for preparing and conducting operations.
Battlefield experiences were gathered, studied, analysed and
converted into directives, instructions and coherent regulations
governing the conduct of war.[3] This practical work paralleled
practical measures the Soviets undertook to mobilize the will and
resources of the nation for war. While ideology remained a strong
ingredient and party control predominated, the Soviets tapped
memories of past "Russian" military glories to inspire the nation. A
pantheon of Russian heroes — Peter the Great, Rumiantsev,
Suvorov, Kutuzov, and others — re-emerged and their memories
were commemorated in new military decorations for Soviet war
heroes. New ranks and titles adorned the new Soviet officer corps
and reinforced the older Soviet discipline even while echoes of
"holy" mother Russia could be heard above the din of battle. If

TABLE 41
TANK ARMIES: 1942

May-June 1942 Type Tank Army

```
     2-3 tank corps
     1-3 rifle and cavalry divisions
       1 separate tank brigade
       1 light artillery regiment
       1 guards mortar regiment
       1 antiaircraft battalion

    strength:  35,000 men
              350-500 tanks
              150-200 guns/mortars
```

Actual Tank Army Composition

3d Tank Army (May 1942)

```
  3 tank corps
  1 motorized rifle division
  2 rifle divisions
  1 separate tank brigade
```

5th Tank Army (June 1942)

```
  3 tank corps
  1 rifle division
  1 separate tank brigade
```

1st Tank Army (July 1942)

```
  2 tank corps
  2 rifle divisions
  1 separate tank brigade
```

4th Tank Army (July 1942)

```
  2 tank corps
  1 rifle division
  1 antitank brigade
  1 separate tank brigade
```

5th Tank Army (Nov 1942)

```
  2 tank corps
  1 cavalry corps
  6 rifle divisions
  1 separate tank brigade
```

the nature of Soviet military doctrine remained constant during wartime, the tone of that doctrine perceptibly changed, driven by the necessity of surviving and attaining victory in war.

Strategy

The foremost strategic problem for the Soviet High Command during the first period of the war was that of conducting a successful strategic defense. Specifically, the Soviets had to halt the German general offensive, deprive the Germans of their initial advantages derived from their surprise offensives and from their superiority in operational and tactical skills; establish defenses along a huge front, including around the major cities of Moscow and Leningrad; and

TABLE 42
MECHANIZED CORPS: SEPTEMBER 1942

Type 1 Mechanized Corps	Type 2 Mechanized Corps	Type 3 Mechanized Corps
3 mechanized brigades (39 tanks each)	3 mechanized brigades (39 tanks each)	3 mechanized brigades (39 tanks each)
1 tank brigade (53 tanks each)	2 tank brigades (53 tanks each)	2 separate tank regiments (39 tanks each)
1 antiaircraft regiment		
1 antitank regiment		
1 guards mortar battalion	(same support as type 1 corps)	(same support as type 1 corps)
1 armored car battalion		
1 signal company		
1 sapper battalion		
1 medical battalion		
1 transport company		
1 repair, reconstruction battalion		

strength: 13,599 men	strength: 14,000 + men	strength: 14,000 men
175 tanks	224 tanks	204 tanks
75 (T-70)		
100 (T-34)		

prepare to conduct critical counteroffensives. All this had to be done over tremendous distances, in spite of tremendous losses in manpower, equipment, territory and the nation's productive base.

The Red Army conducted its strategic defensive operations simultaneously along several strategic directions by using several *fronts* cooperating according to *High Command* plans. This practice clashed with pre-war views which supposed that single *fronts* would be able to conduct strategic defensive operations, and such a departure from pre-war views produced new concepts governing operations by groups of *fronts*. These operations were aimed at inflicting maximum casualties on the enemy, weakening and bleeding his main offensive groups while slowing his offensive, denying him possession of the most important economic and political regions, and creating conditions suitable for the conduct of counteroffensives. Strategic defensive operations raged along frontages from 200 to 800 kilometers to depths of from 100 to 600 kilometers* over a period of from 20 to 100 days. Strategic reserves played a significant role in the strategic defense by establishing new

---

* The German thrusts of 1941 ultimately reached a depth of 400 kilometers. Those of 1942 reached 600 kilometers deep.

defense lines, liquidating enemy penetrations, and providing forces necessary to launch counteroffensives. During this period of the war the *High Command* retained between two and ten reserve armies under its direct control. These reserves were instrumental in slowing and containing the German onslaught, and in launching the winter counteroffensive around Moscow in 1941–42 and the abortive Khar'kov offensive in May 1942. Soviet strategic offensives, usually begun in the form of a counteroffensive, ranged in scope from 50–550 kilometers of frontage to depths of from 50–250 kilometers.[4] All were overly ambitious, and, because of force and logistical inadequacies, they fell far short of expectations. The Soviet High Command still had to learn the art of the possible.

Strict centralization of command and control at the highest level made successful strategic defense possible. Early Soviet attempts to create three separate groups of *fronts* to cover the three main strategic directions (northwest, west, and southwest) failed because of inept command and control during the disastrous operations in the summer of 1941. Even before their initiation, on 23 June 1941 Stalin had created the *STAVKA* of the Supreme High Command (*STAVKA VGK*) to provide "uninterrupted and qualified command and control." By 8 August Stalin reorganized the *STAVKA* with himself as Supreme High Commander.[5] The *STAVKA*, either directly or through its representatives, familiarized commanders of directions and *fronts* with the aims of each operation, provided forces and weaponry, designated missions, and organized cooperation between *fronts* and other large units. It also provided a link between political and military leaders and, as such, provided clear political control over the conduct of the war.

Operational art

In the operational arena, during the first period of war the Soviets amassed considerable experience in conducting *front* and army defensive operations. *Fronts* defended along operational directions under *STAVKA* control while armies defended according to *front* plans. Shortages of men and material forced the Soviets to deploy the bulk of their forces in a single shallow operational echelon with only small reserves (in violation of pre-war concepts) (see tables 43–44). Concentrated German armor supported by aviation easily pierced these shallow, poorly prepared defenses. As Soviet mobilization progressed and weapons production improved, however, the Soviets were able to increase weapons densities and create deeper defenses. By the fall of 1942 Soviet combined

TABLE 43
FRONT OPERATIONAL FORMATION — DEFENSE, SUMMER 1941

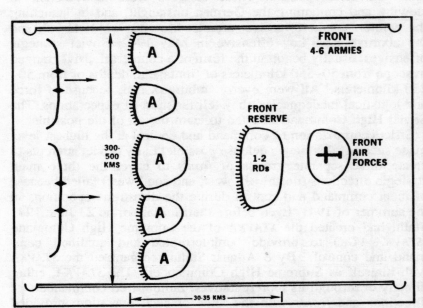

arms armies formed their first army artillery groups, air defense groups, and artillery and antitank reserves (see tables 45–46). The combined arms army's defensive depth increased to as much as 20 kilometers, its average operational density to 10 kilometers of front per rifle division, and the average weapons density to 15–25 guns per kilometer of front. By the end of 1942 army and *front* defensive depths averaged 15 and 30 kilometers, respectively, with the first defensive belt best developed, consisting of battalion defensive regions. The fragmented nature of the defense, however, isolated subunits and hindered maneuver of forces along the front and in its depths.

Throughout the first period of war the Soviets emphasized improvements in antitank defenses which had been ineffective early in the war due to the paucity of weapons and the tendency of commanders to scatter them evenly across the front. Heavy caliber artillery and aviation had been ineffective against enemy armor for

TABLE 44
ARMY OPERATIONAL FORMATION — DEFENSE, SUMMER 1941

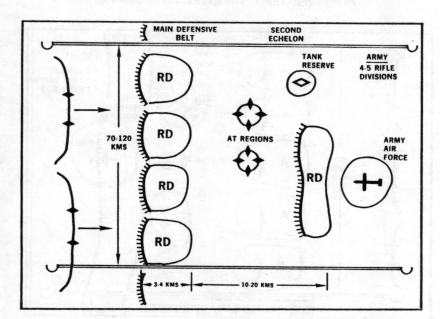

the same reason. Although antitank artillery remained in scarce supply (less than 5 guns per kilometer), by mid-1942 the Soviets began creating antitank regions (strong points) echeloned in depth along likely tank axes of advance. Eventually Soviet attachment of antitank reserves from *front* and army commands to lower command echelons increased the density and mobility of antitank defenses. After the summer of 1941 artillery customarily engaged enemy armor units to supplement other antitank defenses (often in a direct fire role).[6]

Offensive operations conducted during 1941 and 1942 provided the Soviets with the experience upon which to base improvements in their offensive operational techniques. In their largest-scale offensive, the Moscow winter offensive of 1941–42, Soviet *fronts* advanced in sectors from 300–400 kilometers wide and armies in sectors 20–80 kilometers wide, with objectives at depths of 120–250 kilometers for *fronts* and 30–35 kilometers for armies. These objec-

TABLE 45
FRONT OPERATIONAL FORMATION — DEFENSE 1942

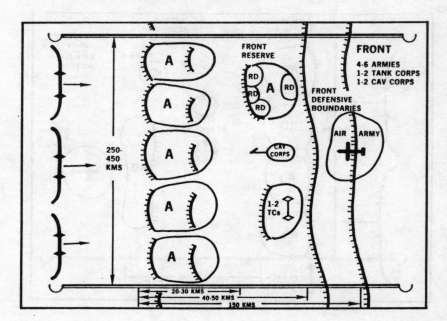

tives were to be secured within a period of 6–8 days. The tendency on the part of Soviet commanders to disperse attacking forces over a wide front prompted *STAVKA* corrective action during the winter offensive. *STAVKA* Directive No. 3 (10 January 1942) required commanders at all levels of command to create shock groups in order to mass forces on relatively narrow frontages in critical sectors.[7] The directive established penetration sectors of 30 kilometers for *fronts* and 15 kilometers for armies. These measures permitted creation of higher artillery densities on main attack directions (from 7–12 guns/mortars per kilometer in summer–autumn 1941 to 45–65 guns/mortars in the summer of 1942).

The offensive operational formation of *fronts* throughout the entire first period of war was single echelon, at first with a two- or three- rifle division reserve, and later with a tank or cavalry corps in reserve (see tables 47–48). Armies also formed in single echelon throughout 1941 (see table 49). In 1942, however, an increase in

TABLE 46
ARMY OPERATIONAL FORMATION – DEFENSE 1942

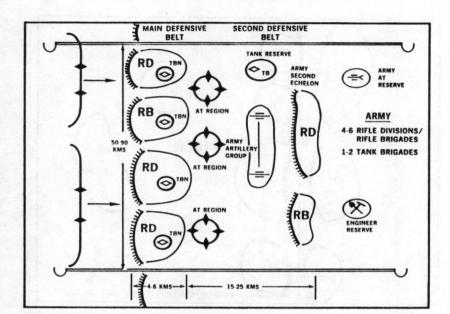

army strength permitted army commanders to deploy their forces in
two echelons with a combined arms reserve; mobile forces (a mobile
group); artillery groups; and antitank, tank, and engineer reserves
(see table 50). As a result, the depth of the army operational
formation increased to 15–20 kilometers and in some instances 30–
40 kilometers.[8]

The operational role of Soviet armor increased both in a defensive role and on the offensive. The Soviets used the small tank
brigades of 1941/42 in concert with cavalry and air assault forces to
stiffen infantry defense, launch counterattacks and spearhead
pursuits. These mobile forces, however, had limited sustaining
power, and they were difficult to resupply and coordinate with
infantry. In 1942 the new tank armies, tank corps, and mechanized
corps provided better means for countering German armored
thrusts and exploiting success while functioning as mobile groups of
fronts and armies. The composition of these fledgling armored

TABLE 47
FRONT OPERATIONAL FORMATION – 1941

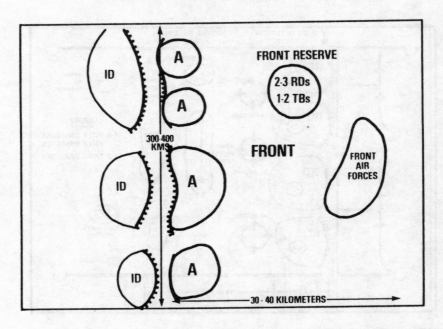

forces, however, was unbalanced because of a marked shortage of mechanized infantry and their strange mixture of hoofbound, footbound, and trackbound forces. Hence, they were difficult to coordinate with other types of forces, they were vulnerable when isolated from their supporting infantry, and Soviet commanders simply had not learned how to use them properly. A special order of the People's Commissariat of Defense (Order No. #325), issued on 16 October 1942, pondered mobile group failures (such as the debacle at Khar'kov in May 1942), directed that tank and mechanized corps be used as single entities for powerful attacks or counter-attacks, and prohibited the fragmented use of those valuable operational formations.[9]

During the first period of war the Soviets attempted to conduct operational deception (*maskirovka*) in accordance with well-defined pre-war views. While their attempts to do so were often unsuccessful, they managed to prepare and implement effective deception plans for their limited offensives at Rostov (December

TABLE 48
FRONT OPERATIONAL FORMATION – 1942

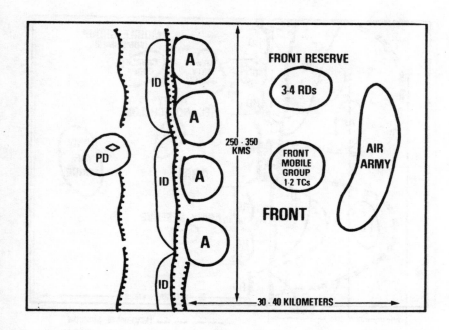

1941), Moscow–Toropets (January 1942) and Barvenkovo–
Lozovaia (January 1942). An effective Soviet operational deception
at Khar'kov (May 1942) fell victim to an even more successful
German strategic deception plan.

Tactics

At the outbreak of war Soviet tactics suffered from the same general
malaise as operational art. Understrength divisions (5,000–6,000
men) defending in extended sectors (14–20 kilometers) were forced
to deploy in single echelon defenses with a depth of only 3–5
kilometers (see table 51). The small reserves had little capability for
conducting sustained counterattacks, and infantry support artillery
groups were weak. Inadequate tactical densities of .5 battalions
and 3 guns/mortars per kilometer of frontage resulted. Division
defenses, subdivided into battalion defense regions, were non-
contiguous and had little engineer support or antitank defenses. By

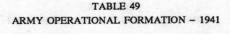

TABLE 49
ARMY OPERATIONAL FORMATION – 1941

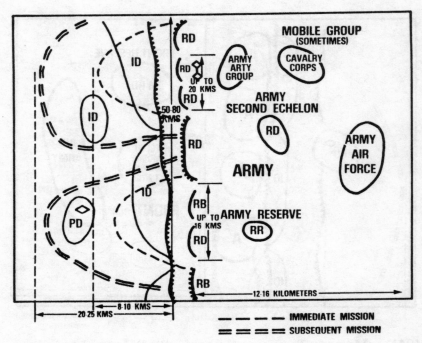

late 1941 more extensive engineer support permitted construction of trenches and the evolution of a truly interconnected first defensive position. Increases in manpower and weaponry further improved the defenses in 1942. Thereafter, divisions began creating second echelons, tank and antitank reserves, and stronger artillery groups (see table 52). The second echelons of rifle regiments and rifle divisions created battalion defensive regions which later would become second and third defensive positions. Meanwhile, division defenses remained shallow (one defensive belt) and weak in anti-tank means. By the end of the first period of war tactical densities had risen to 1 battalion and 20 guns/mortars per kilometer of front.[10]

The realities of combat forced Soviet offensive tactics to deviate from those recommended in pre-war regulations. Rifle divisions at first deployed in two echelon formations recommended by those regulations. This meant that only 8 of the division's 27 rifle

TABLE 50
ARMY OPERATIONAL FORMATION – 1942

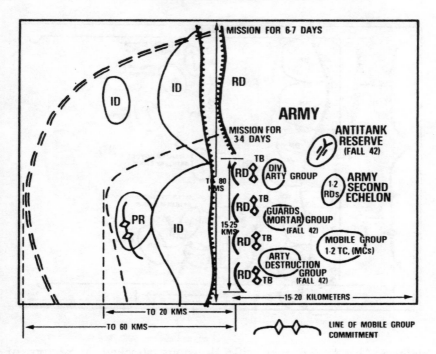

companies actually participated directly in an attack. Because of the general weakness of rifle divisions, this combat formation was futile and vulnerable as well to enemy air and artillery fire. Consequently, Commissariat of Defense Order No. 306, issued on 8 October 1942, required the use of a single echelon combat formation in all units from company to division and the creation of a reserve comprising one-ninth of the force.[11] In effect, this order mandated the forward use of 80 percent of a division's combat power and facilitated achievement of tactical penetrations. However, it also made difficult a division's ability to sustain an attack.

By the winter of 1941–42, rifle divisions, organized in this new single echelon configuration, attacked in sectors 5–6 kilometers wide (on occasions as much as 10 kilometers) to achieve objectives from 5 to 12 kilometers deep (in some isolated instances as much as 20 kilometers)(see table 53). After January 1942, when enemy

TABLE 51
RIFLE DIVISION COMBAT FORMATION – DEFENSE 1942

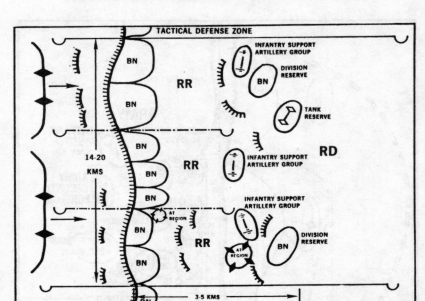

defenses became deeper, rifle divisions attacked in sectors of 3–4 kilometers against objectives 5–7 kilometers deep, which, in reality, took several days to secure (see table 54). Tactical densities increased from 1–2 rifle battalions, 20–30 guns/mortars and 2–3 tanks per kilometer of frontage during the winter of 1941–1942 to 2–4 battalions, 30–40 guns/mortars, and 10–14 tanks per kilometer of frontage in the summer of 1942.[12]

Fire support available for rifle divisions increased with the creation of infantry support artillery groups (PP) and, in some instances, long-range action artillery groups (DD). Centralized artillery preparations conducted before the attack were followed by decentralized artillery fire support of each rifle battalion by one artillery battery during the attack. Armor support for attacking units in 1941 was poor and resulted in heavy tank losses. After the Soviets issued Order No. 325 in October 1942, Soviet commanders used separate tank brigades and separate tank battalions

TABLE 52
RIFLE DIVISION COMBAT DIVISION – DEFENSE 1942

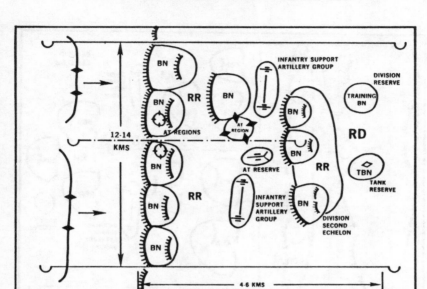

as complete units to support attacking infantry, but only after proper reconnaissance and coordination with appropriate infantry artillery and aviation commanders. After the spring of 1942, rifle divisions also received increased engineer support. Air support, virtually nonexistent before that time, began to grow in the form of pre-attack sorties against enemy defenses and minimal tactical air support for advancing infantry as well.

Conclusion

The first period of war was a harsh and costly experience for the Soviet nation, and the military in particular. In the first six months of war the Red Army lost over 50 percent of its trained peacetime strength. Thereafter, it was faced with the staggering task of conducting operations with a large, although partially trained and poorly equipped, force. In addition to training and equipping a new

TABLE 53
RIFLE DIVISION COMBAT FORMATION – OFFENSE 1941

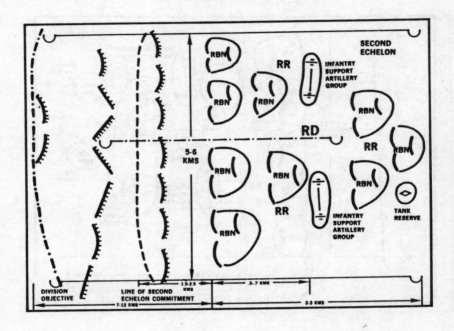

army, the Soviets had to build a new force structure and command cadre for the force. The combat performance of the Red Army pointed out vividly the gap between the promises of 1936 and the realities of 1941. But it was a necessary stage for future victory. The division, army and *front* commanders who emerged in 1942 would lead their units and the Red Army to victory in 1945. The rules, regulations, and theoretical principles which had emerged by 1942 would be adjusted in 1943 and perfected in 1944–45. The military weaponry flowing off Soviet assembly lines in 1942 would flood the theater by 1944 and swamp the best of German equipment by war's end. The prerequisites for eventual victory were established in 1942 and would be capitalized upon in 1943. The best indication of Soviet progress was the offensive that the Soviets unleashed in November 1942 to mark the opening of the second period of war – the offensive at Stalingrad.

TABLE 54
RIFLE DIVISION COMBAT FORMATION – OFFENSE 1942

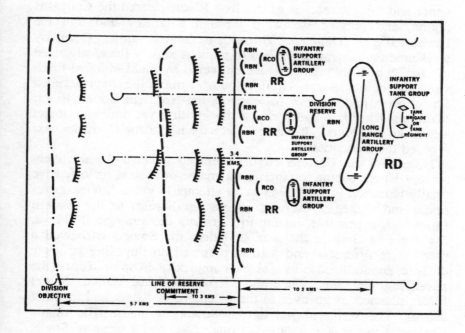

AN ARMY IN TRANSITION (1943)

Context

In November 1942 Stalin, using several *STAVKA* controlled reserve armies, one tank army, and the majority of his new tank and mechanized corps, struck back by surprise at overextended German, Rumanian, Hungarian, and Italian forces in the Stalingrad area. The success of the ensuing operation exceeded Stalin's expectations to encircle and trap the German Sixth Army and a major portion of the Fourth Panzer Army at Stalingrad. This first successful Soviet encirclement operation wrested the strategic initiative from German hands. After the encirclement Stalin attempted simultaneously to reduce surrounded German forces at Stalingrad, defeat German relief attempts, and expand the Soviet offensive to encompass the entire southern wing of the Eastern

Front and, thereby, destroy German Army Group Don. As had been the case in the winter campaign of 1941–42, Stalin was over-optimistic and tried to achieve too much, too soon, with too little. The Soviet offensive reduced the Stalingrad "cauldron," forced the upper and middle reaches of the Don River, cleared the Caucasus region, and pressed westward through Khar'kov and into the Donets Basin (Donbas). Threadbare Soviet armies, lead by weakened tank corps at the end of tenuous supply lines, advanced too far. A brilliant counterstroke delivered by Field Marshal Erich von Manstein's Army Group South* struck the overextended Soviet force and drove it back across the Northern Donets River, liberating Khar'kov and forming the inviting yet ominous Soviet salient around Kursk. It was on that salient that the Germans next focused their attention.

Hitler and the German High Command selected the relatively narrow Kursk sector for their next major offensive, an offensive finally launched in July 1943 in an attempt to crush Soviet opera-tional and strategic reserves, restore equilibrium to the Eastern Front and, if possible, restore to Germany the strategic initiative. For the first time in the war, at Kursk the Soviets eschewed a preemptive offensive and instead prepared an imposing strategic defense, unparalleled in its size and complexity, in order to crush the advancing Germans. Once the German offense stalled, Soviet forces planned to go over to the offensive at Kursk and in other sectors. The script played as the Soviets wrote it. The titanic German effort at Kursk failed at huge cost, and a wave of Soviet counteroffensives rippled along the Eastern Front ultimately driving German forces through Smolensk and Khar'kov back to the line of the Dnepr River. There, in a brilliantly conceived operation during the late fall, Soviet forces suddenly forced the Dnepr River north of Kiev, liberated the city, and created an extensive bridge-head on the right bank of the river. The struggles of mid-1943 marked the beginning of the end for the Germans. Never again would they launch a major offensive. Stripped of a significant portion of their allied forces, increasingly bereft of operational reserves, the Germans could only defend and delay, relying on scorched earth and strained Soviet logistics to impede the Soviet advance and a tenuous defense to further erode Soviet combat capability. Increasingly the Germans hoped Soviet exhaustion and

* Formerly Army Group Don.

depleted manpower resources would produce stalemate or Soviet collapse in the East.

Force structure

The Soviets used 1943 to complete reconstruction of their force structure in accordance with the refined operational concepts enunciated in 1942 orders and directives and incorporated into the 1942 *Field Regulations*. These regulations updated the 1941 regulations and incorporated into one comprehensive document judgments made on the basis of analysis of the experience of the first two years of war. Consequently, force structure changes evolved in tandem with the written regulations which, in turn, reflected the real experience of war (see tables 55–56). In early 1943, while combined arms armies increased in size, rifle corps headquarters were again formed as intermediate control headquarters under armies.* Rifle divisions increased in size and armament while rifle brigades were upgraded to full rifle division strength.

Tank forces also improved significantly (see table 57). Tank and mechanized corps increased in strength, but, more important, in January 1943 the Soviets approved the TOE for a new type of fully mechanized tank army of two tank and one mechanized corps for a total of over 700 tanks each.[13] The five new tank armies created by the summer of 1943 were specifically created to function as *front* mobile groups designated to exploit success. These tank armies, along with the existing tank and mechanized corps at army level, brought to full fruition a force structure capable of implementing the concepts enunciated in 1936 concerning the exploitation of tactical success into operational success. These new tank forces, first unleashed during the Soviet counteroffensives at Kursk, would spearhead Soviet offensive efforts for the remainder of the war.

At the same time, throughout 1943 a host of new supporting units joined the Soviet force structure. Artillery penetration divisions, tank destroyer artillery regiments and brigades, self-propelled artillery regiments and brigades, guards mortar brigades and divisions, "high power" artillery brigades, "special power" artillery brigades, tank penetration regiments and other support units supplemented all elements of the force structure and provided overwhelming firepower superiority over the Germans. In 1943 the

* The number of Soviet rifle corps headquarters increased from 34 on 1 January 1943 to 150 on 1 December 1943.

TABLE 55
RIFLE FORCES: 1943

April 1943 Rifle Army
    3 rifle corps
       7-12 rifle divisions
    4 artillery regiments
      1 gun artillery regiment (152 mm)
      1 antitank artillery regiment (76 mm)
      1 antiaircraft artillery regiment (37 mm)
      1 mortar regiment (122 mm)
    1 signal regiment
    1 line/communications battalion
    1 telegraph company
    1 aviation communications troop

Reinforced by STAVKA units:
    1-2 artillery penetration divisions
      3 artillery regiments
      3 tank destroyer regiments
    3-4 tank or self-propelled gun brigades
    10 separate tank or self-propelled gun regiments
    2 antiaircraft divisions
    1-2 tank or mechanized corps (mobile group)

    strength: 80,000-130,000 men
              1,500-2,700 guns/mortars
              48-497 multiple rocket launchers
              30-225 self propelled guns

December 1943 Rifle Corps
    3 rifle divisions
    1 artillery regiment (122 mm) (optional)
    1 signal battalion
    1 sapper battalion

December 1942 Rifle Division
    3 rifle regiments (4 x 76 mm, 12 x 45 mm)
    1 artillery regiment (12 x 122 mm,
                 20 x 76 mm)
    1 antitank battalion
    1 sapper battalion
    1 signal company
    1 reconnaissance company

    strength: 9,435 men
           (10,670 in guards divisions)
           44 guns
           160 mortars
           48 antitank guns

July 1943 Rifle Division
    3 rifle regiments (4 x 76 mm, 12 x 45 mm)
    1 artillery regiment (12 x 122 mm, 20 x 76 mm)
    1 antitank battalion (12 x 45 mm)
    1 sapper battalion
    1 signal company
    1 reconnaissance company

    strength: 9,380 men
    (same weaponry as December 1942)

TABLE 56
CAVALRY FORCES: 1943

1943 Cavalry Corps
3 cavalry divisions
2 tank regiments (39 tanks each)
1 self propelled artillery
   regiment
1 tank destroyer regiment
1 guards mortar regiment
1 mortar battalion
1 separate tank destroyer
   battalion

strength: 14,000-15,000 men
                 90 tanks/SP guns

1943 Cavalry Division
3 cavalry regiments
(6 x 76 mm, 6 x 45 mm)
1 artillery regiment
   (16 x 76 mm, 8 x 122 mm)
1 reconnaissance battalion
1 antiaircraft squadron
1 engineer squadron
1 signal squadron

strength: 4,700 men
               42 guns
               18 antitank guns
                6 antiaircraft
                  guns

TABLE 57
MECHANIZED AND TANK FORCES: 1943

July 1943 Tank Corps
3 tank brigades (65 tanks each)
1 motorized rifle brigade
1 mortar regiment (36 x 120 mm)
1 antiaircraft regiment
1 self propelled artillery
   regiment (SU-76)
1 tank destroyer regiment
   (20 x 45 mm)
1 tank destroyer battalion
   (12 x 85 mm)
1 guards mortar battalion
1 motorcycle battalion
1 sapper battalion
1 signal battalion
1 armored car battalion
1 transport company
2 repair companies
   (1 artillery, 1 tank)
1 chemical defense company

strength: 10,977 men
               209 tanks
                21 SP guns
               160 guns/mortars
                 8 multiple rocket
                   launchers

December 1943 Tank Corps
3 tank brigades
   (65 tanks each)
1 motorized rifle
   brigade
1 mortar regiment
1 antiaircraft
   regiment
1 self propelled
   artillery
   regiment (SU-76)
1 self propelled
   artillery regiment
   (SU-85)
1 guards mortar
   battalion
1 motorcycle battalion
1 sapper battalion
1 signal battalion
1 transport company
2 repair companies
1 chemical defense company
1 aviation company

strength: 10,977 men
               208 tanks
                49 SP guns
               152 guns/
                   mortars
                 8 multiple
                   rocket
                   launchers

TABLE 57 *(continued)*

September 1943 Mechanized Corps	December 1943 Mechanized Corps
3 mechanized brigades	3 mechanized brigades
1 tank brigade	1 tank brigade
1 self propelled gun regiment (SU-76)	1-2 self propelled artillery regiments (SU-76, SU-85)
1 mortar regiment	1 mortar regiment
1 antiaircraft regiment	1 antiaircraft regiment
1 guards mortar battalion	1 tank destroyer regiment
1 motorcycle battalion	1 guards mortar battalion
1 sapper battalion	1 motorcycle battalion
1 signal battalion	1 sapper battalion
1 medical battalion	1 signal battalion
1 transport company	1 medical battalion
1 repair, reconstruction company	1 transport company
	1 repair, reconstruction co.

strength: 15,018 men
               204 tanks
                25 SP guns
               108 guns/mortars
                 8 multiple rocket
                     launchers

strength: 16,369 men
               197 tanks
                49 SP guns
               252 guns/
                     mortars
                 8 multiple
                     rocket
                     launchers

January 1943 Tank Army	July 1943 Tank Army
2 tank corps	2 tank corps
1 mechanized corps (optional)	1 mechanized corps (optional)
1 motorcycle regiment	1 motorcycle regiment
1 antiaircraft regiment	1 antiaircraft division (64 x 37 mm)
1 tank destroyer regiment	2 tank destroyer regiments
1 howitzer artillery regiment	2 mortar regiments
1 guards mortar regiment	2 self propelled artillery regiments
1 signal regiment	1 guards mortar regiment (same svc spt as Jan)
1 aviation communications regiment	
1 engineer regiment	
1 transport regiment	
2 repair, reconstruction battalions	
1 separate tank brigade or regiment	

strength: 46,000-48,000 men
                 800 tanks (theory)
       450-600 tanks/
                     SP guns (practice)
       500-600 guns/mortars

strength: 48,000 men
       500-650 tanks/
                     SP guns
       550-650 guns/
                     mortars

Soviets also developed procedures for the coordinated use of this burgeoning force structure.

Strategy

The principal strategic aim of the Soviet armed forces in 1943 was to secure and maintain the initiative by using all types of strategic operations (defensive and offensive), by careful employment of field forces on critical strategic directions, and by judicious use of strategic reserves, and by implementing ambitious strategic deception plans. The dominant form of strategic operation was the strategic offensive, exemplified by the two Soviet general counteroffensives conducted at Stalingrad and Kursk, and subsequent development of those counteroffensives. Each counteroffensive, which was launched by a group of *fronts* and directed by a *STAVKA* representative, was larger in scale than any earlier counteroffensive, and each involved simultaneous or successive blows (*udary*) across a broad front. The winter offensive, conducted on the heels of the Stalingrad counteroffensive, involved 4 *fronts* and 18 combined arms armies advancing in a 700–800 kilometer-wide sector to a depth of 120–400 kilometers, while the summer offensive at Kursk involved 10 *fronts*, 40 combined arms and 5 tank armies operating on a 2,000-kilometer front to a depth of 600–700 kilometers.[14] While the winter offensive fell short of its ambitious objectives, the summer offensive succeeded in its aims.

The Soviet 1943 strategic defense at Kursk, unlike that at Moscow in 1941, did not occur along the entire front. Rather, it occurred on one strategic direction and involved a strategic defense by a group of *fronts*. Sufficient time existed to prepare and fully man a deeply echeloned and fortified defense extending over 100 kilometers deep and to prepare a deception plan involving the conduct of diversionary operations and secret movement of reserves. 1943 also saw the rise of a strategically important partisan movement, which disrupted the German rear areas and tied down a considerable number of German troops.

Operational art

Equipped with an almost completely revitalized force structure, manned by an increasingly experienced command cadre, and guided by new regulations which efficiently generalized war experiences, the Soviets used 1943 as an experimental year in the operational realm. Of particular importance was the problem of coordinating the more elaborate forces and evolving operational techniques for their use. The Soviets sought to create a capability to conduct large scale offensive operations on a broad front in order to achieve multiple penetrations of German defenses. To do so the Soviets relied on artful and increasingly concealed concentrations of forces and the use of shock groups. The Soviets employed successful operational deception in numerous operations (for example Kiev, November, 1943) involving extensive use of diversions and simulations to conceal the point of main attack and attack timing and strength. After successful penetration of enemy tactical defenses, mobile groups of armies (tank and mechanized corps) and *fronts* (tank armies) developed the tactical successes into the operational depths. A characteristic of 1943 offensive operations was the decisive conduct of the penetration and the subsequent use of maneuver to effect encirclement of the enemy. Unlike the first period of war, when attack sectors were wide and penetration sectors imprecise, in the second period of war these sectors narrowed and became better defined. *Fronts* attacked in sectors 150–200 kilometers wide and armies in 20–35–kilometer wide sectors. *Front* penetration sectors shrunk to 25–30 kilometers and army penetration sectors to 6–12 kilometers. Offensive operational densities in penetration sectors increased to 2.5–3 kilometers per rifle division and 150–180 guns/mortars and 30–40 tanks per kilometer of front.[15]

Operational formations also matured (see tables 58–61). During the winter offensive of 1942–43, *fronts* deployed in a single echelon configuration backed up by a combined arms reserve; however, the single echelon was stronger than before, sometimes even consisting of a tank army (of mixed composition). Responding to the growth of German defenses, by the summer of 1943 *fronts* formed in two echelons with the *front* mobile group (tank army) following the first echelon on the main attack axis. Combined arms armies during the winter offensive organized in two echelons supported by an army mobile group (tank or mechanized corps). By the summer of 1943 combined arms armies often formed in a single echelon of rifle corps with artillery and antiaircraft artillery groups, mobile obstacle detachments and reserves in order to fulfill the close mission of the *front* at a depth of 60–90 kilometers. On the offense these armies used greater cover and deception, and after October 1942 routinely employed extensive operational reconnaissance before an offensive.

Mobile groups increased in importance and expanded the scope of offensives. Army and *front* commanders usually secretly regrouped their mobile groups and committed them on the first day of the offensive to complete or exploit the tactical penetration. The new tank armies experimented with uninterrupted operations deep in the operational depth of enemy defenses. These first experiences (not always fully successful) served as a basis for subsequent use of tank armies, singly or in combination. In sectors where mobile groups were not available, *front* and army commanders used second echelons to develop the attack, although at a slower pace.

Soviet use of artillery and air support in offensives markedly improved through development of the concepts of the artillery offensive and air offensive. The centrally controlled artillery offensive provided better support of ground troops by subdividing army artillery groups into support groups for first echelon rifle corps. Supporting fires were designed to precede the attack, accompany the attack through the tactical defense, and provide artillery coverage for the advance into the operational depths.[16] The aviation offensive provided similar phasing of air support through-out the duration of the offensive.

During offensive operations the Soviets indulged in significant regrouping of forces to develop success, to switch the impetus of attack to secondary directions, and to defeat German counter-attacks. To an increasing extent they were able to hide this regroup-ing from German intelligence. High attack and pursuit tempos were achieved by the use of task-organized forward detachments which raced ahead of main forces (in particular in advance of mobile groups) in order to secure key terrain features, river crossings and road junctions, and hold them for the main force. While tempos of advance increased and the scale of operations grew, corresponding growth of German defenses continued to limit the scale of Soviet offensive success, as did the systematic German destruction of the regions they abandoned.

With the maturation of defensive principles and techniques in 1943 (both Soviet and German), the nature of Soviet defenses changed. Defensive frontages decreased as the depth of the defenses increased, thus improving defensive operational densities (see tables 62–63). By the summer of 1943 *fronts* defended in sectors 250–300 kilometers wide and the army in sectors of 40–70 kilo-meters. Defensive depths increased to 120–150 kilometers for a *front* and 30–40 kilometers for an army. Resultant operational densities in main defensive sectors amounted to 7–13 kilometers per rifle division, 30–80 guns/mortars and 7–27 tanks/self-propelled guns per kilometer of front. A defending *front* deployed in two echelons, often with a tank army in second echelon. The *front* reserve sometimes included tank and mechanized corps in addition to rifle forces. Combined arms armies and tank armies defended in single echelon formation, supported by artillery and air defense artillery groups, antitank reserves, and mobile obstacle detach-ments. During the organization of a defense following an offensive

TABLE 58
FRONT OPERATIONAL FORMATION – WINTER 1942–1943

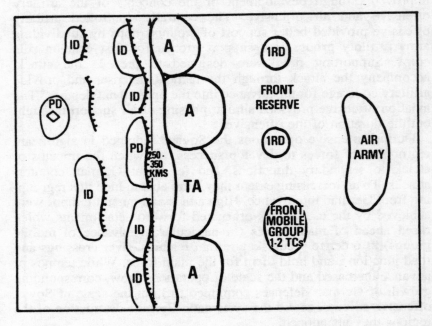

operation, a *front* formed in single echelon with a tank army defending on the main direction.[17]

Antitank defenses matured considerably in the second period of war, a consequence of the increased number of army antitank regions and the presence of distinct *front* and army antitank reserves and mobile obstacle detachments. Antitank densities in main defense sectors grew to 20–25 guns per kilometer of front.[18] The general resilience of defenses also benefited from more extensive and sophisticated use of antiaircraft fire, engineer obstacles, and artillery fire, as well as from more flexible maneuvering on the part of defending units.

Command and control of operational forces improved with the reintroduction of intermediate rifle corps command links and the better use of communications security. Command posts, in particular on the offensive, were deployed closer to operating troops through use of main and reserve command posts, secondary command posts, and observation points.

TABLE 59
FRONT OPERATIONAL FORMATION – 1943

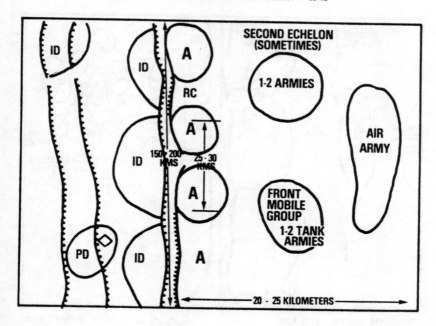

Tactics

During the second period of war Soviet tactics broke away from the linear forms of the earlier war years when forces were more equally distributed across the front, and Soviet commanders began to mass forces in distinct sectors, as well as rely more on secret and rapid maneuver. In accordance with Order No. 306 and the 1942 *Field Regulation*, the Soviets launched the Stalingrad counteroffensive with rifle divisions attacking in single echelon against shallow and relatively weak enemy defenses (see table 64). Rifle divisions on the main attack direction deployed in sectors of 4–5 kilometers (regiment 1.5–2 kilometers; battalion 500–700 meters), sectors which were 1.5 to 2 times wider than had been the case earlier in the war. Reinforced by artillery and infantry support tanks, the division was to achieve an immediate mission at a depth of 4 kilometers and a subsequent mission at a depth of 20 kilometers in the course of one day (the entire tactical depth of the defense). These depths, however, turned out to be excessive and, thus, were rarely achieved.

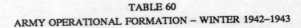

TABLE 60
ARMY OPERATIONAL FORMATION – WINTER 1942–1943

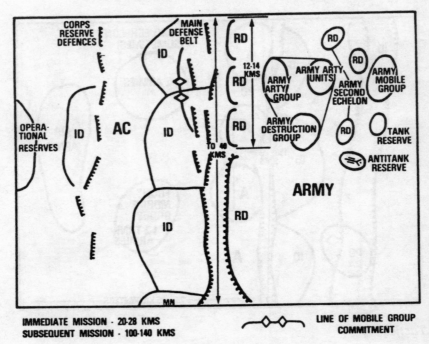

IMMEDIATE MISSION · 20-28 KMS
SUBSEQUENT MISSION · 100-140 KMS

LINE OF MOBILE GROUP
COMMITMENT

By the summer of 1943 enemy defenses were deeper and better prepared (see table 65). Thus, the Soviets decreased rifle division missions, to 3–4 kilometers depth for close missions and 12–15 kilometers depth for the mission of the day. To accomplish these missions, rifle divisions formed in deeper echelons and attacked in narrower sections of 3–4 kilometers width. Thus, tactical densities also increased.[19]

In the second period of war tactical combat involved greater use of maneuver, increased reliance on night operations, and more systematic conduct of reconnaissance. By the summer of 1943 divisions conducted reconnaissance by using reinforced rifle battalions from each first echelon rifle regiment several days prior to the attack to determine enemy dispositions in the first defensive position and to clarify enemy intentions to hold those positions (so as not to waste an artillery preparation on weakly held positions).

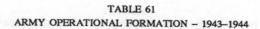

TABLE 61
ARMY OPERATIONAL FORMATION – 1943–1944

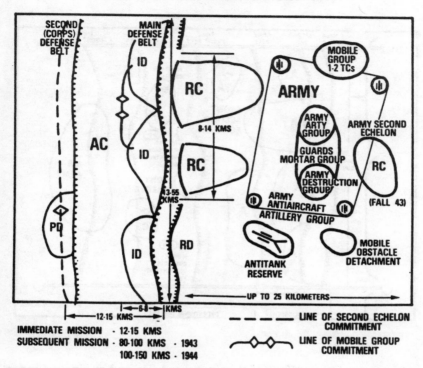

Soviet tactical use of artillery, tanks, and self-propelled artillery became more sophisticated. Although infantry support artillery groups (PP) of divisions supported each first echelon regiment, and long range artillery groups (DD) supported each division and rifle corps, an increasing number of infantry support artillery groups were subordinated directly to regimental commanders. The Soviets also assigned a greater quantity of tanks and self-propelled guns to first echelon rifle regiments operating on main attack directions. Tank brigades and regiments and self-propelled artillery regiments were echeloned in support of rifle divisions and rifle corps from the summer of 1943 in order to provide direct assault and covering fire for advancing infantry units. Engineer support for rifle divisions doubled in 1943 thus improving jumping-off positions, clearance of obstacles, and installation and removal of minefields.

TABLE 62
FRONT OPERATIONAL FORMATION – DEFENSE 1943

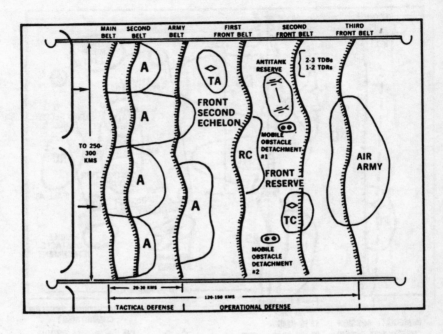

The cumulative effect of this increased fire and engineer support was an improved capability on the part of rifle divisions to overcome the first two enemy defensive positions. However, insufficient numbers of infantry support tanks and the reduced effectiveness of artillery fire at greater ranges left enemy third positions intact. Thus, army mobile groups (tank and mechanized corps) often had to overcome the enemy third defensive position in the first defensive belt, and the entire second defensive belt as well, by attack from the march. Soviet units crossed water obstacles by using makeshift means, or by employing forward detachments to seize bridges and crossing sites from the march.

Tactical command and control improved through greater use of radios, vehicles, aircraft and command points near the front. Armored forces often used special operational staff groups to control mobile operations at great distances. Especially important

TABLE 63
ARMY OPERATIONAL FORMATION – DEFENSE 1943

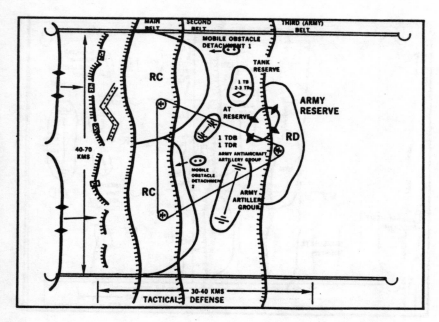

was the practice of assembling all force commanders participating in an operation at a single command post.

By the summer of 1943 Soviet tactical defenses had transitioned from a noncontiguous nature to a dense, deeply echeloned trench defense system providing greater security and more secure maneuver of forces and fire support along the front and in the depth (see tables 66–67). Widths of defensive sectors decreased and depths increased. A rifle corps customarily deployed with two rifle divisions in the first defense belt and one rifle division in the second belt. Rifle divisions defended in one or two echelons and rifle regiments in two echelons. Each was supported by artillery groups, antitank strong points (regions), artillery antitank reserves, and mobile obstacle detachment. A first echelon rifle division (for example, at Kursk) in a main defense sector defended on a front of 8–15 kilometers to a depth of 5–6 kilometers. On secondary directions divisions occupied sectors 25 kilometers wide.[20]

TABLE 64
RIFLE DIVISION COMBAT FORMATION – OFFENSE WINTER 1942–1943

Soviet antitank defenses matured further with the integration of antitank strong points and regions throughout the entire depth of the defense. Separate tank brigades, tank regiments, and self-propelled gun regiments of the rifle division reserve delivered counterattacks or reinforced first echelon regiments by deploying as mobile or fixed firing points. Defense, in general, became more durable and mobile, in terms of both ground units and supporting fires. Above all, integration of all types of units was more thorough. Greater force availability permitted even army and *front*-scale counterattacks in support of defending forces.

Conclusion

The transitional year of 1943 was decisive for the Soviet war effort. Seizing the strategic initiative, the Soviets would never again lose it. By year's end the force structure was virtually perfected. Only minor adjustments would occur in 1944 and 1945. Most important,

TABLE 65

RIFLE CORPS/DIVISION COMBAT FORMATION – OFFENSE SUMMER–FALL
1943

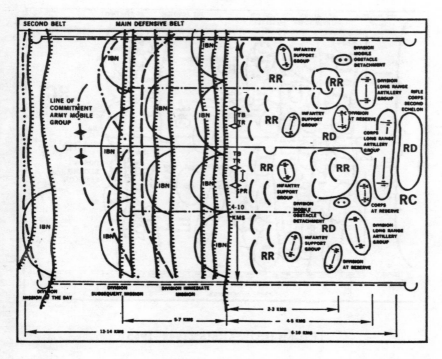

Soviet commanders learned to use their forces. The occasional operational failures of 1943 produced smoother operations in 1944. The patient conduct of the strategic defenses in 1943 (Kursk) insured that ensuing years would be offensive ones, without need to resort to the strategic defense. The offensive operations of 1943 paved the way for the successive offensives of 1944 and the simultaneous offensives of 1945. Operational and tactical techniques tested and smoothed out in 1943 would be refined and perfected in 1944 and 1945. The elementary education the Red Army received in 1941–42 gave way to the secondary education of 1943. In 1944 and 1945 the Soviets would accomplish university-level and graduate study in the conduct of war.

TABLE 66
RIFLE CORPS/DIVISION COMBAT FORMATION – DEFENSE SUMMER–FALL 1943

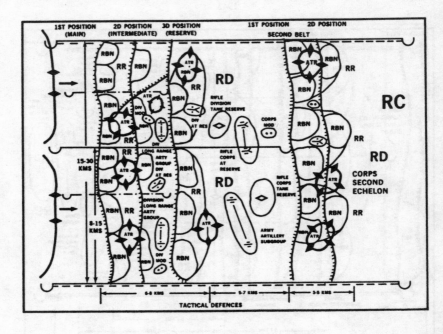

TRIUMPH OF ARMS (1944–1945)

Context

The Soviets opened 1944 with the first of a series of successive strategic offensives which would continue unabated until war's end. The January offensives at the extremities of the Eastern Front against German forces around Leningrad and at Krivoi–Rog and Nikopol', south of the Dnepr River, gave way in early spring to the multi-*front* Korsun–Shevchenkovskii encirclement operation. Unlike the case in previous springs, the Soviets ignored the thaw (*rasputitsa*) and continued a series of successive *front* offensive operations which liberated the right bank of the Ukraine and brought Soviet forces to the Rumanian borders by the end of April. While Soviet armies chopped away at the German northern flank, ultimately driving Finland from the war, a multi-*front* offensive in June 1944, using successive encirclement operations within a

TABLE 67
RIFLE DIVISION COMBAT FORMATION – DEFENSE WINTER 1942–1943

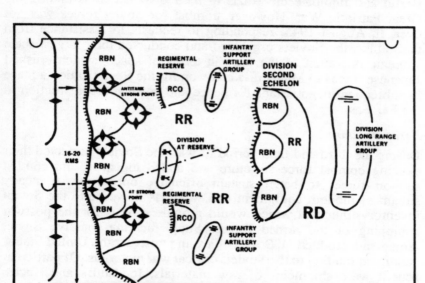

brilliantly conceived strategic deception plan, crushed German Army Group Center in Belorussia and penetrated to the East Prussian borders. A subsequent blow in the Ukraine brought Soviet forces deep into Poland with bridgeheads across the Narev and Vistula Rivers north and south of Warsaw. In August, reflecting Soviet strategic concerns, the Soviets launched a series of successive offensives into and through the Balkans that drove Rumania from the war and propelled Soviet forces into Hungary and Yugoslavia while other Soviet *fronts* continued to grind up German forces in the Baltic region.

The Soviets opened 1945 with a series of simultaneous strategic operations extending from the Baltic to the Balkans. The East Prussian and Vistula–Oder operations propelled Soviet troops to the Baltic Sea and across the Oder River only 40 kilometers from Berlin, while in the south Soviet forces parried a German counter-offensive at Budapest and then continued the advance into Austria.

After conducting operations in February and March 1945 to clear German forces from the flanks of the Soviet main thrust, the Soviets commenced the titanic, almost ceremonial struggle to conquer Berlin and liquidate the Nazis in their own lair, thus ending the Great Patriotic War. However, combat for Soviet forces was not over. In August 1945, responding to requests for assistance from their allies, the Soviets organized and conducted their largest scale strategic operation of the war (in terms of space) which crushed Japanese forces in Manchuria and won for the Soviet Union a place in subsequent negotiations for peace and postwar reconstruction in the Far East.

Force structure

During the third and final period of war, the Soviets perfected their existing combat force structure and added logistical and combat support forces to better sustain offensive operations. A steady stream of modern equipment and weapons flowed into the Soviet inventory, much of which would provide a basis for the postwar equipping of the armed forces. Supplementing massive Soviet armaments production, Soviet allies, in particular the United States, continued sending to the Soviets critical war materials. Of particular benefit were shipments of raw materials, foodstuffs and trucks. Vehicle and truck shipments made possible the motorization of Soviet units, in particular the mobile corps and tank armies. The fact that "Studebaker" and "Willies" have been incorporated into the Russian language speaks for the importance of the material assistance. (Soviet reluctance to admit the importance of the aid in part results from Soviet perceptions that the Allies never accorded the Soviets full credit for their role in the defeat of Germany.)

Combined arms armies, rifle corps, and rifle divisions became more refined in terms of their weaponry, and the earlier occasional attachment of additional artillery, tanks and self-propelled guns to these units became customary in the last year of the war (see tables 68–69). Many of these routine attachments (tank and self-propelled gun regiments and battalions) were integrated fully into post-war unit TOEs. In the last two years of war the Soviets tailored their units more extensively to suit the terrain over which they operated and the enemy they opposed. The Soviet armored and mechanized force structure became more sophisticated with the addition of self-propelled artillery units, additional antitank artillery, and greater engineer support to tank and mechanized corps and tank armies (see table 70). The Cavalry–Mechanized Group became a regular participant in operations where the terrain and weather conditions inhibited operations by regular tank armies.* Combat support units increased in size as the Soviets formed artillery penetration corps, and larger, often mechanized, engineer formations to support strategic operations.

Doctrine

Refined techniques for the creative use of this elaborate force structure appeared in a number of important regulations issued in 1944. These regulations, derived from those of 1942, draw upon the combat lessons of 1943 in order to form a comprehensive view on the nature of operations and the role of all types of forces in those operations. The *Field Regulation* of 1944 (*PU-44*), without specifically resurrecting the earlier watchword of "deep operations," nevertheless stated: "the regulations conceive of tank action as that of a group of direct support for infantry and cavalry and as an echelon for exploiting successes into the strategic depths with the support of powerful aviation."[21] The 1944 regulation's concept of operations and its assignment of tasks to units marked the full realization of the aims of the 1936 *Field Regulation*. A central theme of the 1944 *Regulation* was the achievement of tactical penetrations and the exploitation of those penetrations by mobile groups into the operational (and sometimes strategic) depth of the enemy defense. Other regulations and instructions on specific aspects of military operations supplemented the main 1944 *Field Regulation*.

Soviet military doctrine changed little in substance in the second and third periods of war. The theoretical Marxist-Leninist foundation remained intact as the political focus for doctrinal analysis. While leading military theorists and leaders constructively pondered all aspects of military art and tested the results of their analysis on the battlefield, Stalin retained his dominant position at the "commanding heights" of doctrine. He firmly made all high-level decisions and contributed to Marxism-Leninism-Stalinism by his articulation of the "permanent operating factors" which, he argued, governed the course and outcome of war in general. These factors (listed below) reflected Lenin's earlier broad view of the nature of war and the classic Marxist-Leninist laws of war:

– the stability of the rear;

* A cavalry-mechanized group normally consisted of one mechanized or tank corps and one cavalry corps.

TABLE 68
RIFLE FORCES: 1944-1945

August 1944 Rifle Army	January 1945 Rifle Army
3 rifle corps	3 rifle corps
7-12 rifle divisions	7-12 rifle divisions
1 artillery brigade	1-2 gun artillery brigades
2 gun artillery regiments	2 gun artillery regiments
1 tank destroyer regiment	1 tank destroyer brigade
1 antiaircraft artillery regiment	1 antiaircraft artillery
1 mortar regiment	division
1 engineer/sapper brigade	1 mortar regiment
1 tank regiment	1 engineer/sapper brigade
1 signal regiment	1 signal regiment
1 tank or mechanized corps	2-3 tank brigades or regiments
(optional)	1 tank or mechanized corps
	(attached)

strength: 80,000-120,000 men	strength: 80,000-100,000 men
300-460 tanks	300-460 tanks
1,700-2,000 guns/	1,900-2,500 guns/
mortars	mortars
30-225 SP guns	30-225 SP guns

1944 Rifle Corps

      3 rifle divisions
      1 artillery brigade (guards corps)
      1 artillery regiment (regular corps)
      1 self propelled artillery regiment
      1 guards mortar regiment
      1 antiaircraft artillery battalion
      1 sapper battalion
      1 signal battalion

      strength: 20,000-30,000 men
               750-900 guns/mortars

— the morale of the army;
— the quantity and quality of divisions;
— the armament of the army;
— the organizing ability of the command personnel.[22]

The permanent operating factors, Stalin's legacy to military doctrine, persisted into the postwar years as a veneer overlay on Soviet military thought until critiqued (though never rejected) in the post-Stalinist years. In addition, Soviet military doctrine assumed a more international Socialist character as the Soviet Army began incorporating forces from future Socialist states into its ranks (Polish and Bulgarian armies, and Czech and Rumanian forces), thus presaging the future military cooperation of Warsaw Pact states.

TABLE 68 (*continued*)

<u>December 1944 Rifle Division</u>

3 rifle regiments
  (4 x 76 mm, 12 x 45 mm)
1 artillery brigade
 1 gun artillery regiment
  (32 x 76 mm)
 1 howitzer artillery regiment
  (20 x 122 mm)
 1 mortar regiment (20 x 120 mm)
1 antiaircraft artillery battalion
(12 x 37 mm) (in guards divisions)
1 tank destroyer battalion
  (18 x 45, 57, 76 mm)
1 sapper battalion
1 signal company
1 reconnaissance company

<u>strength</u>: 11,706 men‡
    64 guns
   127 mortars
    12 AA guns
    54 AT guns

<u>June 1945 Rifle Division</u>

3 rifle regiments
  (4 x 76 mm, 12 x 45 mm)
1 artillery brigade
 1 gun artillery regiment
  (20 x 76 mm)
 1 howitzer artillery
  regiment (20 x 122 mm)
 1 mortar regiment (120 mm)
1 self-propelled artillery
 battalion (16 x SU-76)
1 antiaircraft artillery
 battalion (12 x 37 mm)
1 tank destroyer battalion
1 sapper battalion
1 signal company
1 reconnaissance company

<u>strength</u>: 11,780 men‡
    52 guns
    16 SP guns
   136 mortars
    12 AA guns
    66 AT guns

----

‡Rifle Division strengths are by TOE. Actual strength was much
lower, and averaged 3,500-4,500 men per division in 1945.

TABLE 69

CAVALRY FORCES: 1944–1945

<u>1945 Cavalry Corps</u>
3 cavalry divisions
2 tank regiments
1 reconnaissance battalion
1 tank destroyer regiment
1 mortar regiment
1 guards mortar battalion
1 self propelled artillery regiment
1 engineer regiment
1 signal battalion

<u>strength</u>: 18,700 men
   103 tanks, SP guns
   268 guns/mortars
    48 AT guns
    34 AA guns

<u>1945 Cavalry Division</u>
3 cavalry regiments
(6 x 76 mm, 6 x 45 mm)
1 artillery regiment
1 reconnaissance battalion
1 antiaircraft squadron
1 engineer squadron
1 signal squadron

<u>strength</u>: 4,700 men
   42 guns
   18 AT guns
    6 AA guns

TABLE 70
MECHANIZED AND TANK FORCES: 1944–1945

December 1944 Tank Corps

3 tank brigades (65 tanks each)
1 motorized rifle brigade
1 mortar regiment
1 antiaircraft artillery regiment
1 light self propelled artillery regiment (SU-76)
1 medium self propelled artillery regiment (SU-85/122)
1 heavy self propelled artillery regiment (SU-152)
       (in some corps)
1 light artillery regiment
1 guards mortar battalion
1 motorcycle battalion
1 transport company
2 repair companies (artillery, tank)
1 medical battalion (May 1944)
1 sapper battalion
1 signal battalion
1 aviation company
1 chemical defense company

              strength: 12,010 men
                            207 tanks
                             63 SP guns
                            182 guns/mortars
                              8 multiple rocket launchers
                          1,500 vehicles

August 1945 Tank Corps

3 tank brigades (65 tanks each)
1 motorized rifle brigade
1 mortar regiment
1 antiaircraft artillery regiment
1 light self propelled artillery
       regiment (SU-76)
1 medium self propelled artillery
       regiment (SU-100)
1 light artillery regiment
1 heavy tank regiment
1 guards mortar battalion
1 motorcycle battalion
1 transport company
2 repair companies (artillery, tank)
1 medical battalion
1 sapper battalion
1 chemical defense company
1 aviation company

              strength: 11,788 men
                            207 tanks T-34
                             21 tanks IS-2
                             42 SP guns
                            182 guns/mortars
                              8 multiple rocket launchers

TABLE 70 (*continued*)

December 1944 Mechanized Corps

```
3 mechanized brigades
  3 motorized rifle battalions
  1 tank regiment (35 tanks)
1 tank brigade (65 tanks)
1 light self propelled artillery regiment (SU-76)
1 medium self propelled artillery regiment (SU-85)
1 heavy self propelled artillery regiment (SU-152)
       (in some corps)
1 mortar regiment
1 antiaircraft artillery regiment
1 guards mortar battalion
1 motorcycle battalion
1 signal battalion
1 sapper, engineer battalion
1 medical battalion
1 transport company
1 repair, reconstruction company
```

```
          strength:   16,442 men
                         183 tanks
                          63 SP guns
                         234 guns/mortars
                           8 multiple rocket launchers
```


August 1944 Tank Army

```
2 tank corps
1 mechanized corps (optional)
1 motorcycle regiment
1 light artillery brigade
  2 gun artillery/regiments (76 mm)
  1 gun artillery/regiment (100 mm)
1 light self propelled artillery brigade
  3 light self propelled artillery battalions (SU-76)
  1 machine gun battalion
  1 antiaircraft machine gun company
2 mortar regiments
1 guards mortar regiment
1 antiaircraft artillery division
  4 antiaircraft artillery regiments
1 motorized engineer brigade
  2 motorized engineer battalions
  1 pontoon bridge battalion
1 signal regiment
1 aviation communications regiment
1 transport regiment
2 repair/reconstruction battalions
```

```
          strength:   50,000 men
                       1,000 tanks, SP guns
                         850 guns/mortars
```

Strategy

Soviet strategy in the third period of war grew in scope and ambition and took on a more subtle political flavor. With the strategic initiative firmly in Soviet hands, strategic operations became totally offensive, more grandiose, and incessant. While earlier operations occurred on separate strategic directions, by 1944 they took place along the entire strategic front, successively in 1944 and simultaneously in 1945. Each operation was conducted within the context of a deception plan coordinated by the STAVKA which encompassed the entire campaign. These plans successfully concealed both the location and scale of the strategic offensives, and to some extent the timing as well.

By war's end operations by groups of *fronts* involved from 100–200 divisions, up to 2.5 million men, 20,000–40,000 guns/mortars, 3,000–6,000 tanks/self-propelled guns and 2,000–7,500 aircraft. These operations had decisive objectives (usually the encirclement and destruction of large enemy groups), huge scope, high maneuverability, and significant military-political or economic results. They spanned frontages from 450–1,400 kilometers (4,400 kilometers in Manchuria) and thrust to a depth of 500–600 kilometers while destroying as many as 50–100 enemy divisions.[23] Often the political and economic goal of the operation was as important as the military goal, and these goals affected the nature of military operations (operations against Finland, the drive into the Balkans, and the Manchurian offensive).

Strategic offensive operations, conducted under a cloak of deception, sought to achieve multiple penetrations of the enemy front and subsequent rapid encirclement of enemy forces. The Korsun–Shevchenkovskii operation and subsequent operations on the right bank of the Ukraine encircled large German groups. A series of successive encirclement operations in Belorussia in June–July 1944 destroyed German Army Group Center and the Iassy–Kishinev operation encircled and destroyed Rumanian forces and German Sixth Army in Rumania. The East Prussian and East Pomeranian operations pinned large German forces against the Baltic Sea. The pace of Soviet offensive operations increased in accordance with their increased depth to produce rates of advance of 15–20 kilometers per day for rifle units. Armored and mechanized units advanced at even higher rates (up to 100 kilometers per day).

Operational art

Soviet operational art matured with the refinement of operational techniques developed in 1943 and the creation of new techniques during the last two years of war. *Front* operations, an integral part of strategic operations, were conducted to depths of 150–300 kilometers to destroy 16–18 enemy divisions. Armies within the *fronts* attacked to depths of 100–150 kilometers to destroy enemy operational forces (3–6 divisions).[24] During a *front* operation each army conducted one or two successive operations.

The form of *front* operations also matured. During the first two periods of war, *front* offensives had been conducted by several armies attacking on separate directions. In the third period of war, because of increased manpower and weaponry, *fronts* conducted frontal strikes against the enemy center and one or both of the enemy flanks to encircle and destroy multiple enemy groups (Belorussia 1944). Multiple *fronts* also cooperated to achieve larger encirclements. In instances where encirclement operations were impossible or unfeasible, *fronts* supported by heavy supporting fires delivered one or two frontal blows to a great depth, cut up enemy forces, and destroyed them piecemeal (Vistula–Oder 1945). Armies customarily struck one blow against the enemy center or along the enemy flank and advanced into the depth of the defense to cooperate with other armies in encircling enemy forces. By the third period of the war *fronts* could launch, in addition to a main attack, a strong secondary attack and one or two supporting attacks.

The increased strength of *fronts* and greater concentration of forces permitted creation of greater operational densities and increased superiority over the enemy. Major operations achieved operational densities of 200–250 guns/mortars and 70–85 tanks/self-propelled guns per kilometer of frontage and superiorities were attained amounting to 3–5:1 in manpower, 6–8:1 in tanks and artillery and 3–5:1 in combat aircraft.[25]

Operational formations also increased in depth and complexity (see tables 71–72). The *front* operational formation included a strong first echelon; an optional second echelon of one or sometimes two combined armies; a mobile group of one, two or sometimes three tank armies, or in the absence of a tank army, one or two tank corps or one or two cavalry-mechanized groups; strong reserves of all types; and mobile obstacle detachments. The army operational formation was similar, with one or two tank or mechanized corps

TABLE 71
FRONT OPERATIONAL FORMATION – 1944–1945

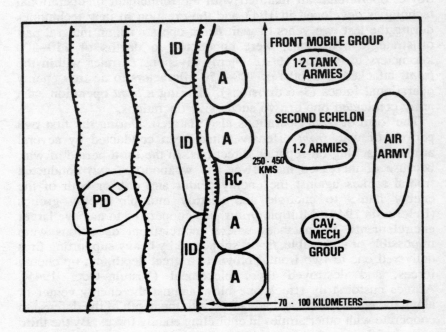

functioning as mobile groups and with army artillery and anti-aircraft groups in support. The depth of the *front* operational formation reached 70–100 kilometers and that of the army 30 kilometers. Operational formations were flexible and tailored to the existing situation. Thus, in Manchuria, two of three *fronts* attacked in single echelon formation, as did the majority of armies. *Front* air armies (generally one) supported *front* and army operations.

Offensive operations began with penetration operations which by 1944 were conducted using shock groups, heavy artillery concentrations, artillery and air offensives, and a greater number of infantry support tanks. By 1945 infantry support tanks were often attached in from company to regimental strength to individual rifle battalions. As a rule the Soviets overcame the enemy's first defensive belt on the first day of operations and the second belt on the second or third day. By the third period of war the penetration of the

TABLE 72
ARMY OPERATIONAL FORMATION – 1945

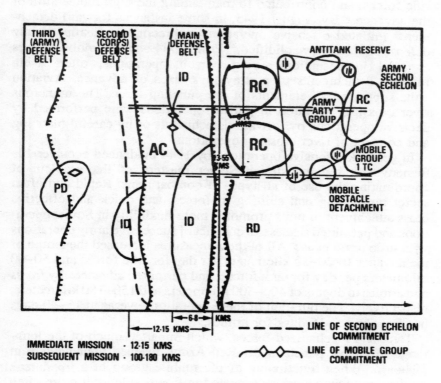

THIRD (ARMY) DEFENSE BELT
SECOND (CORPS) DEFENSE BELT
MAIN DEFENSE BELT
ANTITANK RESERVE
ARMY SECOND ECHELON
ID
RC
ARMY ARTY GROUP
RC
AC
RC
MOBILE GROUP 1 TC
PD
MOBILE OBSTACLE DETACHMENT
ID
ID
RD

←6-8→ KMS
←12-15 KMS→

IMMEDIATE MISSION · 12-15 KMS
SUBSEQUENT MISSION · 100-180 KMS

– – – – LINE OF SECOND ECHELON COMMITMENT
⬦⬦ LINE OF MOBILE GROUP COMMITMENT

enemy's tactical defense was followed by an operational exploitation, the encirclement of the enemy, and the creation of an inner encircling line to choke those entrapped and an outer encircling line to hold off enemy relief attempts (Korsun–Shevchenkovskii). By mid-1944 the outer encircling line continued the offensive while encircled enemy forces were being destroyed (Belorussia, Iassy–Kishinev).

Operational pursuit became important, for it determined the ultimate depth of the operation. While earlier in the war pursuit rates had amounted to 8–12 kilometers per day on distinct directions in close contact with the enemy, by the third period pursuit occurred on a wide front, during both day and night, along separate directions, and at high tempos. Tank armies and tank corps led the pursuit along parallel routes separated by 60–80 kilometers or more from the main rifle forces. Strong tank-heavy task-organized forward detachments led the pursuit and also the advance of main rifle forces, and contributed to maintaining the high momentum of the advance.* By August 1945, in some instances forward detachments initiated offensive operations to preempt or disrupt enemy defenses before they solidified.[26] From 1944 onward, mobile forces engaged in deception during pursuit operations, often using forward detachments to portray false axes of advance. Aviation units supported all elements of the pursuing force. The numerous river crossings required in pursuit operations were performed by decisive operations by forward detachments or by careful planning and conduct of river crossing operations.

In general, offensive operations by 1944 evidenced considerable maneuver and demonstrated Soviet mastery of the problem of coordinating the use of all types of combat arms. Rapid and often secret regrouping and shifting of forces, and quick and effective cross attachment of units promoted more flexibility in Soviet operations and permitted successful conduct of successive army operations with little or no pause. All of these measures increased the tempo of the advance to 20–30 kilometers per day for rifle forces and 50–60 kilometers per day for tank forces, and permitted advances by *fronts* and armies to depths of 400–500 kilometers and 150–180 kilometers, respectively. The duration of these operations averaged 15–20 days per *front* and 5–15 days for armies.

Tank and mechanized forces, which imparted much of the long-range offensive punch to the Red Army, reached their heyday in 1944–45. When functioning as the mobile group of a *front*, tank armies on a few occasions operated in first echelon but more often operated in second echelon. The commitment of tank armies to action created operational armored densities of 30–100 tanks per kilometer of front on main attack directions. By the end of the war separate tank corps operated to a depth of 180 kilometers and tank armies to a depth of 400 kilometers or more. Separate tank corps or mechanized corps, acting as army mobile groups, would complete the penetration of the tactical defense zone to a depth of 25–40

---

* Distinct from advanced guards, forward detachments led the advance with the mission of seizing key terrain features to facilitate the advance of main force units. Later, these detachments also disrupted enemy defenses before they jelled. Tank armies and tank corps used tank corps and tank brigades as forward detachments. Rifle corps used tank brigades and rifle divisions used reinforced rifle battalion, self-propelled artillery battalions or tank brigades.

kilometers, after which tank armies as the *front's* mobile group would develop success to the entire depth of the *front* offensive operation. By 1944–45 a weakening of German operational reserves permitted Soviet tank armies to repulse counterattacks more easily than in the second period of war and, thus, gave the tank armies greater operational freedom. Tank armies conducted pursuit operations rapidly in corps column (pre-combat)* formation led by strong forward detachments deployed to preempt any enemy counteraction. Tank army night operations were particularly effective. Separate tank or mechanized corps covered the flanks of advancing tank armies while forward detachments of advancing rifle forces (reinforced tank brigades, self-propelled artillery battalions, or truck mounted rifle battalions with tanks) linked rifle forces with advancing tank and mechanized forces.

The Soviets achieved efficient command and control of mobile forces operating in extended formation deep in the enemy rear area by using operational groups (forward command points), first echelon staffs (command points), and second echelon command and control (rear command points) posts. To provide continuous command and control during deep offensives, operational groups and first echelon staffs displaced one another in turn.[27] Throughout the war a persistent problem which inhibited the effectiveness of Soviet tank and mechanized units was the absence of an armored personnel carrier. Hence, the Soviets never had real armored infantry.

Aviation support of offensives became more sophisticated in the third period of war. Larger echeloned aircraft attack groups provided continuous close air and interdiction support and concentrated their fire on the most important enemy objectives. Fighters and assault aircraft provided immediate troop support throughout the enemy tactical defense, while bombers and assault aircraft supported forces operating in the operational depths or blocked enemy withdrawal and forward movement of enemy reserves or supplies. Throughout the war, however, air support in the deep operational realm was spotty because of limited airfields, short aircraft combat radii, and limited fuel and ammunition (a result of German scorched earth policies).

Defensive operations decreased in scope and frequency during the third period of war. *Fronts* and armies went on the defense at the end of major offensive operations to resupply and regroup, to repel

* Precombat formation is a march formation from which units can deploy rapidly and fight against an opponent attacking from any quarter.

enemy counterattacks, or to fortify a region just secured. Defenses continued to strengthen at all levels (see tables 73–74). *Fronts* defended sectors 250–350 kilometers wide and armies sectors 30–70 kilometers wide. Operational densities increased to one rifle division per 7–8 kilometers of frontage and 24–36 guns/mortars and 7 tanks/self-propelled guns per kilometer.[28] *Fronts* defended in two-echelon formation with a combined arms or tank army in second echelon and several tank, rifle, and antitank formations in reserve, while armies deployed for defense in one or two echelons. Engineers prepared defenses to depths of 40–50 and 150–180 kilometers respectively for armies and *front*, thus permitting creation of three army defensive belts and one to three additional defensive belts for *fronts* (Lake Balaton 1945). Antitank, tank, artillery, and aviation support for defensive operations improved as well. Second echelon tank or combined arms armies launched *front* counterattacks during defensive operations.

Tactics

Tactical techniques evolved in consonance with improvements on the operational level. Offensive combat by reinforced rifle divisions and rifle corps was fundamental to the achievement of success in tactical battle. Although the personnel strength of rifle corps and divisions was low by 1944 and 1945 (often only 3,000–4,000 men per rifle division), the combat capabilities of these formations increased because of an increase in weaponry. Tactical formations relied on firepower, mass, and maneuver to achieve success rather than just scarce manpower. By the summer of 1944 the rifle division and rifle corps had the mission of penetrating the entire tactical depth of the enemy defense (15–25 kilometers) (see table 75). Since the offensive sectors of corps and divisions shrunk to 4–6 kilometers and 1.5–2 kilometers, respectively, tactical densities rose to 6–8 battalions, 200–250 guns/mortars and 20–30 tanks/self-propelled guns per 1 kilometer of frontage, thus producing a superiority over the enemy of 5–7:1 in manpower, 7–9:1 in artillery and 3–4:1 in tanks.[29] The rifle corps' and rifle divisions' combat formation increased in depth, and regiments, divisions and corps could deploy in one, two or even three echelons depending on existing conditions. By 1944 stronger regimental, division, and corps artillery groups evolved, as did stronger combined arms, tank, and antitank reserves, and mobile obstacle detachments. This increased the flexibility, speed and sustainability of division and corps operations.

Coordination of tactical units, a major problem from 1941–43,

remained a problem in 1944, in particular, because a major part of
the available artillery and armor was immediately subordinate to
the division commander, thus hindering timely fire support at the
battalion level. Organization of regimental artillery groups and
better radio communications helped solve part of the problem. In
addition, by 1945 subordination of tank units down to battalion level
produced more effective armor support.

Techniques for conducting tactical offensive battle improved,
thus permitting units to achieve their assigned missions (not always
done before). After a strong but often varied artillery preparation,
first echelon rifle battalions of rifle division first echelon rifle
regiments, often in tailored assault group configuration, attacked
from prepared jumping-off positions, supported by tanks, aviation,
and artillery. These infantry battalions usually secured the enemy
first defensive position after one–two hours of combat. Because of
likely enemy counterattacks, the rifle regiments' second echelon
infantry battalions assaulted the enemy's second defensive position
and, subsequently, the rifle division's second echelon rifle regiments attacked the third enemy position.

Earlier commitment of rifle corps' second echelon rifle divisions
(or even army mobile groups) often resulted in an even more rapid
advance, although the mobile groups sometimes were heavily
attrited while completing the tactical penetration. Thus, army
commanders preferred to commit the army mobile group after rifle
forces had fully penetrated the enemy tactical defenses. Tanks,
antitank reserves, and mobile obstacle detachments accompanied
attacking units to help repulse enemy counterattacks.

After penetration of the first defensive belt (on the first day), the
army's first echelon rifle corps or, in some instances, the second
echelon corps overcame the enemy second defensive belt (usually
on the second and third day of attack). In some operations, the use
of special attack techniques permitted Soviet forces to overcome
the entire tactical defense zone on the first day of operations
(Belorussia, Iassy–Kishinev, Vistula–Oder). Among these techniques was the use of reconnaissance battalions to secure first
positions and the early commitment of mobile groups (before
commitment of division or corps' second echelons) (Vistula–Oder).
In these instances, army mobile groups overcame the enemy second
defensive belt on the second or third day of the attack.

After successful penetration of enemy defenses and army commitment of its mobile group for exploitation, rifle units joined in the
pursuit, moving in march order led by strong forward detachments,

TABLE 73
FRONT OPERATIONAL FORMATION – DEFENSE 1945

MAIN BELT · SECOND BELT · ARMY (REAR) BELT · FIRST FRONT BELT

A · A · A · A · A

TANK ARMY

RC · RC · RC

TANK DESTROYER UNITS FROM OTHER STRATEGIC DIRECTIONS

MOB #1

FRONT RESERVES

AT RESERVES

AIR ARMY

TC/MC

MOB #2

250-350 KMS

40-50 KMS

150-180 KMS

which advanced up to 25 kilometers ahead of the main rifle force. Day and night pursuit produced offensive tempos of 10–15 kilometers per day in 1944 and 25–30 kilometers per day in 1945. Insufficient motor transport remained the chief obstacle to rapid pursuit by rifle forces and forced those units to improvise. Often rifle divisions conducted an echeloned pursuit with more mobile elements in the lead. During the pursuit, rivers were crossed from the march usually at night on a wide front (3–12 kilometers per division and 6–25 kilometers per corps).[30]

Combat support of rifle divisions and regiments improved in 1944–45. Artillery units resorted to single and double barrages and provided direct fire artillery to smash enemy strong points and provide direct support to advancing infantry. Density of direct fire weapons increased to 20–30 guns per kilometer of front. Infantry support tank units, centralized under division command through 1944, were finally decentralized in 1945. Tank and self-propelled

TABLE 74
ARMY OPERATIONAL FORMATION – DEFENSE 1945

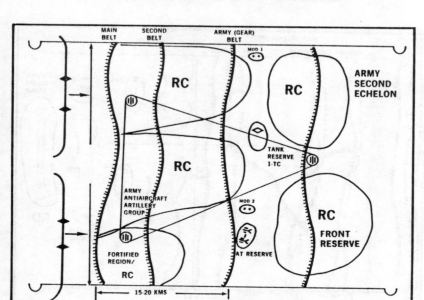

artillery regiments and brigades were attached in company- and battalion-strength to rifle regiment first echelon rifle battalions in order to provide closer, more responsive, fire support. Other separate tank regiments and brigades, under centralized rifle division control, attacked enemy positions at high speed and from the march to benefit from the element of surprise. Air support became more effective when assault aviation units began assigning liaison officers with radios to rifle corps and rifle division command posts to coordinate air support. Prearranged signals were used increasingly to mark the location of advancing units and facilitate air-ground coordination.

Defensive tactics, although receiving less emphasis, improved on techniques first employed in 1943. Defensive sectors decreased with rifle corps defending sectors 15–30 kilometers wide and rifle divisions sectors 6–14 kilometers wide (see table 76). The tactical defense of a rifle corps increased to a depth of 15–20 kilometers, and

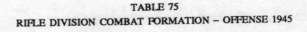

TABLE 75
RIFLE DIVISION COMBAT FORMATION – OFFENSE 1945

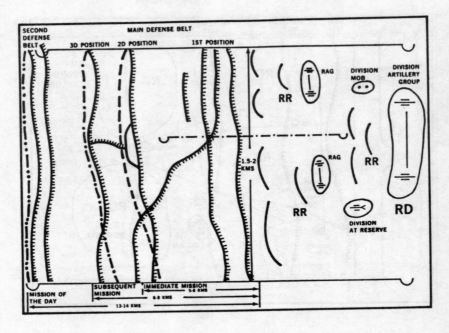

all tactical units (regiments) and formations (divisions, corps) deployed in two echelons. Rifle division first echelon rifle regiments occupied the first and second defensive positions and the second echelon regiment occupied the third defensive position. Two rifle divisions and all attached forces from the rifle corps' first echelon defended the main defensive belt. The rifle corps' second echelon rifle division occupied the second defensive belt and prepared to conduct counterattacks. Supporting artillery groups, antitank reserves, and mobile obstacle detachments raised tactical densities to 0.6–1.5 rifle battalions, 18–30 guns/mortars, 11–14 antitank guns and 2–4 tanks/self-propelled guns per kilometer of front.[31]

During the third period of war logistical support of Soviet forces measurably improved. To overcome logistical problems, hitherto the most serious impediment to offensive operations in light of German scorched earth policies, the Soviets created many new logistical units and a command and control structure to coordinate

TABLE 76
RIFLE CORPS/DIVISION COMBAT FORMATION – DEFENSE 1945

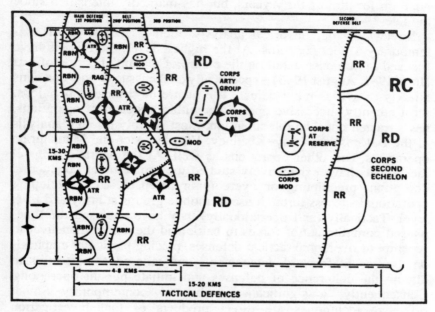

their employment. The Soviets paid special attention to resupply of fuel and ammunition and the maintenance and repair of equipment in critical tank and mechanized formations. Although the Soviets overcame weapons production problems, because of a shortage of trucks the transportation of supplies down to operational and tactical units remained a problem to war's end, in particular when Soviet armies operated in liberated regions.

Conclusion

For the Soviets the third period of the Great Patriotic War has been, and is today, one of the most important periods of their military development. In addition to achieving victory, the Soviets success- fully prepared for and conducted the widest range of operations, in particular offensive operations. Their force structure and regula- tions for its use were more sophisticated than they had ever been, and their command cadre reflected corresponding experience. The intensity and scope of conflict exceeded that of any previous war. Their operational and tactical techniques were well refined. For all of these reasons the Soviets have considered, and still consider, study of that period to be beneficial, if not essential. That study has gone on for almost forty years, but has markedly intensified since the late 1960s.

Review of that historical analysis often is indicative of contemporary Soviet concerns. At the highest level, the Soviets have focused in immense detail on the nature of the initial period of war (June 1941, August 1945) – specifically on the issue of how one wins quickly or avoids rapid defeat. The nature of strategic operations, most recently successive operations within a theater of operations, has attracted considerable attention, most notably through analysis of the Belorussian, Iassy–Kishinev, Vistula–Oder and Manchurian operations, and other operations as well. At the operational level the Soviets have exhaustively studied the problems of conducting deception, preempting or overcoming defenses, and developing operational success through use of mobile groups at army and *front* level. Tactically (and operationally) they have analysed the time-phased commitment of forces to battle and the use of maneuver to preempt or overcome tactical defenses, placing particular emphasis on the use of forward detachments and tailored assault units to disrupt the coherence of defenses and initiate pursuit operations. Consequently, a significant number of contemporary Soviet offensive techniques are direct products of that investigation tempered by contemporary practice, changing technology and field experimentation.

The third period of war for Westerners has been an "unknown war." Few Germans wrote about it, preferring instead to dwell on the more productive years of 1941–43. The Guderians, Mansteins, and von Mellethins, from whose works we have derived our image of Russians, were gone by 1944 and their successors, the Heinricis, Models and Schorners wrote no memoirs (or have had none translated into English). Hence the West remains largely ignorant of that stage of the war and ignorant of the tremendous repository of military knowledge and inspiration the Soviets tap from it.

CHAPTER SIX

OPERATIONAL ART AND THE REVOLUTION IN MILITARY AFFAIRS

THE LAST STALIN YEARS (1946–1953)

Context

Although the Soviet Union emerged victorious in 1945, the problems confronting the nation in general, and the military in particular, were immense. War had wrought extensive economic loss and social dislocation and had taken a heavy toll in human lives. Massive wartime population transfers followed by peacetime adjustment of borders and juggling of peoples, and a sizeable demobilization of armed forces personnel threatened further social instability. These factors combined with wartime popular hopes for postwar liberalization of the totalitarian Soviet state to create a potential for political unrest as well. These largely domestic concerns of Stalin were coupled with his concern over the political nature of the postwar world. By war's end it was clear that a new combination of capitalistic competitor states had emerged – one dominated by the United States. It was also clear that, while war had drained Soviet economic strength and peacetime reconstruction would continue to drain it, war had enhanced the United States' economic potential. American development and use of atomic weapons vividly underscored this point. The preeminent postwar Soviet international concern was to create around the USSR's borders a *cordon sanitaire*, a buffer against future foreign military aggression and the threat of foreign ideas. The ideological imperative of spreading revolution (liberation) and the realities of the principle "to the victor belongs the spoils" justified this policy.

A third problem confronting Stalin was a military one, namely the United States' monopoly in atomic weaponry. Although Stalin publicly denigrated the importance of such weapons (or any single weapon) and continued to do so until his death, he evidenced his concern for such weapons by developing military and technological programs to counter and ultimately end the U. S. monopoly.

Given the realities of 1945 and the potential for political ferment, Stalin worked swiftly even before war's end to ensure continued firm control over the Soviet Union and adjacent territories. He created and sponsored Communist governments in exile complete with military forces (Polish, Czech), and the Red Army entered Eastern Europe with those governments and armies in tow. Once returned to their native lands these exile governments, with Red Army assistance, conducted a process of consolidating "socialist" governments. Within the Soviet Union Stalin carefully eliminated potential challenges to his authority and crushed guerrilla bands operating in territories formerly occupied by Germany. Harsh treatment of Soviet ethnic minorities which had cooperated with Germans and of Soviet prisoners returned from German POW camps was indicative of Stalin's desire to insulate the Soviet Union against any alien ideas or political dissonance.

Doctrine

In the military realm, Stalin firmly controlled all matters, just as he had in wartime. Characteristically, Stalin selected his chief military advisors carefully, making certain no "man on a white horse" would appear to challenge his authority. The leading Soviet wartime military figure, Marshal Zhukov, suffered for his fame by being posted as Odessa Military District Commander in 1946, in virtual exile. A similar fate befell other leading military figures. Stalin had himself portrayed as the architect of wartime victories and the premier military theoretician of the war. Most Soviet theoretical military articles of this time dutifully and understandably echoed those judgments. Stalin's permanent operating factors in war dominated Soviet military doctrine and were often used to explain away the importance in war of such transitory factors as surprise and other Western derived "principles." Although viewed derisively by most Westerners, the overly broad and seemingly basic factors, in essence, summed up the Soviet wartime experience at the national level and provided rationale for avoiding panic over the United States' atomic monopoly.

Western observers have characterized the Stalinist period as one devoid of constructive military debate in the strategic, operational, and tactical realm and as a period of marked retrenchment in military thought, when the Soviet Union refused to recognize the impact of technological change (nuclear weapons) on warfare. Soviet statements made during de-Stalinization after Stalin's death have reinforced this negative view. One critic stated:

> the cult of personality, appearing especially in postwar literature, has had a negative influence on the development of Soviet military science in this period. To please Stalin, the truths of the war were trampled upon. All military success was attributed to him, and the role of military leaders became that of simple functionaries. At the time misfortunes of the war were explained as mistakes of his functionaries – *front* and army commanders. One could not talk about our major failures in the first months of war, much less analyse them ...[1]

The same critic cited as a harmful influence on Soviet military science in the atomic age Stalin's insistence on the validity of the permanent operating factors at the expense of an adequate understanding of the dangers of surprise. Other critics considered Stalin's refusal to analyse the initial period of war equally harmful. Yet these judgments were prompted in part by political considerations, and after de-Stalinization was over more recent Soviet writers (probably also for political reasons) have corrected these judgments, by writing:

> Actually there was no lagging of Soviet military strategy and, furthermore, there was no military weakness of the USSR in that period. The fighting strength of our armed forces, their structure, equipment, and combat readiness, as well as military art, completely corresponded to the requirements of that time and ensured the Motherland's security.[2]

Thus the extreme denigration of Stalin's role in military doctrine is probably as unjustified as the extreme adulation accorded to him during life for his military skill. The written public record during the period 1946–1953 does evidence discussion of the major themes of military science (strategic operations, *front* and army operations, tactics, use of airborne forces, etc.) primarily on the basis of evaluating war experience. The actual record of Soviet political, economic and military accomplishments which had their genesis under Stalin's leadership is impressive. Stalin tackled the problems of rebuilding a nearly destroyed nation, orchestrating socialist revolutions (coups) in eastern European nations, developing nuclear weapons and delivery means, and trying to extend revolution in Europe and Asia, while confronting the overwhelming strategic military superiority of the United States.

Force structure

In the military realm, Stalin maintained, reorganized, and re-equipped a large and formidable ground force capable of deterring potential United States use of nuclear weapons by holding central and western Europe hostage to Soviet ground power. Stalin demobilized Soviet ground forces from a 1945 strength of over 6 million men and over 500 divisions to a force of under 3 million men organized into about 180 divisions.[3] His postwar military reorganization program increased the firepower and mobility of ground force units by introducing new generations of weapons and vehicles into the force structure and by mechanizing a larger segment of those forces (see table 77). In 1946, on the basis of combat experiences in the Berlin and Manchurian operations, he transformed wartime tank armies into mechanized armies with an increased complement of mechanized infantry. Wartime tank and mechanized corps became postwar tank and mechanized divisions, while the brigades of the older corps became regiments in the new divisions. He also strengthened combined arms armies, rifle corps and rifle divisions by adding new tank, self-propelled gun and artillery units to their organizational structure. Force structure changes sought to create units which could fight and survive in the more urbanized terrain of central Europe.

While reforming the most visible element of Soviet military power, Stalin diverted resources from national recovery programs into programs for developing nuclear weapons and delivery systems. His visible concentration in word and deed on improving ground force power distracted public attention from the critical nuclear arena. Feverish activity in the nuclear field, which also involved adroit intelligence work and the cooperation of dragooned German scientists, resulted in production of a Soviet atomic device by 1949, a thermonuclear bomb by 1953, and three new long-range bombers by 1955 (and, by extension, development of a *sputnik* by 1957).

Strategy

Soviet postwar military art reflected fully basic concepts expressed in the field service regulations of 1944 amended by the experience of 1945 operations, in particular the Vistula–Oder, Berlin, and Manchurian operations. Military art emphasized reliance on the offensive, characterized by widespread maneuver and judicious use

TABLE 77
POSTWAR REORGANIZATION OF FORCES

1946 Mechanized Army
    2 tank divisions
    2 mechanized divisions
    1 light artillery brigade
    1 antiaircraft artillery regiment
    1 rocket launcher regiment
    1 motorcycle regiment
    1 engineer brigade
    1 signal regiment
      service units

    strength: approx 60,000 men
                     1,000 tanks

1956 Mechanized Army

    2 tank divisions
    2 mechanized divisions
    1 artillery brigade
    1 antiaircraft artillery division
    1 rocket launcher regiment
    1 reconnaissance regiment
    1 engineer brigade
    1 signal regiment
      service units

    strength: 63,000 men
                     1,200 tanks, SP guns

1946 Mechanized Division

    3 mechanized regiments (32 T-34 each)
    1 medium tank regiment (65 T-34, 21 SU-152)
    1 heavy tank, self propelled gun regiment (21 IS-3, 42 SU-100)
    1 mortar regiment (36 X 120 mm)
    1 howitzer artillery regiment (24 X 122 mm)
    1 antiaircraft artillery regiment (16 X 37 mm)
    1 rocket launcher battalion (8 X 132 mm)
    1 motorcycle battalion (10 T-34)
    1 signal battalion
    1 engineer battalion
    1 medical battalion
    1 transport battalion
    1 headquarters company (5 T-34)

    strength: 12,500 men
               197 tanks (176 T-34, 21 IS-3)
               63 SP guns

TABLE 77 (*continued*)

1954 Mechanized Division

    3 mechanized regiments (34 T-34, 5 PT-76, 11 SU-122 each)
    1 tank regiment (105 T-54, 5 PT-76)
    1 heavy tank/assault gun regiment (46 IS-3, 22 SU-122)
    2 artillery regiments (24 X 122 mm how, 12 X 85 mm guns or
      160 mm mortars each)
    1 antiaircraft artillery regiment (6 X 57 mm, 6 X 85 mm)
    1 rocket launcher battalion (6 X 140 mm each)
    1 reconnaissance battalion (11 T-54, 5 PT)
    1 engineer battalion
    1 medical battalion
    1 transport regiment
    1 signal battalion
    1 chemical defense company

    strength: 15,415 men
                294 tanks (223 T-54, 46 IS-3, 25 PT-76)
                 55 SP guns

1946 Tank Division

    3 medium tank regiments (65 T-34/85, 21 SU-152)
    1 heavy tank, self propelled gun regiment (44 IS-3, 21 SU-152)
    1 motorized rifle regiment
    1 howitzer artillery battalion (12 X 122 mm)
    1 mortar regiment (36 X 120 mm)
    1 antiaircraft regiment (16 X 37 mm)
    1 rocket launcher battalion (12 M-13)
    1 motorcycle battalion (10 T-34/85)
    1 engineer battalion
    1 signal battalion
    1 transport battalion headquarters company (3 T-34/85)

    strength: 10,659 men
                252 tanks (208 T-34/85, 44 IS-3)
                 84 SP guns

1954 Tank Division

    3 medium tank regiments (110 T-54, 5 PT-76)
    1 heavy tank, self propelled gun regiment (46 IS-3, 22
      SU-122/152)
    1 motorized rifle regiment (34 T-54, 11 SU 122/152, 5 PT-76)
    1 artillery regiment (12 X 85 mm guns, 24 X 122 mm how)
    1 artillery regiment (24 X 122 mm how, 12 X 160 mm mortars)
    1 antiaircraft regiment (12 X 57 mm, 12 X 85 mm)
    1 rocket launcher battalion (12 X 240 mm)
    1 reconnaissance battalion (11 T-54, 5 PT-76)
    1 engineer battalion
    1 signal battalion
    1 medical battalion
    1 chemical defense company

    strength: 13,670 men
                451 tanks (380 T-54, 46 IS-3, 25 PT-76)
                 33 SP guns

TABLE 77 (*continued*)

1946 Combined Arms Army

        3 rifle corps
          3 rifle divisions
            or
          2 rifle divisions and
          1 mechanized division
        1 heavy tank, self propelled gun regiment
        1 gun artillery brigade
        1 antitank brigade
        1 antiaircraft division
        1 mortar regiment
        1 engineer regiment
        1 signal regiment

1956 Combined Arms Army

        2-3 rifle corps
          2-3 rifle divisions
          1 mechanized division
        1 heavy tank, assault gun regiment
        1 gun artillery brigade
        1 antitank brigade
        1 antiaircraft division
        1 rocket launcher regiment
        1 engineer regiment
        1 signal regiment

1946 Rifle Corps

        3 rifle divisions
            or
        2 rifle divisions and
        1 mechanized division
        1 artillery brigade
        1 rocket launcher regiment
        1 antitank regiment
        1 antiaircraft regiment
        1 engineer battalion
        1 signal battalion

1956 Rifle Corps

        2-3 rifle divisions
        1 mechanized division
        1 artillery brigade
          1 antiaircraft regiment
          1 artillery regiment
          1 antitank unit
          1 rocket launcher regiment
        1 engineer battalion
        1 signal battalion

TABLE 77 (*continued*)

1946 Rifle Division

    3 rifle regiments (6 X 76 mm SP)
    1 medium tank, self propelled gun regiment (52 T-34, 16
    SU-100)
    1 artillery brigade
       1 gun artillery regiment (24 X 76 mm)
       1 howitzer artillery regiment (36 X 122 mm)
       1 mortar regiment (12 X 160 mm)
    1 antitank battalion (57 mm, 76 mm)
    1 antiaircraft battalion (37 mm)
    1 reconnaissance battalion
    1 engineer battalion
    1 signal battalion
      service units

    strength: 11,013 men
                  52 tanks
                  34 SP guns
                  60 guns

1954 Rifle Division

    3 rifle regiments
    1 medium tank, assault gun regiment (66 T-54, 22 SU-100)
    1 artillery regiment (36 X 122 mm howitzer, 12 X 85 mm guns,
      8 X 160 mm mortars)
    1 antitank battalion (12 X 85 mm)
    1 antiaircraft regiment (24 X 57 mm, 12 X 85 mm)
    1 reconnaissance battalion (11 T-54)
    1 engineer battalion
    1 signal battalion
    1 medical battalion
    1 transport battalion
    1 chemical defense company
    1 artillery observation battery

    strength: 13,335 men
                  82 tanks (77 T-54, 5 PT-76)
                  43 SP guns

of massed armor, artillery, and airpower to effect success on the battlefield. The offensive model was that of 1944–45, although infantry forces were gradually motorized and mechanized, and the last cavalry formations soon faded from the scene. These offensive concepts reflected older deep battle themes, so evident in the 1936 and 1944 field regulations, by stressing that

> offensive combat consists in suppressing the enemy by mighty fire of all means and by a blow in his entire depth of defense, and is conducted by a decisive offensive of the entire combat formation.[4]

In the strategic realm the Soviets emphasized study of the fundamental theme of conducting strategic operations and also devoted time to study of the nature of the strategic defense and how to go over from the defensive to an offensive. In the light of force reorganization, combined arms operations became an important focus of study. In this context the Soviets studied extensively the military art of foreign nations, in particular the United States. Unique postwar conditions, including rapid technological change and increased mechanization of forces, required intensive reflection on wartime strategic operations.

The Soviets assumed a future world war would be an armed clash between two powerful coalitions of states with differing political systems, each fielding armed forces of many millions of men, and each with fully mobilized "economic and morale capabilities."[5] War would involve not only defeat of enemy forces within theaters of war but also the undermining of a nation's economic potential, the occupation of important regions, and the dismemberment of the opposing coalition by forcing its members to unconditionally surrender. Since a number of intermediate military-political missions would have to be accomplished in order to achieve final war aims, it would be necessary to conduct a series of strategic offensive operations. In these strategic operations the ground forces would bear the main burden of struggle assisted by other elements of the armed forces. The Soviets recognized several types of strategic operations, including the strategic offensive, the strategic defense, and the counteroffensive. They considered the strategic offensive, however, to be the most important form.

The Soviets defined the strategic offensive as the

> main and decisive form of strategic operations by the armed forces and that only as a result of it was it possible to defeat the

strategic formation of the enemy armed forces in the theater, capture vitally important territory and finally smash enemy resistance and ensure victory.[6]

The Soviets reckoned the scope of future strategic operations would be in accordance with the scale of 1944 and 1945 strategic operations. Consequently, they envisioned that a strategic operation would encompass one or two strategic directions or a theater of military operations to its entire depth. In larger theaters of war accomplishment of all strategic missions would require two or more successive strategic operations. A strategic operation would involve participation of several reinforced *fronts*, one or two air armies, airborne divisions, military transport aviation, air defense forces, and, in coastal regions, naval forces.

The General Staff would develop the concept for and plan the strategic operation; and determine the composition and formation of forces, the direction of the main effort, the strategic missions of the group of *fronts*, and the approximate timing of the offensive. The width of the strategic offensive sector would range from 400–600 kilometers (two *fronts*) to 800–1,200 kilometers (four *fronts*) with forces concentrated in one or several *front* penetration sectors.[7] Extensive artillery and air preparations would precede the offensive. The artillery preparation would be under *front* control and the air force commander or one of the *front* commanders would control the critical air offensive operation. The air operation, which would last two to three days, would involve one or two air armies, long-range aviation, and national air defense forces. It would seek to achieve air supremacy by destroying enemy tactical air forces in the air or on their own airfields, by destroying airfields, ammunition and POL dumps, and by neutralizing enemy radar systems. The strategic offensive would commence simultaneously with the air operation and would seek to encircle enemy forces or fragment his strategic front by direct attack and destroy his forces piecemeal.[8]

Encirclement operations by groups of *fronts*, the most decisive form of offensive action, would involve two *front* operations along converging directions (as in Belorussia) or one or two *fronts* conducting enveloping attacks to force the enemy against a natural obstacle (sea, mountains) (as in East Prussia). Swift development of the offensive into the depths and toward the flanks would produce the encirclement of enemy strategic groups. Mechanized armies would launch the deep sustained strikes and would cooperate with airborne divisions dropped deep in the enemy rear to complete the envelopment.

Direct attacks by *fronts* deployed on a broad frontage would attempt to achieve multiple penetrations (like Manchuria) and paralyze the enemy's ability to maneuver forces laterally. This would, however, require considerable concentration of manpower and weaponry in the penetration sectors. Both offensive forms (the envelopment or direct attack) would begin with penetration operations conducted by *fronts* and armies. This Soviet view on the nature of strategic operations and internal security requirements dictated the force levels and organization of forces stationed in peacetime central and eastern Europe.

Operational art

Within the context of the strategic operation, the premier operational level organization was the *front* which was designated to perform both operational and strategic missions. *Front* operations would involve a "series of army operations executed either simultaneously or successively." By exploiting the operational capabilities of new weapons, *fronts* would "split the operational structure of the enemy along the front and in the depths into isolated pockets and destroy them one by one ... to encircle and defeat the resisting enemy forces in a given direction with the envelopment of the whole depth of his operational organization."[9] *Fronts*, operating in sectors of from 200–300 kilometers, deployed strong shock groups in one or several penetration sectors of up to 50 kilometers width (see table 78).

The *front's* operational formation would consist of a first echelon of combined arms armies, *front* mobile groups consisting of one or two mechanized armies, a second echelon, frontal aviation, airborne forces (one or two divisions), a *front* antiaircraft group, and a reserve. *Fronts* would employ mechanized armies in first echelon when operating against hasty enemy defenses. *Front* operations had the close mission of penetrating the enemy army group defense on the first day with first echelon armies, then encircling and destroying the enemy forces. Subsequently, the *front* would develop the offensive by committing mechanized armies through 8–12-kilometer sectors on the second day of the operation. The mechanized armies and follow on forces would conduct an exploitation to destroy enemy operational and strategic reserves to a depth of 200 kilometers.[10] Thus, the *front's* operational frontage and depth

TABLE 78
FRONT OPERATIONAL FORMATION – 1946-1953

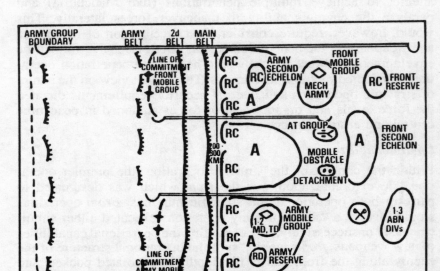

FRONT IMMEDIATE MISSION
ARMY SUBSEQUENT MISSION

of mission increased in comparison with norms of the third period of the Great Patriotic War. The Soviets expected the duration of *front* (and army) operations would be shorter than had been the case in the war years.

Combined arms armies of attacking *fronts* would deploy in 40–50-kilometer-wide sectors and would concentrate their force in penetration sectors 20 kilometers wide (see table 79). An army would deploy with a first echelon of several rifle corps; a second echelon of a rifle corps or several rifle divisions; an army artillery group; an army antiaircraft group; and combined arms, antitank, tank, engineer and chemical reserves. Sometimes an army commander would employ a mobile group consisting of a separate mechanized or tank division. The army's first echelon rifle corps would complete the penetration of the enemy's main defensive zone to the depth of 6–10 kilometers, and the army's second echelon rifle corps would penetrate the enemy second tactical defense zone to a

TABLE 79
ARMY OPERATIONAL FORMATION – 1946–1953

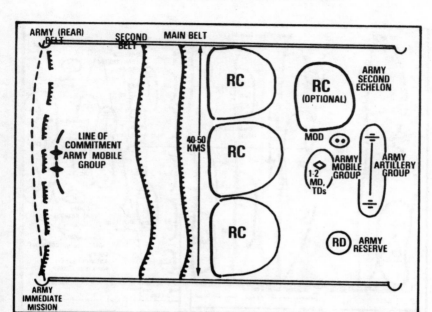

depth of 10–15 kilometers from the front lines, if possible by attacking from the march after a short preparation.[11] Artillery would support the army's advance by firing barrages or successive fire concentrations. Propeller aircraft in small groups would support advancing troops while jet aircraft (because of their speed and command and control problems) struck at enemy centers of resistance ahead of advancing ground troops. Bombers would strike larger centers of resistance in the depths of the enemy defense, including enemy reserves, airfields and other objectives.

Tactics

Tactically, the combined arms army's first echelon rifle corps operating on a main attack direction would attack in a sector up to 8 kilometers wide, and a rifle division within that corps would attack in a sector of up to 4 kilometers wide (see tables 80–81). This would produce tactical densities of 180–200 guns/mortars and 60–80

TABLE 80

RIFLE CORPS COMBAT FORMATION – OFFENSE 1946–1953

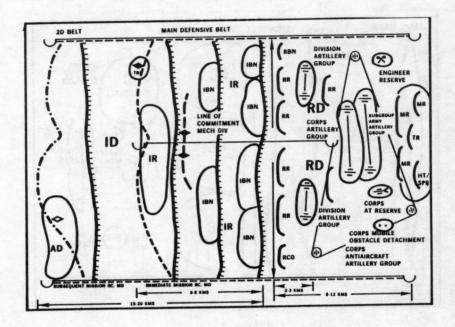

tanks/self-propelled guns per kilometer – numbers close to those of the latter stages of the Great Patriotic War.[12] The artillery and air preparation for the attack would last up to one hour with the artillery firing single or double barrages to the depth of the enemy first defensive positions. First echelon rifle divisions, with the support of infantry support tanks (the integral tank and self-propelled battalion), artillery, and aviation would initiate the attack. On the first day of attack mechanized divisions in the rifle corps second echelon would complete the penetration of the main enemy defensive zone and prepare the way for commitment of the combined arms army's second echelon rifle corps. Thus, the two mechanized divisions in an army's two first echelon rifle corps were a stronger version of the two tank corps used by armies as mobile groups in 1944–45. In addition, combined arms armies had at their disposal a third mechanized division in the second echelon rifle corps.

TABLE 81
RIFLE DIVISION COMBAT FORMATION – OFFENSE 1946–1953

RIFLE DIVISION TANK/SP GUN REGIMENT IN
INFANTRY SUPPORT

Conclusion

Soviet offensive concepts in the first postwar period emphasized employment of strong mechanized forces (mobile groups) echeloned in-depth to overcome strong defenses manned by enemy mechanized forces. Thus, the Soviets stressed heavy firepower and the rapid forward projection of mechanized and heavily armored formations to the depth of the battlefield. The sequential employment of infantry – support tank battalions, mechanized divisions of army first echelons, mechanized divisions of army second echelons, and finally mechanized and tank divisions from the *front's* second echelon mechanized armies provided *narashchivanie* (steady strengthening) of the forward momentum necessary to penetrate initial defenses, grind up enemy mobile operational reserves, and achieve success in the operational depths. The mobile groups of this period were more numerous, stronger and better balanced (in

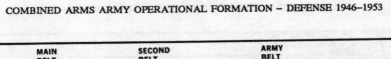

TABLE 82

COMBINED ARMS ARMY OPERATIONAL FORMATION – DEFENSE 1946–1953

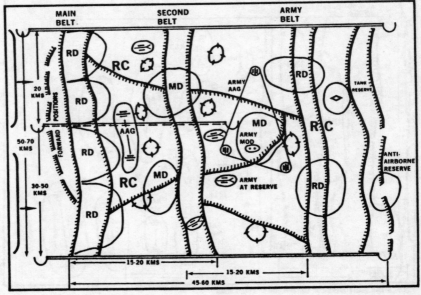

particular in mechanized infantry) than their Great Patriotic War counterparts.

Soviet defensive concepts at both the operational and tactical levels during the first postwar period also built upon the experience of the late war years. Defenses involved deeply echeloned rifle forces occupying defensive positions which integrated considerable engineer, armor and artillery support (see tables 82–84). On the defense, the mechanized army of the *front* and mechanized divisions of the combined arms army and rifle corps performed the active role of counterattacking to destroy any enemy forces which had penetrated the dense defensive network.

Only recognition of new forces on the battlefield could cause the Soviets to consider abandoning their reliance on this time-tested formula for offensive and defensive victory. By the mid-fifties such recognition had occurred simultaneously with and, in part, because of the death of Stalin.

TABLE 83

RIFLE CORPS COMBAT FORMATION – DEFENSE 1946–1953

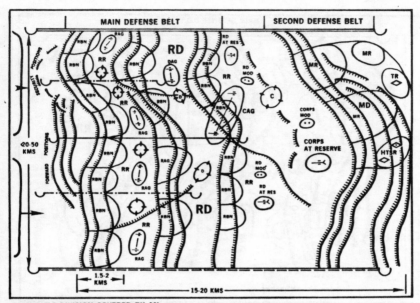

EACH RIFLE DIVISION COVERED BY AN
ANTIAIRCRAFT ARTILLERY GROUP

TABLE 84
RIFLE DIVISION COMBAT FORMATION – DEFENSE 1946–1953

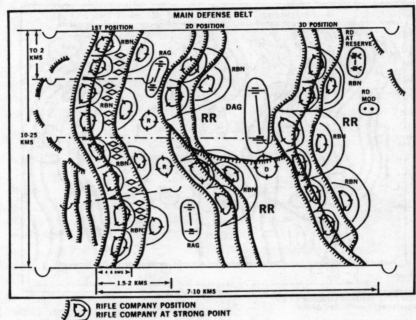

RIFLE COMPANY POSITION
RIFLE COMPANY AT STRONG POINT

INFANTRY SUPPORT SP GUNS, TANKS

THE NUCLEAR ERA AND THE REVOLUTION IN MILITARY AFFAIRS (1953–1968)

Context

The death of Stalin in 1953 and the growing Soviet realization that future war would likely be nuclear had an enormous impact on Soviet military thought and the structure of Soviet military forces. Stalin's demise threw the Soviet leadership into a struggle for power reminiscent of that which had occurred during Lenin's last days and the years immediately following his death. Once again there were two main groups who conducted their struggle within the context of a doctrinal argument focused on the size of armaments and heavy industry expenditures vis-à-vis production to satisfy consumer wants.

G. N. Malenkov, who argued for greater production of consumer goods, wanted military expenditures to be concentrated on the development and production of nuclear weapons and delivery means in order to deter possible American attack, and favored decreased expenditures on massive ground forces. N. S. Khrushchev advocated continued emphasis on conventional armaments, large ground forces and expanded heavy industry. Eventually Khrushchev won a political victory and, hence, the debate. Consequently, until 1960 Soviet ground forces continued to develop at current levels supplemented by steady improvements in nuclear forces. By 1960 however, Khrushchev had co-opted Malenkov's views and had embraced accelerated reliance on nuclear forces at the expense of ground forces, a trend which would endure until well after Khrushchev's ouster from power in 1964.

At a lower level, Stalin's death permitted Soviet military theorists to strip off slowly the veneer of Stalinist principles which had insulated that theory from detailed critical examination and which had prevented more active and open discussion of operational and tactical questions. It also encouraged those theorists to ponder more fully the likelihood and nature of nuclear war. This recognition of the increased importance of nuclear weapons and the enhanced potential impact of surprise attained by initial wartime use of these weapons triggered a basic revision of military theory and wholesale reorganization of the armed forces.

The following period, which lasted until 1960 and which is usually identified as the period of the Zhukov reforms, was characterized by intense Soviet reinvestigation of all areas of military science in the light of technological changes. This study resulted in a thorough reorganization of the armed forces, a redefinition of the role and capabilities of the various arms and services within a new concept of military operations, and accelerated development and fielding of new weaponry. Characterizing these intense debates were a flood of articles in the classified journal *Military Thought [Voennaia mysl']* and in the *Military Historical Journal [Voenno-istoricheskii zhurnal* – founded in 1959]* on topics henceforth little discussed. Among the important themes discussed in early issues of *Military Historical Journal* was that of the nature of the initial period of war. A second wave of changes began in the early 1960s, keynoted by Khrushchev's January 1960 speech, which announced Soviet recognition of a "revolution in military affairs." The second wave represented a full maturation of concepts developed during the first, or Zhukov, phase.

Doctrine

The emergence of a new view of war in general, and of offensive operations in particular, was fundamental to the wholesale changes which occurred after 1953. This new view held that general war would likely begin with or include a nuclear exchange (by strategic aircraft) and would involve use of nuclear weapons on the battle-field. In the late 1950s, however, the Soviets recognized the importance of nuclear weapons, but tempered their assessment of the impact of those weapons on the battlefield. Thus, a leading military theorist noted that "under contemporary conditions the use of weapons of mass destruction in operations can achieve greater success only in combination with artillery fire and aviation strikes." Moreover, "the use of atomic weapons considerably lessens the requirements for artillery in the conduct of an offensive operation, but that new weapon cannot entirely abolish or replace artillery and aviation, which will play a large role in the course of an operation."[13] The same analyst warned that the appearance of new weapons always required careful reassessment of military theory and the development of powerful nuclear weapons made such study essential. Thus, while Khrushchev consolidated his power, Soviet military doctrine began taking cognizance of the nuclear age. The Zhukov force reorganization, which involved the replacement of the cumbersome mechanized divisions and relatively immobile rifle divisions by new motorized rifle divisions, reflected that evolving doctrine.

Khrushchev's 1960 speech signaled his full commitment to the idea that "a revolution in military affairs" had occurred.[14] That "revolution" recognized the preeminence of nuclear weapons in war, elevated the importance of strategy (signified by the establishment of and emphasis on strategic rocket forces) and diminished the importance of operational art (and, by extension, the ground forces). Among the myriad of works explaining the nature of the revolution in military affairs was V. D. Sokolovsky's 1962 book *Military Strategy [Voennaia Strategiia]*. His description of future war echoed Khrushchev's view that "both gigantic military coalitions will deploy massive armies in a future decisive world war; all modern, powerful and long-range means of combat including multimegaton nuclear-rocket weapons, will be used in it on a huge scale; and the most decisive methods of military operations will be used".[15] Sokolovsky maintained that strategic nuclear forces could themselves decide the outcome of war without resort to extended ground operations, and even if ground operations occurred,

> mass nuclear-rocket strikes will be of decisive importance for the attainment of goals in a future world war. The infliction of these assaults will be the main, decisive method of waging war ... armed conflicts in ground theaters of military operations will also take place differently. The defeat of the enemy's groupings of ground troops, the destruction of his rockets, aircraft and nuclear weapons ... will be achieved mainly by nuclear-rocket strikes.[16]

Ground forces would exploit the effects of nuclear strikes, defeat enemy forces, and conquer and occupy territory. In this nuclear context, ground forces would play a distinctly secondary role to strategic rocket forces, and strategy would become more dominant over operational art:

> All this shows that the relationship between the role and importance of armed combat waged by forces in direct contact with the enemy in the zone of combat operations, employing simultaneously tactical, operational and strategic means of destruction on the one hand, and the role and importance of armed combat waged beyond the confines of this zone by strategic means alone on the other hand has shifted abruptly towards an increase in the role and importance of the latter.[17]

This belief in the predominance of nuclear weapons in war persisted even after Khrushchev's ouster from power in 1964. Thus, in 1966

A. A. Strokov noted in his classic work on the history of military art
that the existence of nuclear rockets and the equipping of large units
and formations with them had produced a change in operational art
and tactics. Specifically, the use of such weapons could achieve
strategic results "independently from the conduct of operations and
battles."[18] In general war, operational art was now only an adjunct
to the use of nuclear weapons, although it did retain its importance
in local wars.

Strokov's comments illuminated another aspect of doctrinal
change emerging in the 1960s, which would continue to develop
in subsequent years. Responding to the changing world order,
specifically the breakdown in old colonial empires and the emergence of a "third" world, Khrushchev in 1960 committed the Soviet
Union to support for "wars of national liberation." These wars,
while contributing to instability in capitalist societies, promised
fresh opportunities for the expansion of Socialism, as events in
Vietnam and Cuba had indicated. In subsequent years Soviet
support for these new types of wars would mature from verbal
support, through material support, to the use of advisers and
proxies in selected regions of the world. In essence, this Soviet
policy represented practical implementation of Lenin's description
of revolution in the imperialist stage of development – revolution of
a proletariat of underdeveloped nations against their capitalist
masters. Thus, at the highest levels of military doctrine significant
changes occurred in the post-Stalin years, changes reflected in the
evolving Soviet force structure and in Soviet concepts for conducting war at the strategic, operational, and tactical levels.

Force structure

The first wave of armed force structural changes occurred following
Stalin's death during the initial debates over the nature of future
war. Marshal Zhukov began the reorganization in 1954 and 1955
and his successors continued them after his replacement by Marshal
R. Ia. Malinovsky in 1957. By virtue of the reorganization Zhukov
sought to create smaller, more mobile forces, organized and
equipped to fight better and survive on a nuclear battlefield. Very
simply, the existing large mechanized formations were difficult to
control in fluid combat, and appeared vulnerable to nuclear strikes.
Therefore, Zhukov abolished the ponderous mechanized armies
and mechanized divisions; the less mobile rifle corps and rifle
divisions; and the few remaining cavalry divisions. He created
instead streamlined armored heavy tank armies (comprising tank

divisions) to replace mechanized armies and the more flexible and balanced motorized rifle division to replace both the heavier mechanized division and the lighter rifle division (see table 85). The new combined arms army emerged as a balanced force of tank and motorized rifle divisions, and the tank division was reduced in size as well. The formation of armor-heavy tank armies and tank divisions testified to increased Soviet reliance on the speed and survivability of armored units to achieve success on the nuclear battlefield. The Soviets motorized all units and incorporated new equipment, including rocket artillery, tanks (T-55), tactical missiles, armored personnel carriers (BTR series), and early model surface-to-air missiles into all elements of the force structure. The new mobile ground forces were capable of sustained, flexible, semi-independent operations on the developing nuclear battlefield.

TABLE 85
THE ZHUKOV REORGANIZATION

1958 Tank Army

```
4 tank divisions
1 artillery brigade
1 rocket artillery brigade
1 antiaircraft artillery division
1 reconnaissance regiment
1 pontoon bridge regiment
1 assault crossing battalion
1 signal regiment
2 chemical defense regiments

strength:   1400-1500 tanks
```

1958 Tank Division

```
2 medium tank regiments (102 T-54, 10 X 122/152 mm SPs, 3
  PT-76 each)
1 heavy tank regiment (95 T-10, 3 PT-76)
1 motorized rifle regiment (35 T-54, 3 PT-76)
1 artillery regiment (36 X 122 mm howitzer)
1 antiaircraft artillery regiment (24 X 57 mm)
1 assault gun battalion (32 X 122/152 mm SPs)
1 rocket launcher battalion (12 X 240 mm)
1 reconnaissance battalion (10 T-54, 5 PT-76)
2 sapper battalions
1 signal battalion (5 T-54)
1 motor transport battalion
1 medical battalion
1 chemical defense company

strength:   10,630 men
            95 T-10 heavy tanks
           254 T-54 tanks
            17 PT-76 light tanks
            52 122 mm/152 mm SP guns
```

TABLE 85 (*continued*)

1958 Combined Arms Army
    3 - 4 motorized rifle divisions
    1 tank division
    1 - 3 artillery brigades
    1 antitank artillery brigade
    1 rocket artillery brigade
    1 antiaircraft artillery division
    1 pontoon bridge regiment
    1 engineer regiment
    1 reconnaissance regiment
    1 signal regiment
    1 chemical defense regiment

1958 Motorized Rifle Division

    3 motorized rifle regiments (32 T-54, 3 PT-76 each)
    1 medium tank regiment (99 T-54, 3 PT-76, 10 X 122 mm SP)
    1 artillery regiment (18 X 85 mm guns, 18 X 122 mm how,
      18 X 160 mm mortars)
    1 antiaircraft artillery regiment (24 X 57 mm)
    1 rocket artillery battalion (18 X 140 mm)
    1 reconnaissance battalion (10 T-54, 5 PT-76)
    1 sapper battalion
    1 signal battalion (5 T-54)
    1 motor transport regiment
    1 chemical defense company
    1 medical battalion
    1 artillery observation battery

    strength: 13,150 men
               210 T-54 tanks
                17 PT-76 light tanks
                10 122/152 mm SP guns

   The process of adjusting the force structure accelerated after 1960 in accordance with Khrushchev's views on the preeminent position of nuclear weapons on the contemporary battlefield. Strategic rocket forces, created as a separate type of force in 1960, became the "main and decisive means for achieving the aims of war."[19] The ground force, with its new rocket forces branch, lost its status as an independent command in 1964 by being placed under direct control of the Ministry of Defense, thus signaling its reduced stature (only to be re-elevated to service status in 1967). Concurrently, during 1962 and 1963, the Soviet reduced the size of Zhukov's motorized rifle and tank divisions still further to make them even more mobile and survivable (see table 86). Equipment modernization continued with the introduction of the T-62 tank, antitank guided missiles (ATGMs), infantry combat vehicles (BMP-BMD), and tactical nuclear missiles at division level. The overall strength of the Soviet armed forces fell to 2.5 million men from its 1955 high of 5.76 million and its 1958 strength of 3.6 million.[20] The process of tailoring Soviet operational and tactical units to the nuclear battlefield continued unabated during the mid-60s (see table 87).

Strategy 1953–1960

Soviet strategic theory in the late 1950s treated nuclear war as an important phenomenon, but not one that had as yet produced a full revolution in military affairs. Nuclear weapons were few in number and deliverable only by aircraft. Consequently, the Soviets saw them as a means of increasing the fire power of conventional forces and the effectiveness of existing strategic concepts and forms of operations. Thus, ground forces, assisted by other types of forces, would conduct strategic offensive operations to destroy major enemy forces in a theater of military operations and occupy important political and economic regions. The actual Soviet description of strategic, *front* and army operations changed little from the preceding period; except for an emerging recognition of the growing importance of nuclear fires and the changing capabilities of re-organized and re-equipped ground forces. That recognition increased further with the introduction of intercontinental missiles and greater number of theater nuclear weapons.

By the end of the 1950s, the Soviets still took a cautious view of the impact of nuclear weaponry, and they warned against either overestimating or underestimating its significance. Overestimating nuclear weapons capabilities "could attribute to them the quality of being able to secure victory in war in a minimally short period" while underestimating their impact could adversely effect other proven operational techniques.[21] The Soviets admitted, however, that "nuclear weapons are one of the basic means of attacking the enemy during the conduct of operations. All other existing weapons have improved their capabilities to such an extent as to correspond in their combat characteristics to the requirements of modern war."[22] As a consequence,

> the means of massive destruction, the varied military weaponry, the motorization and mechanization of the army, the presence of air assault forces and the achievements of aviation have created new material prerequisites for the conduct of opera-

TABLE 86
FORCE REORGANIZATION OF 1961–62

1962 Tank Army

    3-4 tank divisions
    1 mixed artillery brigade
    1 rocket artillery brigade
    1 antiaircraft artillery brigade
    1 rocket launcher regiment
    1 pontoon bridge regiment
    1 assault crossing battalion
    1 engineer regiment
    1 signal regiment
    1 radio relay battalion
    1 line construction battalion
    1 intelligence battalion
    1 chemical regiment

    strength: 1100-1500 tanks

1961 Tank Division

    2 medium tank regiments (101 T-54, 10 X 122/152 mm SPs)
    1 heavy tank regiment (95 T-10, 3 PT-76)
    1 motorized rifle regiment (35 T-54, 3 PT-76)
    1 artillery regiment (54 X 122 mm how)
    1 antiaircraft artillery regiment (24 X 57 mm SP)
    1 assault gun battalion (32 X 122/152 mm SP)
    1 rocket launcher battalion (12 X 240 mm)
    1 reconnaissance battalion (10 T-54, 10 PT-76)
    1 sapper battalion
    1 signal battalion (3 T-54)
    1 medical battalion
    1 chemical defense company

    strength: 10,857 men
                 95 T-10 heavy tanks
                 253 T-54 tanks
                 22 PT-76 light tanks

1962 Combined Arms Army

    4 motorized rifle divisions
    1 tank division
    1 mixed artillery brigade
    1 antiaircraft artillery brigade
    1 antitank artillery brigade
    1 rocket launcher regiment
    1 rocket artillery brigade
    1 assault crossing battalion
    1 chemical defense regiment
    1 signal regiment
    1 pontoon bridge regiment
    1 line construction battalion
    1 intelligence battalion
    1 engineer regiment
    1 radio relay battalion

TABLE 86 (*continued*)

1961 Motorized Rifle Division

```
3 motorized rifle regiments (32 T-54, 3 PT-76)
1 medium tank regiment (101 T-54, 10 122 mm/152 mm SP)
1 artillery regiment (18 X 100 mm gun, 36 X 122 mm how, 18 X
  160 mm mortars)
1 antiaircraft artillery regiment (18 X 57 mm, 18 X 57 mm
  SP)
1 rocket artillery battalion (18 X 140 mm)
1 reconnaissance battalion (10 T-54, 10 PT-76)
1 sapper battalion
1 signal battalion (3 T-54)
1 motor transport battalion
1 chemical defense company
1 medical battalion
1 artillery observation battery

strength:   13,767 men
               219 T-54 tanks
                22 PT-76 light tanks
                10 122/152 mm SP guns
```

tions on a large scale, to a considerable depth and with more decisive aims than in the last war ... Soviet military science proceeds from the belief that modern war is characterized by the unfolding of armed conflict on land, in the air, and on the sea simultaneously in many theaters of military operations. That war will involve widespread use of atomic weapons and other means of massive destruction, jet aircraft flying at great heights, at speeds greater than sound and at long distances, as well as various rockets including intercontinental ballistic missiles. *Nevertheless*, Soviet strategy does not overestimate the new weapons. The massive use of atomic weapons by no means excludes the conduct of forms of ground force, air and naval operations in future wars. Without these types of armed forces and without their proper cooperation it is impossible to conduct war successfully.[23]

Strategic operations in the late 1950s involved the preparation and conduct of "deep and complex, simultaneous and consecutive operations of different types and scales" conducted by *fronts* consisting of tank and combined arms armies and airborne forces supported by the air force and fleet.[24] Operations would be more maneuverable, and nuclear weapons would eradicate the clear distinction between front and rear. Initially, the Soviets integrated nuclear weapons into existing strategic defensive concepts. By the late 1950s, however, the appearance of nuclear rockets had

TABLE 87

FORCE REORGANIZATION OF 1963–1968

1963 Motorized Rifle Division

    3 motorized rifle regiments (31 T-62, 3 PT-76 each)
    1 medium tank regiment (93 T-62, 3 PT-76)
    1 artillery regiment (18 X 122 mm gun how, 18 X 152 mm gun
    how, 28 X 160 mm mortars)
    1 rocket artillery battalion (18 X 140 mm)
    1 FROG battalion (4 FROGs)‡
    1 antitank battalion (100 mm gun, ATGM)
    1 antiaircraft battalion
    1 reconnaissance company (10 PT-76)
    1 signal battalion
    1 sapper battalion
    1 chemical defense company
    1 artillery reconnaissance battery

    strength: 11,013 men
                186 T-62 (some with T-54/55) tanks
                 22 PT-76 light tanks

1968 Motorized Rifle Division

    3 motorized rifle regiments (31 T-62, 3 PT-76 each)
    1 medium tank regiment (95 T-62)
    1 artillery regiment (54 X 122/152 mm)
    1 rocket artillery battalion
    1 FROG battalion
    1 antitank battalion (100 mm, ATGM)
    1 antiaircraft battalion
    1 reconnaissance company
    1 signal battalion
    1 sapper battalion
    1 chemical defense company
    1 artillery reconnaissance battery

    strength: 10,500 men
                188 T-62 tanks

1968 Tank Division

    3 medium tank regiments (95 T-62, 3 PT-76 each)
    1 motorized rifle regiment (31 T-62, 3 PT-76)
    1 artillery regiment (54 X 122 mm how)
    1 reconnaissance battalion (5 PT-76)
    1 antiaircraft battalion
    1 FROG battalion
    1 rocket launcher battalion
    1 signal battalion
    1 chemical defense company
    1 artillery reconnaissance battery

    strength: 9,000 men
                316 T-62 tanks
                 17 PT-76 light tanks

‡FROG - free rocket over ground

confirmed the "illegitimacy of a strategic scale defense".[25] Consequently, defense as a form of combat operation would occur only on an operational and tactical scale, on secondary directions, and in secondary theaters of military operations.

Operational art and tactics 1953–1960

In the operational and tactical realms, the period 1953–1960 was one of transition. Earlier techniques for the conduct of offensive and defensive operations persisted although forces were reorganized to enable them to better survive on the nuclear battlefield. *Front* and army operations would seek to achieve their objectives by the conduct of a series of consecutive operations into the depths of the enemy defense to achieve successive missions (see tables 88–94). With the full mechanization and motorization of all ground forces the Soviets dropped the term mobile group. The exploitation function of the mobile group remained however, and was now

TABLE 88

FRONT OPERATIONAL FORMATION – 1958–1962

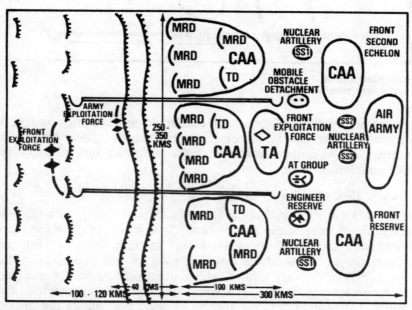

IMMEDIATE MISSION   – 150 - 270 KMS
SUBSEQUENT MISSION – 400 - 550 KMS

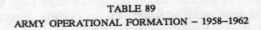

TABLE 89
ARMY OPERATIONAL FORMATION – 1958–1962

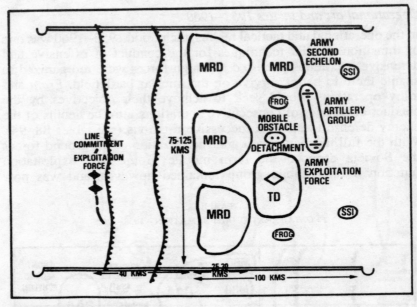

IMMEDIATE MISSION · 70 KMS
SUBSEQUENT MISSION · 270 KMS

performed by tank divisions of combined arms armies and tank armies of *fronts*. On the increasingly fragmented nuclear battlefield motorized rifle units themselves could perform a limited exploitation function.

Strategy 1960–1968

While older operational concepts endured, coexisting with nuclear weapons, Soviet theorists worked feverishly to develop less ambiguous strategic, operational and tactical concepts for the ground forces. By the time Sokolovsky gave full definition to the "revolution in military affairs", those concepts had finally received more complete definition. His work *Military Strategy* provided the context within which other authors defined the role of the armed forces in war – which by definition would be nuclear. Having granted to strategic rocket forces the key role of deciding the

TABLE 90
MOTORIZED RIFLE DIVISION COMBAT FORMATION – OFFENSE 1958–1962

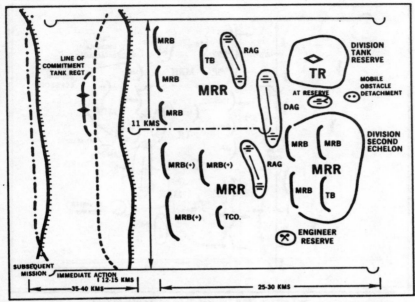

AGAINST A PREPARED DEFENSE

MOTORIZED RIFLE DIVISION MISSION OF THE DAY—55-60 KMS

ultimate outcome of war, Sokolovsky said that ground operations, if required, would be conducted in close concert with nuclear strikes. With the use of nuclear strikes, "great possibilities are created for waging extensive mobile offensive operations with the aid of highly mobile mechanized troops."[26] War would likely begin with a nuclear exchange. Ground operations would occur against this nuclear backdrop, and theater ground forces would have the mission of mopping-up enemy theater forces after the devastating nuclear exchange. Ground operations would involve use of mobile tank and motorized rifle formations, supported by nuclear fires of rocket forces, conducting deep operations at a high rate of speed, often on multiple axes, in order to exploit the effects of nuclear strikes, defeat enemy forces, and conquer and occupy territory.

The appearance of nuclear weapons and their proliferation on

TABLE 91
MOTORIZED RIFLE DIVISION COMBAT FORMATION – OFFENSE 1958–1962

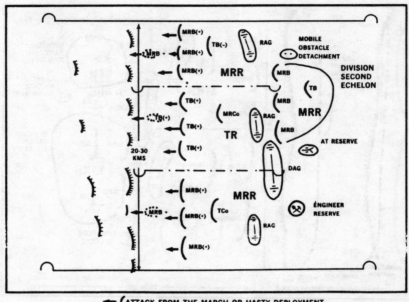

← (ATTACK FROM THE MARCH OR HASTY DEPLOYMENT
← ⦂ FORWARD DETACHMENT (OPTIONAL)

AGAINST A HASTY DEFENSE

the battlefield increased the vulnerability of conventional ground forces, required their dispersal on the battlefield, thus negating the old definition of mass, and increased the importance of maneuver by mobile, self-contained operational and tactical units. Concentration of forces to conduct the classic frontal penetration operation, "gnawing through" the defense, became folly; and the Soviets rejected the idea of set-piece battle conducted in carefully patterned arrays.[27] The comparative invulnerability of armor to nuclear strikes, the speed of armored units, and the growing importance of speedy success in initial offensive operations prompted the Soviets to place greater emphasis on the use of tank units in first echelon at every level of command. Thus, the classic function of exploitation forces (mobile groups) blurred a bit. Exploitation could now occur initially in any operation after nuclear strikes by use of reinforced tank units in first or second echelon.

TABLE 92
FRONT OPERATIONAL FORMATION – DEFENSE 1958–1962

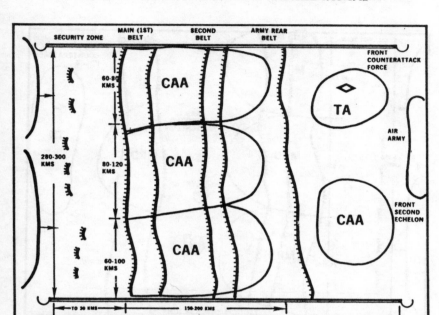

On the strategic level, strategic rocket forces, long-range aviation and nuclear missile submarines would strike the economic base, the nuclear delivery means, the armed forces, and the very seat of political power of potential enemy nations. Thus, rocket forces, able to achieve principal strategic aims in a relatively short period of time, broadened the arena of war. Consequently, ground forces, equipped with their own operational-tactical and tactical rockets would perform the lesser role of destroying enemy forces and nuclear weapons and occupying enemy territory within a theater of war. In contrast to earlier wars, however, the ground forces would exploit the results of strategic rocket strikes to fulfill their missions more rapidly and decisively. *Fronts*, still viewed as strategic-operational units, would conduct strategic offensive operations in cooperation with airborne forces to fulfill strategic missions within the theater of military operations. The rapidity of the operation

TABLE 93
COMBINED ARMS ARMY OPERATIONAL FORMATION – DEFENSE 1958–1962

within the fluid environment of nuclear war dictated direct control of these strategic operations by the General Staff (*STAVKA*).

The threat of nuclear attack on the Soviet Union elevated the defense of the homeland to the level of strategic operations. *PVO Strany* [national air defense] forces received the mission of defending important economic, political, military, and population centers against enemy attack. To supplement active strategic defense measures, a more passive civil defense program was instituted as a facet of strategic defense. With the inclusion of missile firing submarines into the Soviet military force, the realm of strategic operations broadened to include the sea. Above all other strategic considerations, the Soviets intensely analysed the nature of the initial period of war, which loomed more prominently in an age of potential surprise nuclear attack.

TABLE 94
MOTORIZED RIFLE DIVISION COMBAT FORMATION – DEFENSE 1958–1962

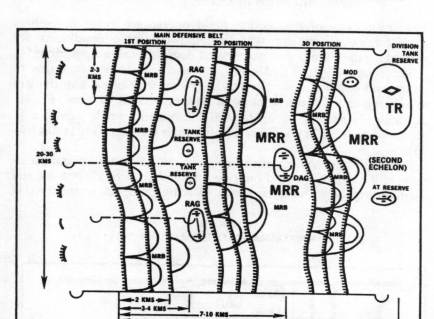

Operational art 1960–1968

If nuclear weapons occupied center stage after 1960 in the strategic realm, they also dominated the field of operational art. Precisely stated, "the main means of destruction in operational large units of all types of armed forces are rocket-nuclear weapons." The outcome of battles and operations

> depends in large measure on the results of nuclear strikes. The capability of simultaneous and sudden attack with nuclear rocket and conventional means on the entire depth of the enemy's operational formation on land and sea theaters of military operations, regardless of whether they are attacking or defending, and also of destroying objectives in the deep enemy rear has acquired very important meaning. Skillful use

of rocket-nuclear weapons secures in a shorter period than in previous wars, the infliction of large enemy losses, the destruction of important objectives and groupings, and the creation of a favorable correlation of forces.[28]

The complexity of conducting rapid operations in the dangerous environment of nuclear war "created favorable conditions for perfecting the theory and practice of deep offensive operations."

The scope of *front* and army operations increased in terms of tempo and depth of operations as a consequence of the requirement to achieve more decisive aims in shorter periods of time. *Fronts*, attacking in sectors of up to 400 kilometers, would advance to depths of up to 300 kilometers to fulfill their missions (see tables 95–96).

Although the requirement to concentrate forces on critical directions still existed, it could only be accomplished by dispersing and fragmenting large units to avoid creating compact formations in

TABLE 95
FRONT OPERATIONAL FORMATION – 1968

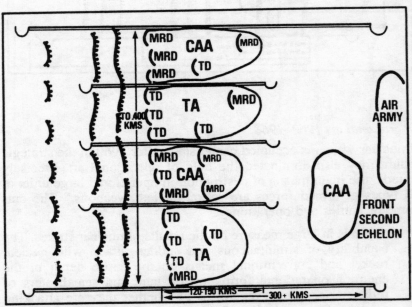

IMMEDIATE MISSION · 300 KMS
FINAL MISSION · 800 KMS

restricted spaces vulnerable to nuclear fires and then concentrating forces rapidly, at the last moment in critical attack sectors. Likewise, it was no longer necessary to establish high operational densities of artillery. Use of nuclear weapons and timely concentration of the most maneuverable forces (tank) on decisive directions provided necessary superiority over a defending enemy.

A *front* offensive would begin with nuclear attacks on main enemy groups, in particular against enemy nuclear delivery means. Ground forces would launch simultaneous attacks along decisive and secondary directions to support the main attacks. Attacking *front* forces would be supported by air armies, by the nuclear strikes of operational-tactical and tactical rocket forces, and by *front* aviation. The primary initial task was to destroy enemy atomic artillery, rocket units, and tactical aviation to the operational depth of the defense. Because of the enemy nuclear threat, Soviet *front* forces would find it necessary to deploy a considerable distance from the front lines and then launch their attack after an approach

TABLE 96
ARMY OPERATIONAL FORMATION – 1968

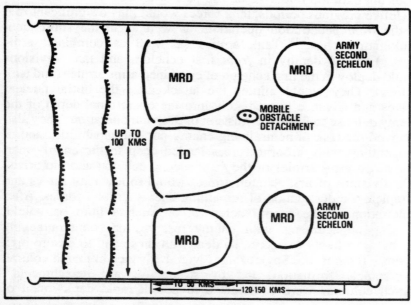

IMMEDIATE MISSION · UP TO 100 KMS
SUBSEQUENT MISSION · UP TO 300 KMS

march from the rear area. While the Soviets maintained that *fronts* could deploy in a variety of formations, the extended two echelon configuration offered better dispersion and lessened the risk of damage from nuclear attack. Tank armies, because of their mobility and strength, would attack from *front* first echelon, particularly if enemy defenses were weak.

Penetration of prepared enemy defenses would avoid "gnawing through" the defense in narrow penetration sectors. Instead, nuclear strikes would blow holes in the defense through which tank and motorized rifle divisions of first echelon armies, in march formation, would pass as rapidly as possible. Thus, *front* and army attack sectors were wider than in previous years (up to 400 kilometers for *fronts* and up to 100 kilometers for armies). The *front* offensive would develop along separate operational directions using maneuver to a maximum in order to strike enemy units' flanks and rear. Because of the absence of a dense linear front, flexible maneuver of artillery fires and nuclear strikes would fill the gaps between units. Airborne units would exploit these nuclear fires and assist in encircling enemy formations.[29] Consequently, the *front* offensive became a complex of fragmented and separate battles requiring extreme initiative on the part of all combat leaders.

Unlike previous periods, tank forces would play a significant role in the *front* penetration operation, as well as in the subsequent exploitation phase.[30] Tank armies (as well as combined arms armies) would deploy in *front* first echelon, and tank divisions would deploy in the first echelon of combined arms armies (and tank armies). They would initiate the attack after the initial nuclear strikes and advance immediately into the operational depth of the enemy defense to fulfill the mission of the *front* operation. They also received the task of neutralizing enemy nuclear capabilities and of cooperating with airborne forces landed deep in the enemy rear. Combined arms armies of the *front* second echelon and motorized rifle divisions of first echelon armies would follow tank forces and complete the destruction of remaining enemy ground forces. After penetration of the enemy defenses, on such a fluid battlefield, meeting engagements with enemy reserves or counterattacking forces were likely to occur. To deal with these and to ensure high advance tempos, the Soviet forces would advance in march column (pre-combat formation) led by strong forward detachments.* March columns were constructed to permit rapid deployment of

* Pre-combat (or pre-battle) formation is a march configuration of a unit from which the unit can engage the enemy, regardless of what direction he attacks from.

tank-heavy forces into required operational or combat formations to fend off enemy attack from any direction.

Another variant of offensive and pursuit operations involved meeting an enemy force which occupied prepared positions on good defensible terrain and which was supported by nuclear artillery, rockets, air and antitank and antiaircraft missiles. In such a configuration enemy infantry and armored divisions would be deployed in depth with only covering forces located in forward positions. The Soviets would attack these defenses with nuclear rockets, air strikes, and concentrated conventional artillery fire while tank units (battalions, regiments and divisions), coordinating with the nuclear strikes and air support, would penetrate the defense from the march.

Soviet military theorists believed that *front* and army offensive operations were most effective if conducted simultaneously along several operational directions to split the enemy force and destroy each part in piecemeal fashion. The Soviets would concentrate nuclear strikes and the largest offensive forces by last minute moves on the most critical attack directions. Continuous high intensity operations conducted to the depth of the enemy defense would be complex and would involve the following measures:[31]

- systematic struggle with enemy nuclear delivery means;
- destruction of opposing units by nuclear fires;
- engagement of enemy reserves;
- engagement of counterattacking enemy forces;
- continuous support of advancing forces by aviation;
- continuous engineer and chemical security for advancing forces;
- development of the offensive in daytime and nighttime.

The necessity for a rapid offensive tempo would require forces to advance primarily on tanks and in armored personnel carriers supported by necessary fires. These forces would use intervals and gaps in the enemy operational defense to strike the enemy's flanks and rear, to cut up, surround, and destroy those enemy units.

Modern development of airborne forces provided them with a capability of conducting operational air landing operations in support of offensive *front* and army operations. Airborne forces would exploit nuclear strikes and fulfill such missions as seizing areas containing enemy nuclear units and operationally important objectives not overcome by other means such as river crossings, bridgeheads, mountain passes, etc. Air landing operations could be successful if enemy antiaircraft fire was suppressed and if Soviet forces had a marked superiority over the enemy. Larger operational drops (multi-regimental, divisional) would occur late in an operation in coordination with the advance of large, exploiting, tank forces, while smaller drops (battalions or regiments) would support the advance of tactical units.[32]

Depending on how war began, defensive operations could occur initially, during pauses in offensive operations, or along secondary directions. As in earlier periods, defensive operations would seek to economize forces, win time, defend territory just seized, repulse counterattacks by superior enemy forces, or provide respite when nuclear attack means had been expended. However, the Soviets altered considerably defensive techniques used in earlier years. Defenses would be more dispersed in width and depth and would be erected along important directions. Rocket forces, engineer obstacles, and mobile forces would cover the gaps between units by both fire and maneuver. Defenses would be anti-nuclear and thus would involve maximum use of cover, concealment, and defensive measures against chemical and nuclear attack. Air defenses would be heavy over firing positions, command and control centers, airfields, and rear objectives; and the Soviets placed considerable emphasis on antitank defenses, in particular the use of antitank guided missiles. Effective defense could best be conducted using heavy nuclear and conventional rocket artillery, air counter-preparations, and armor-heavy counterattacks cooperating with airborne assaults deep in the rear of penetrating enemy units. *Fronts* and armies would defend primarily in two echelon operational formations with tank units deployed in second echelon from where they could launch counterattacks.[33]

The revolution in military affairs drastically altered the nature of air support in both offensive and defensive operations. Until 1959 air operations had still involved a struggle for air superiority in the form of the air offensive. With the growth in importance of nuclear rockets, however, the meaning of air superiority and the nature of the air offensive changed. Now the destruction of enemy nuclear rocket and nuclear air forces became the principal mission of air forces (and of rocket forces as well). The Soviets armed *front* and long-range aviation, as well as fighter aviation, with more capable bombs, rockets, and guns. The longer ranges of Soviet aircraft permitted air operations to cover the *front* rear areas and the deep enemy rear. In addition, *front* aviation could better cooperate with *front* air defense units in defending Soviet forces. The most important mission of *front* aviation became the destruction of smaller enemy mobile targets, primarily nuclear delivery means. Long-range aviation performed such missions as conducting reconnaissance, transporting troops and equipment, and evacuating casualties. *Front* air defense forces, in conjunction with *PVO Strany* forces, organized air defense in the *front* sector during the air offensive and subsequent combat operations.[34]

The nature of operations in nuclear war placed a high premium on nuclear and chemical defense, on radio-electronic combat, and on mobile, survivable command and control systems. Nuclear and chemical defense units appeared at every level of command, and equipment for such defense proliferated in the force structure. Training strongly emphasized chemical and nuclear defense, decontamination, and operations across contaminated zones. Radio-electronic combat, conducted at all levels, focused on the critical objectives of disrupting enemy command and control, in particular command and control of nuclear delivery units. Simultaneously, it sought to protect friendly communications. The increased dynamism and scope of operations dictated creation of new, more flexible command and control systems and required commanders and staffs to prepare, implement and alter plans more rapidly.

The nuclear battlefield also placed a premium on timely collection and dissemination of intelligence. Hence, new types of mobile command posts evolved at all levels, often located in armored vehicles and in aircraft and helicopters. Dense, redundant communications nets linked headquarters at each level of command using radios with greater range and accuracy. Computers assisted rapid communications between rocket units, aircraft, ships, and major land command posts. Logistical measures to support the more intense and complicated operations involved increased emphasis on resupply of fuel and ammunition to front line units. The threat of nuclear interdiction produced an emphasis on building peacetime stocks in the forward area, creating high bulk delivery of required materials forward (pipelines) and creating a more formidable transport aviation capability.

Tactics 1960–1968

Just as nuclear warfare caused a revolution in operational art, it also had a considerable impact on tactics and the nature of battle. Many of the same features that characterized changing operations also applied to tactics, including:

- recognition of the preeminence of nuclear strikes;
- emphasis on the mission of combined arms formations, units and subunits to exploit nuclear strikes, to complete the destruction of enemy forces, and to occupy important regions;
- use of nuclear fires to fulfill tactical missions, in addition to conventional fires, maneuver and shock action;
- attack by mobile formations and units on separate directions, coordinated as to aim and timing;
- focus on destroying enemy nuclear reserves;
- use of maneuver to exploit nuclear strikes, develop the attack and secure objectives;
- stress on the importance of maneuvering nuclear fires;
- recognition of the increasing impact of surprise on successful combat and emphasis on the significance of closer cooperation between combined arms units;
- recognition of the need for dispersed combat formations of divisions, regiments and battalions so as to avoid destruction of several battalions by a single nuclear strike;
- concentration of forces accomplished by massing fires and by last minute movement under tight security;
- attack from assembly areas in the depth rather than from close jumping-off positions;
- attack in precombat formation with or without an artillery preparation;
- attack at high tempo along separate directions, deploying for combat only when necessary;
- emphasis on use of tank forces, or motorized rifle forces reinforced by tanks, in first echelon.[35]

Offensive tactics involved combat in larger sectors to greater depths. Tank and motorized rifle divisions would deploy in one or two echelons, depending on the nature of the defense, and would attack in sectors 10–20 kilometers wide with regiments advancing in 5–8-kilometer sectors and battalions in sectors 1.5–2 kilometers wide (see tables 97–98).[36]

Regiments would also form in one or two echelons and would attack with battalions advancing in pre-combat column formation. After the delivery of initial nuclear strikes, lead battalions of first echelon divisional regiments would advance on separate directions into the enemy defenses using gaps blown by the nuclear strikes. The attack would develop at different rates along different directions as battalions and regiments liquidated enemy resistance or

TABLE 97
MOTORIZED RIFLE DIVISION COMBAT FORMATION – OFFENSE 1968:
AGAINST A PREPARED DEFENSE

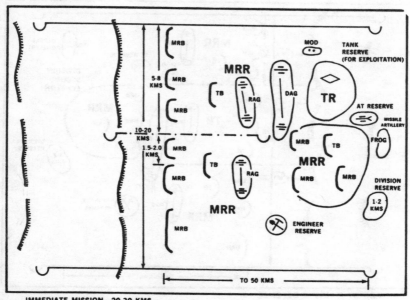

IMMEDIATE MISSION—20-30 KMS
MISSION OF THE DAY—100 KMS
CONCENTRATION IN ATTACK POSITION AT LATEST POSSIBLE TIME

repulsed counterattacks. The uneven development of the offensive would permit greater use of maneuver to envelop, outflank, and surround portions of the enemy forces. Tactical airborne assaults (battalion or regimental strength) and assaults by helicopter-lifted motorized rifle battalions would assist the advance of ground forces.[37] Once the enemy tactical defense had been penetrated, forward detachments would lead division pursuit operations, disrupting enemy attempts to create new defense lines, seizing key terrain, and maintaining the momentum of the attack. Second echelons would build up the force of the attack, replace destroyed units, change the direction of the attack, or assist in pursuit operations. Tank divisions of armies and tank armies of *fronts* would develop the success of tactical operations and without a pause would seek to achieve *front* missions.

TABLE 98
MOTORIZED RIFLE DIVISION COMBAT FORMATION – OFFENSE 1968:
AGAINST A HASTY DEFENSE

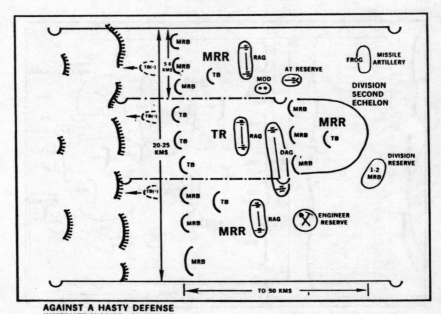

AGAINST A HASTY DEFENSE
IMMEDIATE MISSION—30-40 KMS
MISSION OF THE DAY—100 KMS
FORWARD DETACHMENTS (OPTIONAL)

The tactical defense would change in consonance with the operational defense, and become less dense and more mobile. Deeply echeloned units would occupy wider sectors (battalion 3–5 kilometers, regiment 8–12 kilometers, division 16–30 kilometers) and tank units usually would deploy in second echelon to maneuver and conduct counterattacks (see table 99).[38]

Nuclear and conventional fires, mobile obstacle detachments, and fixed engineer obstacles would fill inevitable gaps in the defense. Chemical, antitank, and nuclear defenses received considerable attention, especially in battalion training. Tactical operations, in general, increased the battlefield demands on all forces, but in particular on officers at lower command levels, who would have to operate efficiently and with a high degree of initiative.

TABLE 99
MOTORIZED RIFLE DIVISION COMBAT FORMATION – DEFENSE 1968

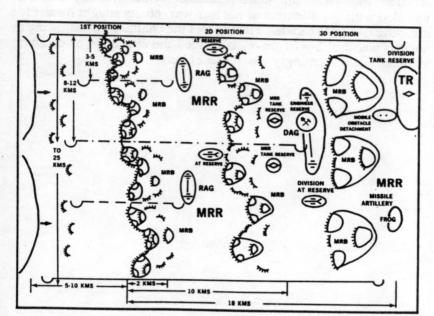

Conclusion

The revolution in military affairs caused far-reaching changes in all aspects of Soviet military doctrine. Commitment to the single option of nuclear war (reminiscent of the United States' strategy of massive retaliation) elevated the stature of strategic rocket forces, increased the importance of strategy, and reduced emphasis on operational art and tactics. The Soviet force structure shrank, especially the ground forces within that force structure. The requirement to conduct all operations within a nuclear context forced Soviet commanders to break with long-standing principles concerning massing of forces, formation of forces, timing of operations, and the provision of fire support. The revolution forced Soviet theorists to review intensely all of the techniques for war and, at the same time, subjected to doubt the validity of studying past experiences, in particular those of the Great Patriotic War. In essence, the revolution injected insecurity and uncertainty into the realm of Soviet military doctrine, a situation compounded by the supposed fact that future war would inevitably be nuclear. The reaction was swift and understandable. While military theorists wrestled with the dilemma of nuclear war, others sought means for escaping from its shackles. Having met the challenge of adjusting to nuclear warfare, Soviet theorists tackled the challenge of escaping its deadly and seemingly inevitable effects.

CHAPTER SEVEN

REFINEMENT OF THE REVOLUTION IN MILITARY AFFAIRS

BACKGROUND

During the early 1960s the Soviet Union conceded that a "revolution" had occurred in military affairs, brought about by the dominance of nuclear weaponry in contemporary warfare. This "revolution" recognized the destructive power of nuclear weapons, and, more important, the fact that the new weapons had an impact on strategic and operational matters as well as tactical. N. S. Khrushchev acknowledged this realization in 1960, and subsequently Soviet military doctrine, force structure, and military science reflected the impact of that "revolution." Marshal V. D. Sokolovsky's 1962 book *Military Strategy* perhaps best articulated the Soviet view of war in this new period. In brief, Sokolovsky stressed that war would be nuclear from the outset. Hence the conventional preoccupation with operational art and tactics faded in importance, and war at the strategic level became all-important. Soviet acknowledgment of "single option" nuclear war prompted wholesale force reorganization and marked the emergence of the strategic rocket forces as the most important element of the Soviet military forces. However, even during the "single option" period not all Soviet military theorists reconciled themselves to the reduced stature of the Soviet ground forces in future war.

Although Khrushchev fell from power in 1964, the "single option" conception of global nuclear war continued to dominate Soviet military thought for several years. As early as the mid-1960s, however, subtle changes began to occur to threaten that dominant view.[1] Preoccupation with the strategy of thermonuclear war began to erode and Soviet theorists began to display renewed interest in questions of operational art and tactics. An early manifestation of this trend was a revival of interest in research and writing on operational themes, past and present. On the basis of this research, Soviet military theorists focused on distinct themes spanning the strategic, operational and tactical realms, themes relevant to nuclear as well as conventional war. General and specific works on military art investigated precise ground force operational and tactical techniques (albeit in a nuclear context). The sheer detail unearthed by these investigations distinguished them from earlier works written during the zenith of the revolution in military affairs. Included in this new category were Reznichenko's classic work *Tactics*, Sidorenko's *The Offensive*, Savkin's *The Basic Principles of Operational Art and Tactics*, Babadzhanian's *Tank and Tank Forces*, and Bagramian's text for officers, *History of War and Military Art*. All paid lip service to the assumption that general war would be nuclear, but all also dwelt at length on the techniques of ground operations in far more detail than their predecessors.[2] During this period the Soviets continued their intense investigation of the nature of the initial period of war (*nachal'nyi period voiny*) which had been a focal point of study since 1958.

In these works and in others, caveats began appearing to qualify the Soviet belief that general war would inevitably be nuclear. In his 1968 revision of *Military Strategy*, Sokolovsky qualified his 1962 statement that "armed combat in ground theaters of military operations ... will be achieved mainly by nuclear rocket strikes" by transforming this blunt statement into a question:

> But in essence, the argument is about the basic method of conducting future war: will it be land war with the use of nuclear weapons as a means of supporting the operations of ground troops [the pre-1960 view], or a war that is essentially new, where the main means of solving strategic tasks will be the nuclear rocket weapon? The theory of military art must give an answer to such important questions as: what types of strategic action will be used in nuclear war, and what form military operations must take.[3]

Sokolovsky's tentative answer was that theater operations would occur, but that on the battlefield "the decisive role will be played by fires of nuclear weapons; the other means of armed combat will utilize the results of nuclear strikes for the final defeat of the enemy."[4] Bagramian, in his *Military History*, more succinctly commented, "while working out the means of conducting war in the nuclear situation, Soviet military science has not excluded the possibility of conventional combat."[5] Subsequent Soviet works of the same generation included the same qualification.

Meanwhile, Soviet military analysts intensified their research on operational matters and produced comprehensive studies on virtually every aspect of the Soviet Army's operational and tactical experience – most dealing with the Great Patriotic War (in particular its later stages). As if to highlight these new concerns, the Soviets in 1965 published an anthology of works written by preeminent pre-World War II Soviet military theorists. The work, entitled *Questions of Strategy and Operational Art in Soviet Military Works 1917–1940*, with a preface by M. V. Zakharov, Chief of the Soviet General Staff, signaled the rehabilitation of the purged generation of Tukhachevsky and evidenced renewed interest in deep operations (*glubokie operatsii*) and the techniques necessary to achieve them.[6] The following year the Soviets published P. A. Kurochkin's detailed study on army operations, *The Combined Arms Army in the Offensive*.[7] Writings during the period 1968 to 1972 seemed to reflect patient and deliberate study of the issue of the nature of war and operations. While Reznichenko, Savkin, Sidorenko and others enunciated official doctrine, still others continued generating articles and works focusing on the theory and practice of strategy, operational art and tactics in the Second World War and speculating on the contemporary relevance of those practices. The periodicals *Military Thought* and *Military-Historical Journal* published extensive studies on the World War II and postwar trends in military art. By the mid-1970s, the number of major studies investigating virtually every aspect of military art, in historical and contemporary contexts, reached flood proportions. A. I. Radzievsky built upon Kurochkin's studies of combined arms operations. I. E. Krupchenko, P. A. Rotmistrov, A. I. Radzievsky and O. A. Losik surveyed in detail armored warfare and the evolution of Soviet tank forces, while I. I. Lisov, and later D. S. Sukhorukov, resurrected the long obscured experiences of Soviet airborne forces. Soviet logistics lessons learned and the future direction of the rear services in supporting theater operations were addressed in S. K. Kurkotkin's 1977 study. In addition, Radzievsky edited a multi-volume study of tactics by combat example at every combat level from platoon through division.[8]

The intense and ongoing concern for operational art and tactics, paralleled by Soviet restructuring of the armed forces to improve their operational capabilities, has elevated the importance of these levels of military art from their relative position of neglect in the early 1960s to major areas of contemporary concern. Over the last decade and a half, the total subservience of operational art and tactics to the overall considerations of nuclear war has lessened to a remarkable degree. Even the seemingly mandatory nuclear context for the discussion of these levels is often absent. Thus, in 1979, Marshal V. G. Kulikov could write, "successful operations by formations and units of the armed forces, or branches of the armed forces, and of specialized forces, especially during combat using conventional weapons, retain their importance."[9]

During this revival of concern for operational art and tactics, all aspects of military art underwent investigation. Certain topics, however, have received greater attention than others. During the 1970s, the Soviets formulated the concept of *protivoiadernyi manevr* (anti-nuclear maneuver).[10] First expressed in defensive terms in the early 1970s, throughout the late 1970s the Soviets ceased making direct reference to the term "anti-nuclear maneuver." However, they continued verbally to describe the function and moreover, they described it in an offensive context.

Soviet study of operations in their Great Patriotic War provided the inspiration and the model for contemporary maneuver forces. Specifically, the wartime mobile group and forward detachments seemed to be the ideal types of forces suited to conduct anti-nuclear maneuver both at the operational and the tactical levels. These concepts and forces provided the basis for the emerging concepts of operational maneuver by operational maneuver groups (OMG) and tactical maneuver by forward detachments, which by 1980 had reached full articulation. In time, it was evident the Soviets would field such forces.

Simultaneously, the Soviets deemphasized the importance of operational second echelons (at the *front* and army level) because of their potentially increased vulnerability to nuclear strikes, and began to emphasize the concept and utility of employing multiple operational maneuver forces and reserves at these levels. In essence, the Soviets postulated the early concentration of the bulk of their forces well forward, and the early commitment into combat of numerous operational maneuver forces along multiple axes. Tactical maneuver forces were designated to pave the way for the advancing operational maneuver forces and to lead the advance of main force units, as well. Today the concept of anti-nuclear maneuver provides a cornerstone for Soviet operational and tactical techniques designed to pre-empt, preclude, or inhibit enemy resort to nuclear warfare. As articulated in 1987 by V. G. Reznichenko "the continuous conduct of battle at a high tempo creates unfavorable conditions for enemy use of weapons of mass destruction. He cannot determine targets for nuclear strikes exactly and, besides, will be forced to shift his nuclear delivery means often."[11] The Soviets have tentatively decided that even greater emphasis on this type of maneuver is also a partial remedy to countering enemy use of high precision weaponry.[12] To capitalize fully on the effects of maneuver, the Soviets believe that they must reduce planning time and execute command and control more crisply. This will require increased emphasis on the use of cybernetic tools, including automation of command and expanded reliance on tactical and operational calculations (nomograms, etc.).

Among the topics attracting greatest attention was that of the nature of the initial period of war. This had been a subject of contemporary concern since 1958, and renewed interest was evidenced by the publication in 1974 of S. P. Ivanov's book, *The Initial Period of War*, and numerous other articles.[13]

Drawing heavily on research done on the theme "the initial period of war" or, specifically, what a nation's army must do to win rapid victory or avoid precipitous defeat, the Soviets have concluded that the principal prerequisites for victory are the surprise conduct of rapid operations by forces concentrated well forward. Hence, the Soviets tend to eschew preliminary large scale mobilization (the primary indicator of impending war) and to argue for employment of a single strategic and operational echelon supplemented by numerous tailored operational and tactical maneuver forces. Even tactically, by 1987 Soviet writers were able to argue "there arises the problem of defining the optimal structure for the first and second echelons at the tactical level. With the enemy using high precision weapons, the role of the first echelon has to grow. It must be capable of achieving a mission without the second echelon (reserve)."[14]

Operational and tactical combat in the Soviet's view "embraces simultaneously the entire depth of the combat formation of both contending sides."[15] As a result, combat missions are no longer described in linear fashion by the seizure of lines. Instead missions call for the securing along multiple axes deep in the enemy's defense of objectives whose seizure "undermines the tactical stability of the enemy defense."[16] At the tactical level, specifically designated and tailored maneuver forces – usually forward detachments – perform this function, while tailored operational maneuver forces do likewise at the operational level.[17]

This offensive posture may significantly alter traditional concepts of echelonment, not only by reducing the number of ground echelons but also by supplementing the ground echelon with a vertical echelon which will add greater depth to battle. According to Reznichenko,

> One can propose that, under the influence of modern weapons and the great saturation of ground forces with aviation means, the combat formation of forces on the offensive is destined to consist of two echelons – a ground echelon, whose mission will be to fulfill the penetration of the enemy defense and develop the success into the depths, and an air echelon created to envelop defending forces from the air and strike blows against his rear area.[18]

In essence what has emerged is a Soviet concept of land-air battle juxtaposed against the US concept of AirLand battle.

Since the revival of the terms "deep battle" and "deep operations" in the mid-1960s, these topics have become a major focus of study along with all the techniques necessary to realize deep operations. In 1975, Marshal Zakharov underscored the importance of the latter stating: "the theory of deep operations has not lost its significance today. It can serve as a basis for the creative work of command cadres when resolving the many-sided and complex problems of today."[19]

As an adjunct to their concentrated study of deep operations, the Soviets have emphasized: the value of the offensive; the importance of surprise and deception, the utility of encirclement operations and exploitation; the necessity to deploy efficiently and to regroup forces flexibly for combat; methods for solving the problem of effecting and developing penetration of defenses; the requirements associated with sustaining large theater combined arms forces; and the nature and conduct of meeting engagements. Soviet authors have accorded special attention to operational maneuver performed by mobile groups and tactical maneuver by forward detachments and have investigated in detail virtually every aspect of past mobile operations. In recent works the Soviets have focused on the conduct of the defense during offensive operations, a probable reaction to U.S. development of AirLand Battle doctrine. Among the myriad of operations the Soviets have selected for special study have been the Belorussian Operation (June 1944), the Vistula–Oder Operation (January 1945) and the Manchurian Operation

(August 1945), all of which they consider relevant to contemporary operations.

FORCE STRUCTURE

While the focus of Soviet theoretical writing has shifted toward the operational and tactical, significant changes have taken place in the Soviet ground force structure (after its reinstatement as an independent service in 1967) (see table 100).[20] These changes, begun in the early 1970s and still continuing, have increased the size of the mobilized force structure and have improved the mobility and firepower of all units. The cumulative effect of change has been an overall build-up in conventional forces and an increase in the force capability of forward-deployed forces paralleled by a reduced peacetime readiness posture of forces within the Soviet Union. While the overall size of the ground forces has remained relatively stable, the number of combat divisions in the force structure has risen from 150 (in 1968) to about 220 (roughly the size of the force structure in 1958).[21] More important, the strength of these divisions and divisional firepower have increased significantly. This has markedly increased the combat capability of forward area divisions which are kept at full combat strength in peacetime. At the same time, the Soviets have reduced the peacetime readiness status of divisions within the Soviet Union, a probable indication that the Soviets have deemphasized the feasibility and importance of classic total pre-war force mobilization and reinforcement, that traditional portent of impending war. Consequently, the Soviets have improved their capability to conduct rapid selective mobilization to reinforce forward area forces prior to war and have improved the capabilities of all divisions when they are mobilized. The Soviets still emphasize flexibility and speed in whatever type of mobilization they conduct. Soviet ideas on the initial period of war stress the idea of creeping up to conflict, with a major effort being made to conceal pre-mobilization moves. The existence of back-up forces can be used either to intimidate other powers from entering a struggle or to reinforce the initial attacking forces. Increasing the overt readiness status of forces within the Soviet Union may also be an important way of signaling resolve in a pre-war period.

As early as 1972 Soviet theorists noted the basic requirement for a more carefully articulated force structure. V. Ye. Savkin wrote "The difference in composition of troops operating on the axes of the main attack and on other axes probably will be less sharply

TABLE 100
FORCE STRUCTURE: 1987

<u>1987 Motorized Rifle Division</u>
    3 motorized rifle regiments (1 BMP-equipped, 2 BTR-equipped)
      (40 T-62/-64/-72/-80, 37-43 BMP-1/2, 18x122 mm each)
    1 medium tank regiment (94 T-62/-64/-72/-80)
    1 artillery regiment (36 x 122 mm how, 18 x 152 mm how, 18-
      122 mm MRL)
    1 SSM battalion (4 FROG/SS-21)
    1 antitank battalion (12 x 100 mm, 9 AT-5 launcher vehicles)
    1 SAM regiment
    1 reconnaissance battalion
    1 separate tank battalion (51 T-62/-64/-72/-80) (validated
      version-40)
    1 signal battalion
    1 engineer battalion
    1 medical battalion
    1 materiel support battalion
    1 chemical defense battalion
    1 helicopter detachment/squadron

    <u>strength</u>: 12,890 men
                272 T-62/-64/-72/-80 (validated version-261)

<u>1987 Tank Division</u>
    3 tank regiments (94 T-62/-72/-80, 37-43 BMP-1/2, 18 x 122
      mm each)
    1 motorized rifle regiment (BMP) (40 T-62/-64/-72/-80
      18 x 122 mm)
    1 artillery regiment (18 x 152 mm, 36 x 122 mm, 18 x 122 mm
      MRL)
    1 SSM battalion (4 FROG/SS-21)
    1 SAM regiment
    1 reconnaissance battalion
    1 signal battalion
    1 engineer battalion
    1 medical battalion
    1 materiel support battalion
    1 chemical defense battalion
    1 helicopter detachment/squadron

    <u>strength</u>: 11,470 men
                322 T-62/-64/-72/-80) tanks

<u>1987 Combined Arms Army</u>
    2 - 4 motorized rifle divisions
    1 - 2 tank divisions (tank or mechanized corps)*
    1 separate tank regiment or tank/mechanized corps (150x
      tanks)
    1 SSM brigade
    1 artillery brigade
    1-2 SAM brigades
    1 engineer regiment/brigade
    1 pontoon bridge regiment
    1 assault crossing battalion
    1 chemical defense battalion
    1 radio relay battalion
    1 separate radio relay battalion
    1 signal regiment

TABLE 100 (continued)

```
1 materiel support brigade
1 attack helicopter regiment
1 intelligence battalion
1 early warning battalion
1 long-range reconnaissance company
1 radio and radar intercept battalion
1 general purpose helicopter squadron
1 air assault battalion
  rear services
```

1987 Tank Army**
```
2-4 tank divisions
1-2 motorized rifle divisions
1 SSM brigade
1 separate tank regiment or tank/mechanized corps
1 artillery brigade
1-2 SAM brigades
1 signal regiment
1 engineer regiment/brigade
1 pontoon bridge regiment
1 assault crossing battalion
1 chemical defense battalion
1 separate radio relay battalion
1 materiel support brigade
1 attack helicopter regiment
1 early warning battalion
1 long-range reconnaissance company
1 radio intercept battalion
1 general purpose helicopter squadron
1 air assault battalion
  rear services
```

* Tank or mechanized corps configured as an operational maneuver group or as an army forward detachment would consist of 2 or 3 tank brigades, 2 motorized rifle brigades and tailored support units with a strength of 350–450 tanks. These experimental units were referred to by the intelligence community as "New Army Corps" or NACs, and are now called "Unified Army Corps."

** A tank army configured as an operational maneuver group could contain 3–4 tank or mechanized corps with 1,000–1,400 tanks.

expressed than was formerly the case. The main troop groupings will be distinguished more in the qualitative sense than in numbers."[22] Throughout the 1970s and into the 1980s the Soviets carefully analysed contemporary warfare (Vietnam, 1973 Israeli–Arab War, the Falklands War, and the war in Lebanon) and noted the impact of new weaponry on combat (for example, ATGMs). Through a series of major exercises (Dnepr – 1967, Dvina – 1970, Iug – 1971 and others) the Soviets tested concepts, forces, and new equipment mixes.

Reflecting that experimentation, the Soviets fielded a broad array of new weaponry to match the requirements of the times (ATGMs, armored vehicles, tanks, self propelled artillery, mobile bridging, etc.). A variety of supporting functional units evolved to meet the same new combat demands. Air assault battalions and brigades now provide a new vertical dimension to both operational and tactical maneuver and may be supplemented in the future by air assault units at division level and by even larger, more capable divisional-size air assault corps.

The Soviets have increased the size and firepower of motorized rifle divisions by increasing their personnel strength from 10,500 men to almost 13,000 men, their tank strength from 188 to 272 tanks (in forward-area divisions), and their artillery strength by the addition of self-propelled artillery, new mobile antiaircraft missile systems and other new weapons systems to give motorized rifle divisions increased capability for sustained mobile operations.[23] In size, the contemporary motorized rifle division is reminiscent of its 1958 predecessor. Simultaneously, tank divisions have grown to a more limited extent but have become more balanced by an increase in the strength of motorized rifle forces within the division. Thus, both the motorized rifle division and the tank division have more balanced fire and maneuver capabilities. Logistics for divisions has been strengthened substantially both through increases in lift and force structure changes and through the establishment of a rear service command and control system that more effectively integrates materiel support into combined arms operations.

Armies have also gained in sophistication and combat capability. Some tank armies have added one or more motorized rifle divisions to their likely wartime configuration, and the older heavy tank/self-propelled gun regiments (later heavy tank regiments) of armies now have become separate tank regiments (probably the nucleus of wartime tank or mechanized corps designated to perform the role of army forward detachment).[24] Armies are equipped with sufficient helicopter assets to lift into combat at least one air assault battalion. At *front* level, the existing heavy nuclear punch has been supplemented with the addition of a heavy artillery brigade (and new nuclear tube artillery at army as well); an air assault brigade complements potential *front* use of conventional airborne divisions; and a special operations (reconnaissance-diversionary (*razvedyvatel' naia-diversionnaia*)) brigade* is assigned to perform

---

* Often the term "Spetsnaz" is associated with Soviet special operations forces. It derives from the Russian term *voiska spetsial'nogo naznacheniia* (forces of special designation). Some care should be taken in its use, however. Although Western analysts

a wide variety of sabotage and commando-type missions in the enemy deep rear areas.[25] By virtue of these structural improvements the Soviets have improved their forces' mobility, firepower, sustainment, and, perhaps most important, their ability to engage enemy nuclear delivery means while conducting deep operations.

MILITARY DOCTRINE

All of these organizational changes, set against the backdrop of changing Soviet published views, strongly suggest a basic shift in the Soviet view of war. While the Soviets still consider nuclear war to be a strong possibility, they have increasingly displayed a hope that war can be kept conventional in the early stages, or perhaps even throughout its entirety. They have concluded that the existence of a strategic or tactical nuclear balance on both sides (or a superiority on their side) may produce in the enemy a reluctance to use nuclear weapons, a sort of mutual deterrence that increases the likelihood that conventional operations will remain conventional and become decisive. At a minimum, the Soviets have prepared themselves to fight either a nuclear war or (unlike the 1960s) a conventional war in what might be termed a "nuclear-scared" posture. This Soviet version of "flexible response" emphasizes the necessity for expanding and perfecting combined arms concepts. Foremost among new concepts are those involving operational and tactical techniques (in essence, anti-nuclear maneuver) that could assist in preventing nuclear conflict by inhibiting an enemy's ability to respond with nuclear weapons even if he wished to, while enhancing the chances of rapid success on the battlefield in the initial period of war. Hence, the Soviets have developed warfighting approaches designed to pre-empt enemy nuclear use by the early destruction of enemy nuclear systems and by the rapid intermingling of friendly and enemy forces.

Reflecting this emerging Soviet view on the dual option for fighting war, most theorists have abandoned the obligatory reference to a nuclear context, and instead carefully distinguish between the two types of conflict. Thus,

> in nuclear war, if it is unleashed by aggressive countries, simultaneous nuclear strikes on the enemy and skillful

---

use the term to describe special operations forces, the Soviets use it to describe a variety of formations to include special engineer formations, special radio-technical units and experimental formations or formations with temporary and/or specialized functions, as well as special operations formations.

exploitation of the results of those strikes is most important. During combat with only conventional weaponry, skillful concentration of superior forces and weaponry is required to deliver blows on selected directions and also rapid dispersal of those forces after fulfillment of the combat missions.[26]

This assertion from an article on operational art by Marshal V. G. Kulikov and other articles on offensive operations, *front* operations, army operations and tactics appear in the authoritative eight-volume *Soviet Military Encyclopedia*, published between 1976 and 1980. They illustrate changing views by clearly delineating between nuclear and conventional operations. In addition, they stress the increased capabilities of all types of ground units, the growth in the scope of the offensive, and the increased dynamism of battle. Articles in professional military journals have reiterated the distinction even more clearly. A 1982 article by N. Kireev in the *Military-Historical Journal* described the changing view of war and combat. After recounting measures and techniques used to operate in nuclear warfare, the author wrote:

Since the beginning of the 1960s our military theory and practice conceded the conduct of combat using only conventional means though under constant threat of enemy use of nuclear weapons. This circumstance dictated the necessity of determining modes of employment of tank units and subunits in penetrating a well-prepared enemy defense in conformity with the new demands. A large number of demonstrations, tactical and other exercises, as well as military scientific conferences, were conducted. The experience of penetration of a deliberate enemy defense obtained during the years of the Great Patriotic War began to be more extensively utilized.[27]

To underscore the full development of this new Soviet view, M. A. Gareev, in a 1986 critique of the works of Frunze, disputed Sokolovsky's earlier view and fully articulated the difference between nuclear and conventional war.[28]

While developing military doctrine that seemed to meet the challenge of escaping from the dangerous grasp of nuclear war, the Soviets have continued to build up global military capabilities and have put into practice a more active policy to realize Soviet aims in the Third World, the periphery of traditional great power lands, a region from which the capitalist nations obtain much of their economic sustenance. Expanding on Khrushchev's declaration of support for wars of national liberation, Soviet attempts to influence the course of events in the Third World came to embrace a spectrum of military, political, and economic measures which, by the end of the 1960s, included ambitious military assistance efforts for selected countries in the Middle East, Africa, and Latin America. Military presence in underdeveloped regions was reflected in the proliferation of military advisers in many Third World nations and the use of Soviet proxy advisers and combat forces in Ethiopia and Angola. Coupled with the announcement of the Brezhnev Doctrine (1968), in which the Soviets reserved the right militarily to maintain the socialist system where it already existed, a more active Soviet global stance sought to aid "progressive governments" against imperialism, increase Soviet influence, and deny the West access to resources either through creation of socialist states or by manipulating disorders in critical regions to paralyse normal economic activity and trade. At the same time, the publication in 1976 of Admiral Sergei Gorshkov's *Sea Power of the State*, marked an overt acknowledgment of the fact that the Soviets had embarked on a naval construction program to create an oceanic navy capable of better projecting Soviet power overseas in tandem with the already burgeoning Soviet merchant marine. The 1979 edition of the same work made it clear that Soviet naval presence, while a valuable political tool, was not independent of the war plans of the Soviet General Staff, which retained the duty of formulating all operational plans for the Soviet Armed Forces, whether the branches of those forces acted jointly or independently.[29]

These trends, reinforced by other motives, encouraged direct Soviet military involvement in Afghanistan, an invasion presumably launched in accordance with the Brezhnev Doctrine. Significantly, the invasion marked the first active incursion of Soviet forces beyond their own borders and the Soviet Bloc proper since the end of 1945 (except for the wartime joint Allied occupation of Iran and joint United States–Soviet occupation of Korea in the immediate postwar years). Soviet intervention in Afghanistan was a *coup de main* aimed at changing the character of a Soviet-sponsored regime by intimidation and the use of internal collaborators. It just so happened that there was also an armed anti-communist resistance in the field at the time. Soviet international activity was made possible in part by United States' overcommitment around the globe and a Soviet sensing that the nuclear deadlock and general fears of global nuclear war left more room for maneuver at the local war level.

Recent Soviet pronouncements regarding the "defensive" nature of their military doctrine represent a sophisticated new stage in how the Soviets perceive the course of the revolution in military affairs.[30] By emphasizing "defensiveness" and "prevention of war" the Soviets capitalize on current global political realities to accent the political aspects of a doctrine which by definition has always been inherently defensive. By stressing "prevention of war" the Soviets further develop their view that nuclear war by virtue of its destructiveness to all parties, is unthinkable and hence avoidable. In essence the "new" definition of Soviet doctrine articulates an intent *to prevent nuclear war*. As such the new definition finds its corrollary in Soviet proposals for arms reductions, particularly in the nuclear realm and, in the extreme, the creation of nuclear free zones and the outright abolition of nuclear weapons.

Soviet postulation of a "defensive" military doctrine also responds, in the military-technical realm, to a new phase in the technological revolution − a technological revolution in conventional weaponry which in many ways promises to make new high precision conventional weapons as lethal as their nuclear counterparts. This new reality has prompted intensive Soviet study of future strategy, operational and tactical concepts and techniques.

Ultimately the degree to which Soviet doctrine is "defense" will be evidenced by real developments in Soviet force structuring and theoretical and practice work in the more mundane realms of strategy, operational art, and tactics.

MILITARY STRATEGY

As Soviet military doctrine has changed, so also has the Soviet view of military strategy. The Soviets have, for the past fifteen years, addressed two fundamental military problems reflecting the realities of the times. The first of these is the problem of overcoming contemporary defenses, whether those defenses are in the Far East (China) or in Central Europe (NATO). This problem is a long-standing one made more complex by technological changes, in particular the development of modern, more lethal antitank and other precision-guided weapons. Consequently, the Soviets have studied their own experience (1941−45), the experiences of the 1973 Arab−Israeli War, other contemporary conflicts, and a series of key experimental exercises. The second problem is that of nuclear warfare, or, specifically, how alternatively either to avoid it, preempt it, or conduct it. The Soviets recognize the possibility that a major war may become nuclear, but at the same time they have sought ways to avoid nuclear conflict (nuclear freeze, renunciation of first use, nuclear free zones, etc. in the political realm) and have developed operational and tactical concepts both to inhibit the enemy's resorting to nuclear weapons and to reduce the effectiveness of those weapons if they are used. Thus, former Chief of the General Staff N. V. Ogarkov has written regarding the Soviet declaratory policy of no first use:

> Soviet military strategy assumes that a world war may be started and conducted for a certain period of time with conventional weapons alone. The expansion of military operations however, can result in its escalation into a general nuclear war, with nuclear weapons, primarily strategic, as the main means of conducting it. Soviet military strategy is based on the position that the Soviet Union, proceeding on the basis of the principles of its policy, will not be the first to employ such weapons.[31]

While expressing a Soviet desire to keep hostilities conventional, Ogarkov warns any aggressor of the consequence of resorting to nuclear warfare, stating: "Any possible aggressor should clearly understand, however, that it will be the target of an annihilating answering strike in the event of a nuclear missile attack against the Soviet Union or the other countries of the Socialist community." Such statements are part of the struggle for retention of the initiative during the initial period of war through deterring an opponent and limiting his options by political means.

Recent pronouncements by Gorbachev and Defense Minister Iazov regarding the "defensiveness" of Soviet doctrine and Soviet actions regarding arms limitations (particularly nuclear) are further political manifestations of Soviet desires to denuclearize future warfare, should it occur, as well as to soften the impact on Soviet military preparedness of the technological revolution in conventional weaponry.

In the event such a policy fails to deter nuclear war, the Soviets have prepared themselves for the worst through study of several distinct areas fundamental to the conduct of general war. The Soviets have intensely examined the nature of nuclear war and have spent immense time and resources to train and equip their forces to operate successfully in a nuclear environment.

However, it remains a clear Soviet intention to achieve theater objectives without the use of nuclear weapons by either side, and Soviet efforts to develop concepts and forces capable of meeting this goal have been extensive as well. The Soviets have studied in considerable detail the operations of their forces in the Great Patriotic War, especially during the initial stages and the third period of the war, focusing on operational and tactical techniques that could assist in preventing enemy recourse to nuclear weapons while better preparing Soviet forces to win should those weapons be used.[32]

As a result the Soviets have reaffirmed their faith in the preeminence of the offensive in producing victory, although they recognize that conditions surrounding the outbreak or course of war may require integration of a defensive phase or temporary defensive actions in some sectors into the overall strategic offensive plan. They believe that armor, as but one element of a combined arms team, still plays a significant role in successful offensive operations. Their analysis of successful combat in past "initial periods of war" has led them to several conclusions. First, those nations succeed which quickly bring overwhelming force to bear on the enemy. The effectiveness of that force is magnified if the enemy is not given time to prepare his defenses fully. Maximum force can best be generated and projected forward if applied simultaneously across a broad front by only the first strategic echelon. The application of such a force in such a manner can generate rapid penetration into the depths of the defense along numerous directions, create total paralysis in enemy command and control systems, and result in reduced enemy capability or willingness to respond with nuclear weapons.[33]

Second, in initial and subsequent operations in a potentially nuclear war, the Soviets categorically rule out the conduct of setpiece battle by forces deployed in deeply echeloned and densely patterned arrays which are highly vulnerable to nuclear and conventional strikes (the Western stereotype of Soviet echelonment).[34] Thus, the Soviets have altered traditional concepts concerning mass and concentration and have continued to stress flexible echeloning techniques. Echeloning will meet the requirements of specific combat conditions (the nature of enemy defenses, depth of objectives, terrain etc.), and mass and concentration will be achieved by rapid movement of forces from dispersed positions and by shifting of fires rather then by traditional assembly of forces in dense arrays prior to an operation. Soviet study of the last period of the Great Patriotic War has led them to conclude that many of the techniques developed in that period are applicable today in spite of changing technology. On the basis of their study the Soviets believe that surprise is absolutely essential for victory: strategically regarding timing; and operationally and tactically, regarding the form, location, and nature of the offensive.[35] Moreover, they believe wartime strategy is inexorably related to political conditions existing before and during the initial period of war.

The Soviets have also analysed the nature of modern defense, in particular that of NATO, its coherence, the time it takes to form and, most important, the time ramifications of political decision-making.[36] They understand how formidable the NATO defense would be if fully in place. Although they still credit NATO with the ability to conduct a mobile defense, one must assume they understand the forward positional nature of the defense, its limited depth, and its lack of mobile operational reserves. Given the real and potential problems associated with timely establishment of NATO defenses, the Soviets realize that, if hard pressed, and if given the opportunity, NATO may choose to go nuclear. Thus, a cardinal tenet of Soviet planning (supported by their research into operational and tactical techniques) is a recognition of the necessity of preempting the defense or disrupting its full deployment or, failing in that, preempting the use of or minimizing the effects of nuclear weapons.[37]

Based upon these conclusions, in the event of war the Soviets would seek to achieve surprise by using deception to a maximum extent while politically trying to undermine the unity and resolve of the coalition itself. They would attempt to preempt or disrupt strategic (theater) defenses and preempt the use or limit the effectiveness of enemy nuclear weapons and precision-guided munitions (PGMs) by launching a massive ground offensive, by emphasizing early neutralization of enemy nuclear delivery means, and by attacking, using operational and tactical techniques designed to disrupt enemy command and control and produce paralysis and confusion in enemy ranks. A clear Soviet focus would be to force the capitulation of one or more of the weaker members of the enemy coalition. To accomplish these ambitious aims the Soviets must keep forward-area forces in a high state of readiness, furnished with first-rate equipment. Combat forces must be backed up by a logistical capability sufficient to sustain operations for the duration of the initial strategic and – because the potential for protracted operations is recognized – until the defense industrial sector is fully mobilized and producing key materiel and equipment (i.e., 60–90 days). The Soviets must achieve parity or superiority in the strategic and tactical nuclear realm, and because of the necessity to effect speed and surprise, they must abandon large-scale advanced mobilization and reinforcement of forward area forces prior to war. Forward area forces must be capable of attacking on short notice with only limited redeployment and regrouping. Maximum use of cover and deception is essential, and forces must be structured for and capable of conducting high speed deep operations. The Soviets feel they have achieved the bulk of these prerequisites.

The Soviets assert that a war which is nuclear from the outset will begin with strategic operations by nuclear forces. The initial strategic nuclear exchange − theater or global − will be massive and will affect all levels of war. In this nuclear variant the strategic nuclear exchange and subsequent exchanges will be accompanied by theater strategic operations. The theater strategic operation, in concept, is a framework for understanding how a nation achieves its strategic military objectives by armed force in continental theaters. Its scope is a direct function of aim. It can involve coherent use of all types of forces in multiple theaters to win a global war, or it can take more limited form to achieve more modest goals. Thus, it provides a context for operations which requires thoughtful balance between aims and the forces used to achieve aims. On one end of the spectrum, the theater strategic operation in multiple TVDs (Russian *teatry voennykh deistvii* [theaters of military operations] or in current DOD parlance, TSMAs [theaters of strategic military action]) can involve the mobilization of the nation's entire force to achieve global and theater aims by successive strategic operations; at the other end of the spectrum in a single remote theater, the theater strategic operation can involve the selective application of force to achieve lesser intra-theater objectives. As such, the concept is simply a refinement of previous Soviet thought on strategic offensive operations and is by no means a new subject.

The Soviets will conduct theater strategic operations with "the forces of several *fronts*, according to a single concept or plan within continental Theaters of Military Operations (TVDs)." High commands of forces in each TVD [TSMA] or a TVD representative assigned from the *STAVKA* will coordinate operations of all land, air and naval forces within the theater "under the continuous control of the High Command."[38] The most important feature of a strategic offensive operation in a nuclear context is the delivery of massed nuclear fires. Subsequent offensive operations by *fronts* will seek to achieve the final destruction of the enemy and secure the most important regions. Regardless of whether nuclear weapons are used, the theater strategic operation in a major continental TVD

[TSMA] will involve *simultaneous* and *successive* operations by *fronts*, each of which "can conduct two or more *front* operations in succession, with brief pauses and even without pauses."[39] In addition to initial and subsequent operations by *fronts*, a theater strategic operation in a continental TVD [TSMA] can include: "on coastal directions, initial and subsequent operations by fleets, air defense, airborne landing, naval landing, combined landing and other operations, as well as nuclear missile and air strikes."[40] Thus the theater strategic operation in its fully developed form includes:

— nuclear strikes of strategic nuclear forces;
— air operations;
— anti-air operations;
— *front* operations;
— naval fleet operations;
— landing operations.

The initial *front* operations will have

> decisive importance. They will be distinguished by surprise, by decisive aims and operations from the very beginning by large spatial scope; by high dynamism, by massive use of forces and weapons to destroy the most important objectives, by participation of large quantities of various types of armed forces, by intense radio-electronic combat, and by the complexity of command and control and rear area support.[41]

Forces within the theater of war (TV) will seek to achieve rapid victory by conducting successive *front* operations without pause in the theater's TVDs [TSMAs]. A first strategic echelon will consist of combat-ready forces (*fronts*) within the TVD [TSMA] (primarily forward) backed up by a second strategic echelon and a strategic reserve consisting of *fronts* (and in some cases individual armies) mobilized within the Soviet Union on the basis of the strength and status of each military district.[42] Stronger peacetime military districts will provide second strategic echelon forces and weaker districts will provide reserves. The strategic offensive will probably rely for success on the use of first strategic echelon forces to preserve strategic surprise by avoiding more than essential pre-hostility mobilization and reinforcement. The Soviets will commit second strategic echelon forces and reserves to combat either in the event the first strategic echelon fails to achieve its aims and a protracted conflict occurs or in the event an offensive against well-prepared defenses is necessary.

The deployment of forces by each TVD [TSMA] command is carried out in accordance with the existing situation. In a nuclear context, or in the likely context of an offensive launched against unprepared or partially prepared defenses the Soviets will tend to array their *fronts* in single echelon with a combined arms reserve (one or two armies). Echelonment will increase in depth in direct proportion to the increased strength of the defense and in consonance with Soviet capabilities to conceal offensive preparations. Throughout the process the Soviets will seek to capitalize on both surprise and strength. They recognize that the former is most critical and that achievement of surprise itself multiplies a favorable correlation of forces.[43] An offensive against a fully prepared defense will require more substantial deployment of second strategic echelon forces (*fronts* or armies) into the forward area prior to commencement of hostilities. Large-scale strategic airborne or amphibious operations can support the conduct of a strategic offensive in the initial stages by strikes against more vulnerable objectives on enemy flanks, where their use could detract from the main enemy defensive efforts, or against targets of major political or economic value. Large scale airborne or amphibious operations could also be used in the later stages of a successfully developing offensive to administer the *coup de grâce* against already beleaguered enemy forces. Smaller scale airborne or amphibious assaults will support a ground offensive throughout its entire duration.

OPERATIONAL ART: *FRONT* AND ARMY OPERATIONS

Today, the Soviets believe that future war, with or without the use of nuclear weapons, will be war by maneuver. Their military solution to the problem of the lurking presence of nuclear and other modern weaponry is, characteristically, a dialectical synthesis of the new and the old — of operational and tactical techniques developed in the 1960s and 1970s to meet nuclear realities combined with time honored methods of large scale operational and tactical maneuver developed in the Great Patriotic War. The resulting synthesis envisions Soviet forces operating in a nuclear-scared configuration employing operational and tactical maneuver in the critical initial period of war to pre-empt and overcome quickly enemy defenses, to paralyze the enemy's ability to react, and to win rapid victory within carefully defined political limits.

On the offensive, through the means of focused operational and tactical maneuver, Soviet forces will attempt to pre-empt, disrupt, or crush forward enemy defenses; penetrate rapidly into the depths of the enemy's defenses along numerous axes; and, by immediately intermingling their own and the enemy's forces and by other direct actions, deprive the enemy of the ability to respond effectively with nuclear or high precision weapons. As Soviet maneuver unfolds into the depths, consequent paralysis of enemy command and control will ultimately produce paralysis of his will to resist and, hence, his final defeat.

The Soviets have clearly articulated this view since the mid-1970s. M. M. Kir'ian, describing an army penetration operation in 1976, wrote, in a nuclear environment

> formations [divisions] advance on their axes of attack from areas where they had restored their combat effectiveness and decisively move forward. In favorable conditions the offensive can be begun by forward detachments.[44]

If nuclear weapons are not used,

> The security zone [covering force area] is overcome by forces of the first echelon formations [divisions] after powerful air and artillery strikes on the most important objectives to the entire depth of the enemy defense. Forward detachments from each division destroy covering and security subunits [battalions] of the enemy and secure important objectives and areas in the forward defensive positions. Their operations are supported by artillery fire and air strikes in cooperation with operations by tactical air assault forces. Having overcome the covering force area, the forward detachments, supported by first echelon forces, penetrate the forward defensive positions from the march. If there is no possibility of creating conditions for the advance of the main force, the positions are overcome after a suitable preparation.[45]

To emphasize the role of tactical maneuver, a 1977 source noted:

> An important role in the achievement of a high offensive tempo can be played by forward detachments, prepared and aimed at specific objectives ... By their daring and enter-prising operations and skillful envelopment of strong points, they can rapidly fulfill their mission.[46]

A 1982 work describing recent tactical methods noted:

> Their [the forward detachments] principal mission was to

capture and destroy weapons and control facilities for barriers of fire established in this [security] zone, aggressively penetrate and capture tactically important installations and positions, with the objective of creating the requisite conditions for the main forces to advance to the forward edge of the enemy's main defensive area and penetrate it.[47]

A 1988 article rounded out these descriptions by adding:

Modern combined arms battle is fought throughout the entire depth of the enemy combat formation, both on the side's contact live [FLOT] and in the depth, on the ground and in the air.[48]

Consequently, the fragmented nature of battle will result in "mutual wedging of units and subunits, which will have to operate independently for a long time."[49] The synthesis of these views is that tactical and operational maneuver forces, committed to combat in great number and as early as possible, will provide the motive force for Soviet offensive operations at the tactical and operational levels of war.

These concepts were developed in the 1970s and early 1980s when tactical nuclear weapons posed the greatest potential threat on the battlefield. In the mid-1980s the Soviets have recognized the growing threat of high precision weaponry and other high technological weapons systems. Their initial response has been to accentuate those trends of the 1970s by stressing heavier single echelons, more rapid tactical and operational maneuver, and greater tactical flexibility by small units. One author has noted that, although basic offensive principles still apply, greater premium would have to be placed on the importance of surprise actions, maneuver of subunits and fires, sharp and continuous cooperation, skill in concealing from the enemy one's intentions, and firm continuous command and control.[50] Another has added "the revived capabilities of the battalion, and the increased significance of independent operations of subunits, naturally places great demands on the commander."[51] These and similar assertions indicate an increased Soviet concern for tailoring more carefully at the battalion and regimental level and a concomitant concern for more initiative and flexibility on the part of their commanders at these levels.

Given these developments, *fronts* will conduct operations within the scope of the strategic operations of a TVD [TSMA] command. In cooperation with other *fronts*, with aviation and, where possible, large naval formations, *fronts* will operate along one strategic or several operational directions (axes) under a single concept or plan to destroy large enemy forces and secure important territory. The increased scale of *front* operational capabilities has resulted in wide *front* attack sectors (250–350 km – although decreased from those of 1960); and deeper *front* objectives than in earlier years (up to several hundred kilometers).[52] The *front's* operational formation, depending on the nature of combat and the depth and continuity of the enemy defense, will include one or two echelons, an exploitation force (operational maneuver group), groups of rocket forces and artillery, *front* aviation, air defense forces, special operations (diversionary) forces, air and amphibious assault forces, antitank reserves, mobile obstacle detachments, a complex and widely deployed logistic infrastructure, and various reserve and support groups.[53] The scope of a *front* operation will include: the destruction of enemy objectives by nuclear or conventional fires; initial and successive offensive operations of first echelon armies (or defensive as required); introduction into battle of the *front* exploitation force (operational manuever groups) and second echelon armies (if formed) or reserves; air operations; air defense operations; operations by airborne, amphibious, special operations forces, and air assault brigades; and supporting operations of various types.[54]

Against an unprepared or only partially prepared defense, the Soviets will commit the bulk of *front* forces into action on a broad front after a limited preparation period (see tables 101 and 102).[55] Concentration of *front* forces for the attack will occur at the last possible moment in areas remote from the front line and final commitment of forces into combat will be on a time-phased basis, probably at night. A single echelon of armies at *front* level will provide maximum force to the initial attack, impart forward momentum necessary to carry the offensive through main enemy defenses, and reduce the risk of enemy nuclear response by quickly intermeshing Soviet forces with those of the enemy in depth along several axes. Coincidentally, this also reduces the effectiveness of enemy deep attacks and interdiction. The *front* exploitation force (OMGs, or operational maneuver groups), consisting of one or two reinforced tank armies, will deploy by dispersed divisions (tank or mechanized corps) in the close rear of first echelon forces in proximity to the sector of most likely penetration and will be committed to develop the offensive from the first to the third day of the offensive, depending on its progress. Exploiting tank armies

TABLE 101
FRONT OPERATIONAL FORMATION – 1987:
AGAINST AN UNPREPARED DEFENSE

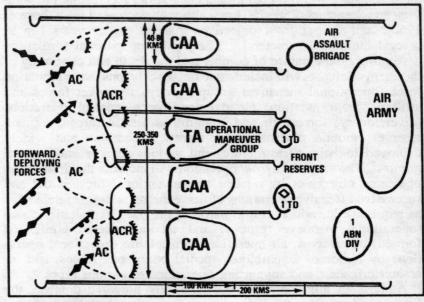

IMMEDIATE MISSION · 350 KMS
FINAL MISSION · 800 KMS

will normally attack in two columns of tank divisions (tank or mechanized corps) each organized into regimental (brigade) columns advancing in pre-combat (pre-battle) formation. A forward detachment of reinforced tank battalion (brigade) size will precede the advance of each tank division (corps).

Against hasty enemy defenses lacking operational reserves the Soviets could deploy one or more tank armies in the *front* first echelon and, thus, lead the attack with the exploitation force (OMG) and its lead forward detachments. In either case, airborne units up to regimental strength or the *front* air assault brigade will conduct operations in concert with the advancing *front* exploitation force at operational depths of 80 to 100 kilometers.

Front forces will seek to advance on a maximum number of directions, many of them deliberately traversing inhibiting terrain, and will conduct continuous day–night operations. Air offensive

TABLE 102
FRONT OPERATIONAL FORMATION – 1987:
AGAINST A PARTIALLY PREPARED DEFENSE

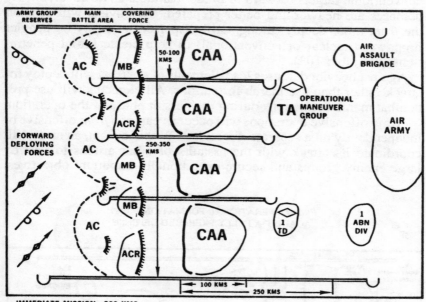

IMMEDIATE MISSION—300 KMS
FINAL MISSION—700 KMS

and anti-air operations, coordinated by the TVD command, will accompany the ground offensive primarily to neutralize enemy nuclear delivery means and gain control of the air. In addition, *front* special operations forces, committed in small teams, deployed prior to or during hostilities, will conduct reconnaissance and strike nuclear, economic, command and control, and political targets to the depths of the enemy rear in order to paralyze the enemy's ability to respond to the offensive. This form of *front* offensive presumes rapid success against enemy tactical defenses and the necessity of fighting numerous meeting engagements, in particular, by advancing exploitation forces against deploying or reinforcing enemy operational or tactical units. Hence, the Soviets have placed heavy emphasis on training for that type of combat.

The single echelon *front* offensive operation is designed to attain swift victory against unprepared or partially prepared forces occupying (or trying to occupy) relatively shallow defenses (less than 40 kilometers deep) and lacking significant operational reserves. This type of operation also lessens the likelihood of enemy nuclear response and denies the enemy large nuclear or conventional targets forward or in the rear area. If, however, enemy defenses are heavier and better prepared, the Soviets will echelon the *front* more deeply (though still dispersed) and rely on heavier firepower (nuclear or conventional) to help create initial penetrations (see table 103).

Against heavier defenses lead elements of the *front* will deploy for attack rather than use march formations. All elements will use pre-combat march formations during the pursuit phase of the operation.

Army offensive operations will occur as part of a *front* offensive or independently on a separate direction.[56] Within a *front*, an army will coordinate its attack with the assaults of other armies to destroy large enemy groups and secure operationally important objectives.

TABLE 103
FRONT OPERATIONAL FORMATION – 1987:
AGAINST A FULLY PREPARED DEFENSE

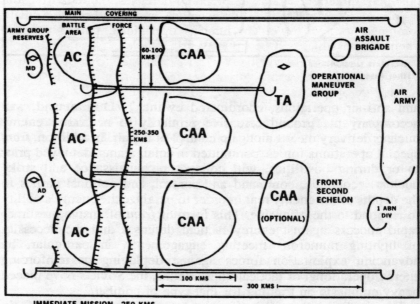

IMMEDIATE MISSION—250 KMS
FINAL MISSION—600 KMS

As was the case with the *front*, the increased capabilities of armies and their improved maneuverability have produced large attack sectors (up to 100 kilometers) and increased depths of mission. Within an army attack sector the *front* commander will designate the direction of the army main attack. An army usually will conduct one main attack against a prepared defense and several against a partially prepared defense.

The army will adopt an operational formation which reflects the concept of the operation and the nature of the defense. The operational formation will include: a first echelon (combined arms formation); an exploitation force (operational maneuver group); a second echelon and/or a combined arms reserve, artillery groups, air defense forces, air assault forces, antitank reserves, mobile obstacle detachments, and specialized reserves. Against an unprepared or partially prepared defense, the army will create a strong first echelon consisting of its motorized rifle divisions (see tables 104 and 105) and will employ an army forward detachment to lead its attack.

The army will position a tank division (tank or mechanized corps) in the immediate rear of the first echelon to exploit along the most expedient direction (against unprepared defenses, the tank division or corps can be deployed in first echelon), and it will create a small combined arms reserve. (In nuclear operations, tank divisions, whenever possible, will be in army first echelon.) A separate tank regiment (tank or mechanized corps) assigned to army control will operate as the army forward detachment, initially, or after penetration of the enemy defense.[57] The *front* air assault brigade will support the operations of the army forward detachment operating on a main *front* attack direction (at a depth of 40–100 kilometers), or an army air assault battalion (helicopter-lifted) will provide similar support at lesser depth. Against heavier defenses, armies will create heavier second echelons and delay commitment of the forward detachment and the army exploitation force until late on the first or the second day (see table 106).

Deeper enemy defenses will also require commitment of heavier fire support for a longer duration preceding and during the attack.

During the attack the army first echelon will penetrate the defense (if possible in pre-combat column march formation) using the army and divisional forward detachments to overcome covering zones and penetrate the defense, destroy enemy first echelon forces and reserves, engage enemy nuclear delivery means (with fire and forward detachments), and initiate pursuit of enemy forces.[58] The

TABLE 104
ARMY OPERATIONAL FORMATION – 1987:
AGAINST AN UNPREPARED DEFENSE

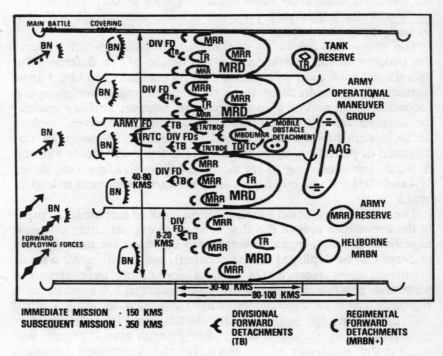

IMMEDIATE MISSION · 150 KMS
SUBSEQUENT MISSION · 350 KMS

DIVISIONAL FORWARD DETACHMENTS (TB)

REGIMENTAL FORWARD DETACHMENTS (MRBN+)

army forward detachment will lead the army attack along the most critical axis in the army offensive sector. It will push its advance to a depth of from 40 to 80 kilometers, that is, completely through the entire depth of the enemy's tactical defenses to preempt or disrupt those defenses. Army main force divisions, each led by its own forward detachment, will complete destruction of enemy tactical defensive forces and secure the commitment into the penetration of army exploitation forces.

The army exploitation force (OMG), marching in pre-combat formation in columns of regiments (brigades), will develop success into the operational depth, overcome subsequent enemy defense lines, engage reinforcing enemy forces in meeting engagements, repulse counterattacks, and pave the way for commitment of the *front* exploitation force in cooperation with an air assault force of

TABLE 105
ARMY OPERATIONAL FORMATION – 1987:
AGAINST A PARTIALLY PREPARED DEFENSE

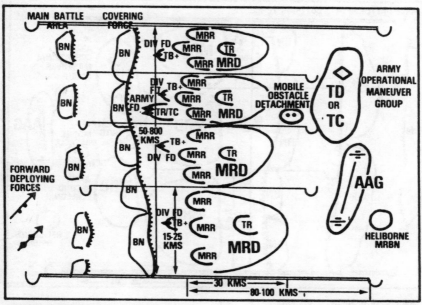

IMMEDIATE MISSION · 120 KMS
SUBSEQUENT MISSION · 300 KMS

front or army. The army second echelon and/or reserve will replace destroyed first echelon elements, reinforce the first echelon, and liquidate bypassed enemy forces. Army penetration and pursuit operations will seek to use encirclement operations as much as possible.

During the exploitation, forward detachments and operational maneuver groups provide a means for maintaining the forward momentum of the entire force. They insure continued fragmentation of enemy forces, pre-empt or overcome intermediate enemy defenses, and destroy the equilibrium of redeploying enemy reserves. All the while, forward detachments provide the essential linkage between operational maneuver forces and main forces, and lend cohesiveness to the entire offensive. Throughout the offensive, tactical air assaults ranging from company to brigade strength

TABLE 106
ARMY OPERATIONAL FORMATION – 1987:
AGAINST A FULLY PREPARED DEFENSE

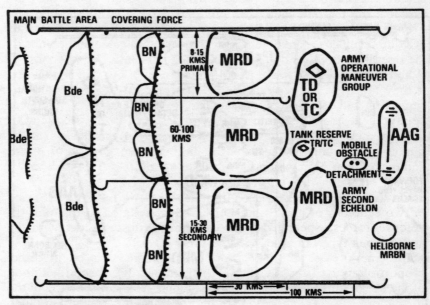

IMMEDIATE MISSION · 100 KMS
SUBSEQUENT MISSION · 250 KMS

cooperate with maneuver forces. Air assault forces with their vertical fire support means (helicopters) constitute an air echelon, which supplements existing ground echelons.[59] The Soviets strongly believe requisite offensive success can be achieved only against an unprepared or partially prepared defense. Throughout the offensive, Soviet forces will undertake measures to defend against enemy chemical and nuclear strikes and radio-electronic combat.

Fronts will conduct defensive operations in cooperation with other *fronts* and other service forces, under a single TVD concept or plan; to defend a separate strategic or several operational directions; to secure key regions or objectives; to disrupt enemy offensive activity and inflict on him maximum casualties; to win time; and to create conditions conducive to resumption of the attack by Soviet forces. The *front* defensive operation will be part of a strategic operation in a TVD [TSMA] or an independent operation, and it will involve: fire suppression of the enemy as he moves toward and occupies jumping-off positions; a counter-preparation; defensive operations of first and sometimes second echelon armies; *front* counterattacks; supporting operations (air, special operations, air assault); and the repulsion of amphibious assaults in coastal regions. *Fronts* will undertake defensive operations under enemy pressure or voluntarily. "A *front* defense is constructed to achieve the aims of the operation both with and without the use of nuclear weapons."[60] When nuclear weapons are used, their greatest effect will be realized if they are used against enemy assault forces while they are concentrating and deploying for an attack. Soviet/Warsaw Pact planners believe that PGMs have raised new issues for the conduct of defensive operations. That is, the PGMs have given defenders the opportunity to change radically the battlefield correlation of forces and make a rapid transition to offensive operations. This is clearly a subject of intense Soviet investigation.

On the defense, the *front* operational formation will contain one or two echelons of armies, artillery groups, aviation formations, air defense forces, specialized forces, mobile obstacle detachments and various types of reserves (see table 107).[61]

In general, the depth of *front* echelonment will be in direct proportion to the strength of the enemy attack. Increased likelihood of the use of nuclear weapons will also increase the dispersion of the formation. If a single echelon formation is used, a strong combined arms reserve will be formed. In a conventional defense, maximum fire will be inflicted on advancing enemy units to block a penetration and force the enemy to commit his reserves. *Front* second echelon or reserve units, usually armor-heavy, will reduce enemy penetrations by fire and attacks on his flanks. In a nuclear defense, defending forces will use nuclear fires against the deploying enemy or against an enemy penetration preparatory to launching a counterattack. The Soviets will renew offensive operations after successful completion of a defense.

Armies will defend as part of a *front* operation, or independently, to achieve objectives similar to those of *fronts*. Armies will form in one or two echelons, artillery groups, air defense groups, antitank and specialized reserves and mobile obstacle detachments (see table 108).[62]

Depth of army defensive echelonment will depend on enemy strength and the nature of war, although in general, forces will be dispersed as much as possible. The army's first echelon, consisting

TABLE 107
FRONT OPERATIONAL FORMATION – DEFENSE: 1987

FIRST ECHELON   SECOND ECHELON

FRONT COUNTERATTACK FORCE

60-120 KMS

CAA

TA

200-350 KMS

CAA

CAA

CAA

AIR ARMY

30 KMS   150-200 KMS

TO 400 KMS

of motorized rifle divisions, will inflict as much damage as possible on the enemy. The second echelon, or combined arms reserve (of tank and/or motorized rifle divisions) will engage penetrating enemy forces or air assault forces, hold on to key lines or regions, and launch army counterattacks seeking to cut off enemy forces and penetrate into their rear areas.[63] Nuclear and/or conventional fires will support every phase of the defense. The Soviets will pay particular attention to engineer preparation of the defense, to concentration of artillery, antiaircraft and antitank fires, and to defense of forces from chemical and nuclear attack.

TABLE 108
COMBINED ARMS ARMY OPERATIONAL FORMATION – DEFENSE: 1987

TACTICS: CORPS AND DIVISION OPERATIONS*

Significant changes have occurred at the tactical level since the late 1960s, particularly concerning the conduct of offensive operations. Specifically, offensive tactics retain the dynamic, fluid and rapid nature of the early 1960s, but today a study of techniques used in the Great Patriotic War and introduction of new weaponry in greater quantities has strengthened the force and sustainability of the attack. While force tactical frontages and depths have decreased somewhat from the early 1960s, they still exceed corresponding norms for the war years. Soviet tactical theory "provides for forces

*The Soviets define the corps as the highest tactical or operational-tactical formation of the armed forces, depending on its type and function in combat. A corps subordinate to army would be tactical; a corps operating as a forward detachment would be operational-tactical; and a corps serving as an OMG would be operational. Presently, there are no combined arms corps subordinate to armies.

operating in conditions involving both the use of nuclear weapons and the use of only conventional weapons."[64] Conventional operations, however, will be conducted in a nuclear scared posture. Thus, tactical operations will involve task organized forces in relatively dispersed formations relying on rapid maneuver to achieve tactical success. Contemporary Soviet tactics place a high premium on flexible, automated command and control, close cooperation between forces, and initiative on the part of commanders at all levels.

Divisions, regiments and battalions will conduct operations under army control. Their combat formations will reflect the nature and depth of the defense and the operational plan of the army commander. Divisions will normally form with one or two echelons, artillery groups, antiaircraft forces, antitank, engineer, combined arms, and specialized reserves, and mobile obstacle detachments.[65] In certain types of operations, divisions will field forward detachments whose operations will be coordinated with battalion-size, tactical heliborne assaults.[66] As a rule, single echelon formations (of regiments, battalions and companies) will be employed to overcome a hasty or ill-prepared defense or defenses lacking depth (see tables 109 and 110).

In addition, forward detachments and tactical air assaults will be used more extensively and aggressively against weaker defenses. On a nuclear battlefield, a single echeloned, offensive formation will both reduce force (especially division) vulnerability to nuclear attack by quickly enmeshing opposing forces and strengthen the shock value and depth of the initial penetrations. While dispersion, characteristic of deep echelonment, will provide some protection against nuclear strikes, it will also weaken the power of the initial attack.

However the Soviets echelon their forces at the tactical level, in a nuclear environment they will stress the use of tanks well forward at every level of command. Army first echelon motorized rifle and tank divisions will attack from positions to the rear of the front lines in pre-combat march column configuration, led by armor-heavy, forward detachments (reinforced tank battalions or brigades) at division level and reinforced motorized rifle battalions at regimental level. The attack will proceed without a halt through gaps in the enemy defenses created by nuclear fires. Tactical operations will seek to penetrate tactical defenses to a depth of 30–40 kilometers along numerous axes on the first day of combat to facilitate commitment of army exploitation forces into the operational depths (on day one or two). Battalion-size heliborne assaults will provide a vertical dimension to the operations of the divisional forward detachment and will occur at depths of up to 50 kilometers.

In a conventional but nuclear-scared configuration, army motorized rifle (and in some instances tank) divisions, supported by strong aviation (helicopter) and artillery strikes on the entire depth of the defense and led by forward detachments, will advance rapidly to overcome the enemy covering zone and main defensive positions.

> Forward detachments of each division will destroy enemy security and covering units and secure important objectives and regions in the forward defense positions. Their action is supported by artillery fire, aviation strikes and operations by air assault units. Having overcome the security belt, forward detachments, supported by other first echelon units, from the march, will penetrate the forward defense positions.[67]

A reinforced tank battalion (brigade) usually will serve as the division's forward detachment, while a reinforced, motorized rifle battalion will perform the same function for motorized rifle regiments. The forward detachments could advance at night prior to the advance of the division main forces in cooperation with the army forward detachment. The division forward detachment's mission will be to cut through the covering force sector and penetrate into the main forward defensive positions to a depth of 20–50 kilometers

> to capture and destroy weapons and control facilities for barriers of fire established in this zone, [effect] aggressive penetration and capture of tactically important installations and positions, with the objective of creating the requisite conditions for the main forces to advance to the forward edge of the enemy's main defensive position and penetrate it.[68]

Extensive logistical reorganization has occurred within the division to enable it better to support forward detachment operations.

While the division forward detachments preempt or disrupt the continuity of enemy defenses in cooperation with battalion-size heliborne assault landings in main attack sectors, forward detachments of each first echelon motorized rifle regiment, also advancing in pre-combat formation, will attack along separate axes with missions similar to those of the division's forward detachment, only at lesser depths.

Division main forces will advance in regimental columns in pre-

TABLE 109
MOTORIZED RIFLE DIVISION COMBAT FORMATION – 1987:
AGAINST AN UNPREPARED DEFENSE

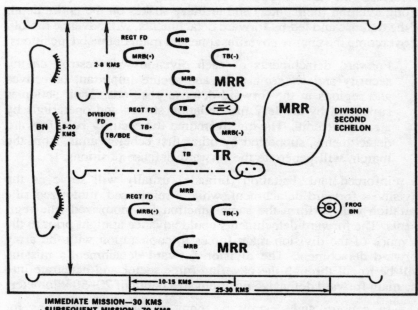

IMMEDIATE MISSION—30 KMS
SUBSEQUENT MISSION—70 KMS

combat formation or in march order in order to engage the defense and capitalize on the disruption caused by the forward detachments. Artillery and helicopters will provide fire support for forward detachments and divisional main forces throughout the duration of the attack. After completion of the penetration, army and division forward detachments, as originally designated or reconstituted, will continue the advance at maximum speed. Thus,

> defensive lines deep in the enemy's defense were to be overrun without a halt, in dispersed approach march formation, and sometimes in march columns as well. Penetration was to be accomplished primarily by advanced guards or forward detachments, while the main forces were to penetrate this defense at a rapid pace ...[69]

TABLE 110
MOTORIZED RIFLE DIVISION COMBAT FORMATION – 1987:
AGAINST A PARTIALLY PREPARED DEFENSE

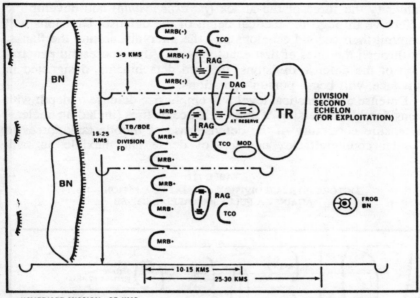

IMMEDIATE MISSION—25 KMS
SUBSEQUENT MISSION—60 KMS

Divisions may rely solely on forward detachments, main forces, and army forces to begin the exploitation into the operational depth, or divisions may create in advance an exploitation force of reinforced regimental strength from its second echelon (tank regiment or perhaps a reinforced motorized rifle regiment equipped with BMPs) to begin the pursuit.

In the event enemy defensive positions are well prepared, occupied in great depth (more than 40 kilometers), and backed up by operational reserves, Soviet tactical offensive preparations will be more elaborate (see table 111).

A phased artillery and air preparation of varying duration will suppress enemy artillery fire and strike at critical enemy positions, command and control points, and supply points. After the preparation, the division will attack, probably in two echelons, unless nuclear response is imminent. First echelon regiments, cooperating closely with tanks (serving in support fashion for rifle battalions) will penetrate tactical enemy defensive positions without a halt while detailing specific battalions (from the regimental second echelons) to destroy bypassed enemy units. The second echelon, advancing in pre-combat formation, will follow the first echelon to intensify the force of the attack (*narashchivanie*) and develop the offensive through the tactical depth of the defense. Divisions will commit their second echelons into the intervals, around the flanks, or through the lines of first echelon units. After successful penetration of the defense divisions, forward detachments, designated in advance, will begin pursuit operations.

Defense at the tactical level will emphasize defense in depth with considerable dispersion of units, reliance on fires (including nuclear) to ensure continuity of the defense, use of mobile tank forces to launch counterattacks, creation of dense and flexible antitank

TABLE 111

MOTORIZED RIFLE DIVISION COMBAT FORMATION – 1987:
AGAINST A FULLY PREPARED DEFENSE

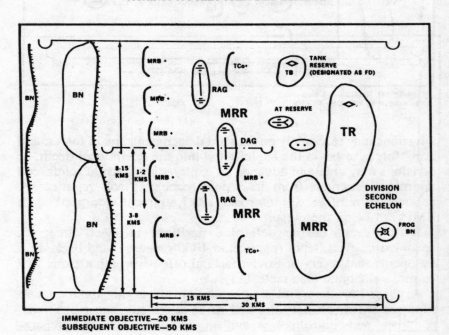

IMMEDIATE OBJECTIVE—20 KMS
SUBSEQUENT OBJECTIVE—50 KMS

defenses, formation of complete and redundant air defense coverage, establishment of engineer defensive barriers (trenches, minefields, etc.) and strict measures involved to defend forces against the effects of nuclear and chemical fires. Divisions, formed in two echelons of regiments, will defend sectors of from 20–30 kilometers to a depth of 15–20 kilometers (see table 112).[70]

CONCLUSION

Since the late 1960s the Soviets have continued to wrestle with the dilemma of nuclear war. Recognizing that nuclear war could devastate the victor as well as the vanquished, the Soviets have sought ways to produce alternatives to nuclear catastrophe, should the unlikely necessity for general war arise. The tentative solution they have reached is based on the chess-like premise that the nuclear power of a potential enemy can be stalemated, permitting Soviet forces to achieve theater objectives without enemy use of nuclear strikes. Soviet nuclear parity or superiority at both the strategic and

TABLE 112
MOTORIZED RIFLE DIVISION COMBAT FORMATION – DEFENSE: 1987

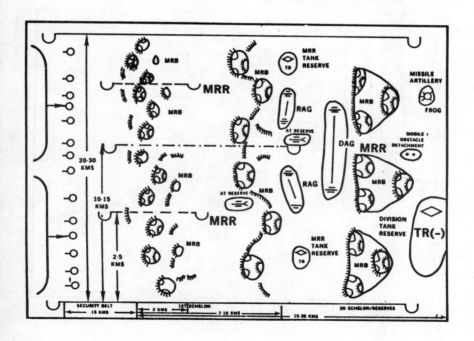

theater (tactical) levels create the basic prerequisite for stalemate and result in the increased likelihood of war remaining conventional. As additional insurance, the Soviets have developed, on the basis of in-depth analysis, strategic concepts and operational and tactical techniques that would make an enemy decision to use nuclear weapons (if he wished to do so) even more difficult. This has been accomplished by the development of capabilities to achieve strategic objectives in the theater using conventional weapons only.

Confronted with the looming presence of new high technological conventional weaponry, the Soviets are seeking to extend the solutions they developed to deal with the dilemma of nuclear weapons to the realm of new conventional weaponry as well. Whereas in the 1970s the Soviet solution remained in the military-technical area of doctrine, today it has spread to the political dimension. The scope and subject of the Soviet military studies are apparent, and their results emerge more clearly every day. Study goes on, and as it does techniques will continue to evolve.

CHAPTER EIGHT

PERSPECTIVE ON THE FUTURE

BACKGROUND

Dynamism and continuity have characterized the evolutionary nature of Soviet military doctrine. There is every reason to believe that, despite recent pronouncements, it will continue to evolve in the same manner. Soviet doctrine identifies the principal adversary as imperialism, the main proponent of which is the United States. Ideological assumptions and the dynamic of the Marxist–Leninist dialectic dictate that wars (struggle and competition) will occur both between capitalist (imperialist) states themselves and between those states and underdeveloped, exploited nations. While doctrine and self-interest contend that the Soviet Union and revolutionary states be defended against attack by imperialism, the same imperatives suggest that wars suited to loosening the grip of imperialism in the world and weakening its economic, political and social foundations are altogether proper and just. Thus the Soviet Union is ideologically and practically committed to maintaining military power sufficient for the achievement of its political objectives. In the present and future contexts, the Soviets seek the ability to dominate escalation at each level so that they can intimidate or deter opponents. If they fail to intimidate or deter they feel they must be able to fight and win at all levels of potential war: strategic nuclear, theater nuclear, theater conventional, local, short wars, and protracted conflicts. Simultaneously, the Soviets seek methods to deter or avoid the inevitably catastrophic (and perhaps unnecessary) damage of general nuclear war. To maintain their strength the Soviets must fully exploit science and technology to master the new technological revolution, politically educate their population, and organize all aspects of state power to generate and maintain military strength. Simultaneously, they are adjusting doctrinal tenets to help achieve that end.

The litany of new doctrinal terminology eminating today from the Soviet Union, which includes such concepts as "prevention of war," "defensiveness" and "reasonable sufficiency" probably indicates an overriding Soviet concern for reducing the likelihood of future nuclear war. It reflects, as well, Soviet response to harsh technological and economic realities which threaten the Soviet's ability to compete globally as other than a military power.

Soviet fixation on avoiding nuclear war is consistent with Soviet policies in the 1970s and represents a strategic and global version of operational and tactical anti-nuclear maneuver concepts. The Soviets believe the international climate is receptive to accepting reduction of nuclear arsenals. The goal remains partial or full renunciation of nuclear war as a viable military option.

In the economic and technological realm the Soviets desire *peredyshka* [breathing space] in the stormy military-technical race which Soviet technology and economic strength are ill suited to contest. Ultimately, only time and concrete Soviet actions in the strategic, operational, and tactical levels of military science will indicate the degree to which Soviet military doctrine, and hence political goals, have evolved.

Militarily, in the Soviet view, the irreconcilable natures of the competing socialist and capitalist systems dictate that general war between them would become a struggle for the future existence of the two systems. The totality and finality of such a war are determining factors in overall Soviet national strategy and resulting military strategy. Sober realities temper Soviet attitudes toward the conduct of war in general, and, by extension, affect Soviet operational art and tactics. This understanding is most clearly evidenced in Soviet preparedness and concern for the "initial period" of war − a period crucial for achieving quick victory or forestalling rapid defeat. Soviet sensitivity to the exigencies of war has been intensified by the accelerated pace of technological change in the second half of the twentieth century. Technological change not only makes the initial period of war loom larger in importance, but also affects all other aspects of military doctrine. Soviet recognition of this major factor's impact on the highest and lowest levels of military doctrine was articulated by an increasingly visible Chief of the General Staff Marshal N. V. Ogarkov, who wrote in 1982:

> Analysis of the development of military art in the post-war also allows us to select a number of general, characteristic objective laws, among which the following may be named:
>
> − First, on the development of military affairs, the scientific-technological revolution has ever growing influence, present-

ing increased demands for qualitative characteristics in military technology and weaponry, and on searching out new methods and forms for conducting combat actions.

— Second, the tempo of development of military technology and weapons is increasing, the time intervals between qualitative leaps in development in various areas of military affairs are being shortened, which in turn tells on the development of military affairs as a whole.

— Third, the significance of strategic means of conducting war is growing, means which today are able directly to influence its course, and consequently also operational/strategic control organs.

— Fourth, the processes of controlling troops and forces are becoming more complicated, which demands an approach new in principle for organizing structurally efficient systems of control and equipping them with the necessary modern control technology.

— And finally, the air sphere in combat actions and operations is acquiring an ever growing role, which gives modern operations a three-dimensional, deep character.[1]

Within this context, the Soviets will continue to study intensely the nature of war and methods for its preparation and conduct. They will do so with a keen eye on technological change, seeking to harness technology to their military ends. While the Soviets will fashion and field new systems and develop operational tenets for their use, they will also continue to emphasize the possible and practical. The Soviets have also learned from experience the pitfalls of embracing radically new systems without proper testing or without possessing doctrine for their use. They will rely on practical systems that work and absorb new technologies incrementally, in tandem with developing doctrine. Only in those most critical areas, having immediate impact on the outcome of war (the initial period), will the Soviets seek to insure that their technological achievements match or exceed those of the West.

MILITARY STRATEGY

The Soviets will consider carefully the scope and range of future war in all of its manifestations. At the highest level, they have clearly acknowledged the importance of the cosmos (outer space) by referring to it in their definition of strategic operations and by undertaking systematic study of the impact of the cosmos on every level of operations. At the lowest level on earth, they will continue to develop concepts for the extended struggle with imperialism in the Third World, a struggle developing and fulfilling Khrushchev's promise of support for wars of national liberation. In the Third World, the Soviets will seek the ability to wage war according to its broadest definition (economic, political and social) while improving their capability to influence the outcome of war militarily, if it assumes the form of outright conflict. In addition, they will continue to amplify and refine the Brezhnev doctrine to affect more directly the fortunes of the Socialist bloc.

Further, Soviet military developments in the strategic, operational, and tactical arenas will reflect Soviet beliefs concerning the changing nature of war. This means a continued and perhaps intensified Soviet concern for the nature of future war and theater strategic operations conducted within a conventional context.

Continued Soviet study of the nature of the initial period of war (*nachal'nyi period voiny*) will focus on determining methods for achieving rapid victory in offensive war and for avoiding surprise attack and defeat by a potential enemy. The Soviets appreciate the benefits of strategic surprise and know the indicators associated with impending hostilities. Hence, on the offensive, in order to avoid detection and achieve surprise, the Soviets will employ methods to cloud or totally mask the most vivid indicators. Chief among the indicators are visible force mobilization and other manifestations of strategic deployment of forces, which are subject to detection by an ever-widening array of sophisticated technical surveillance means. The Soviets recognize the ambiguities of the Indications and Warning (I & W) process and will undertake measures to confuse that process. To confound or avoid surveillance, the Soviets will seek to create strategic concentrations of forces in peacetime and will resort only to selective or covert mobilization prior to the outbreak of hostilities.* In accord with tradition and past experience, the Soviets will rely on strict planning security, draconian security measures to cover movement, movement of forces at night and in adverse weather, and the assembly of forces secretly or under the guise of exercises or normal troop rotation.

---

* The Soviets have conducted covert limited mobilizations in preparing for the invasion of Afghanistan and during the 1980–81 Polish crisis, among other instances.

Peacetime organization of Soviet forces probably masks actual wartime force configuration, and the Soviets could well possess (or adopt in the future) a system for the forward storage of unit equipment (similar to POMCUS) to facilitate more rapid mobilization and expansion of combat forces in the forward area and to meet the necessary wartime force requirements.[2]

The Soviets are likely to employ massive deception (*maskirovka*) measures to cover strategic deployment. Their intent would be to mask the scale and scope of offensive preparations, the timing of the attack, and the precise location of main attack regions. By doing so successfully the Soviets could, to some extent, mask intent to attack as well. Deception means could run the gamut from political measures designed to cover intent to a variety of other measures designed to cover scale, scope and location of attack. Such measures could include sophisticated ones such as the exploitation of existing exercise patterns, the use of a large-scale announced exercise or a false troop rotation, or such mundane but previously effective means as night movement, movement in inclement weather or movement under the cloak of extensive physical camouflage.

Drawing heavily on research done on the theme "the initial period of war" or, specifically, what a nation's army must do to win rapid victory or avoid precipitous defeat, the Soviets have concluded that the principal prerequisite for offensive victory is the surprise conduct of rapid operations by forces concentrated well forward. Hence, the Soviets have tended to eschew preliminary large scale mobilization (the primary indicator of impending war), and have argued for employment of a single strategic and operational echelon supplemented by numerous tailored operational and tactical maneuver forces.

In addition to their concern for secret mobilization and undertaking other measures associated with strategic deployment, the Soviets recognize the importance of sustainment in a theater offensive operation, either if surprise is achieved or if it is not. In their study of previous initial periods of war (such as August 1914 and June 1941), they have noted that the lack of an ability to sustain operations was a major contributing factor to the failure of the strategic offensive. They have concluded that it is necessary to stockpile logistical materials in the forward area and to create means for moving essential materials forward to combat units as the offensive develops. Such measures will include the forward storage of logistical materials (fuel and ammunition) and major end items of combat equipment (tanks, guns) far beyond the immediate peacetime needs of forward area forces, and the creation of special supply means (such as tactical oil pipelines) to push those supplies as far forward as possible.

The nature of theater strategic operations (primarily offensive but also defensive) is, and will continue to be, a subject of major concern for the Soviets.[3] Specifically, the Soviets will attempt to bridge the inevitable gap between what they hope and think they can achieve (theory) and what their forces actually can achieve (practice). This requires a careful definition of their own forces' capabilities vis-à-vis their opponent (correlation of forces) and a careful matching of those strategic plans with actual force capabilities. Presently, the Soviets are intensely studying their past experience with strategic operations and the sequencing of various operational phases within the overall strategic offensive.[4] They will juxtapose the data they derive from this analysis of past experience against technological changes in weaponry and equipment to generate a wide range of strategic norms. These norms, a distillation of experience, represent what can reasonably be achieved by a given force under given circumstances. The Soviets, of course, have used a similar system to derive operational and tactical norms.

Parallel to their study of strategic operations is extensive Soviet study of successive operations, in essence, study of the sequencing of operations necessary for a strategic force to achieve its strategic objective. The Soviets studied successive operations in the 1920s and 1930s, practiced successive operations in the Second World War, and fostered an analysis of these practices in the 1950s. After a hiatus in the 1960s, when nuclear combat seemed to negate the value of successive operations, the Soviets have resumed study of the subject, most recently in a theater-strategic context. In addition to their concern for the timing and planning of a strategic operation, the Soviets will seek to conduct successive operations at theater and *front* level without recourse to the interruptions of operational pauses.

As a by-product of their study of strategic offensives, the Soviets have created a TVD [TSMA] command structure to control the operations of several *fronts* within key sectors of the theaters of war. They will continue to refine that TVD structure with emphasis on more effective command and control relationships both with the *STAVKA* (high command) level and with the operating *fronts* within the TVD itself. Their preeminent aim at all levels of command is to reduce planning time and shorten the decision-making cycle during the conduct of the offensive by comprehensive study and use of

automation of command, mathematical formulae, and calculations
and nomograms of various types.

OPERATIONAL ART AND TACTICS

At the operational and tactical levels the Soviets will concentrate on
achieving a capability for conducting continuous *front* (and army)
operations as a part of the unfolding strategic offensive. Soviet
concern for conducting rapid operations will be reflected by
continual emphasis on operational maneuver within the *front* and
army designed to preempt defenses or, failing in that intent, to
penetrate quickly or to bypass principal enemy defensive positions.

The Soviets recognize two principal realities of modern combat.
The first is the changing nature of the modern battlefield, the
principal feature of which is the increased urbanization of terrain, in
particular, in a European context. The second reflects the changing nature of combat forces characterized by the emergence of
precision guided weapons, the growth of antitank weaponry, and
the appearance of the helicopter as a potent weapon on the conventional battlefield. These two realities combine to make the
achievement of offensive aims ever more complicated.

The Soviets are developing doctrinal techniques and a force
structure capable of dealing with these two realities of contemporary
combat. Concurrently, they recognize a third reality, the imperative of maintaining a capability for conducting operational maneuver.
As in the past, that means instilling in a portion of their force
structure a quality that distinguishes it from other forces and permits
it to accomplish successfully those tasks associated with operational
maneuver. In the past the superior mobility and firepower of mobile
forces (the mobile groups) vis-à-vis footbound infantry permitted
mobile forces to conduct operational maneuver. That distinction
disappeared, to some extent, when all forces became mobile (hence
the term mobile group became obsolete).

Nevertheless, the necessity of performing operational maneuver
remained throughout the 1950s, reappeared in the 1970s, and
retains significance today. The logical questions now are: what
qualities must forces possess to perform operational maneuver,
how extensive should those forces be, and what operational and
tactical techniques should they use? The Soviets have begun to
answer these questions. Careful task organization and tailoring of
units to improve unit range of operations, firepower, sustainability,
and survivability can provide units with the ability to conduct

operational maneuver. So can improved planning techniques, tightened command and control, automation of command, and exploitation of the vertical dimension of operational maneuver (such as integration of helicopter fire support and use of air-mobile forces in conjunction with advancing ground maneuver forces).[5] The Soviets strongly believe that as the numbers of high precision weapons proliferate on the battlefield, requisite offensive success can be achieved only against an unprepared or partially prepared defense.

Foremost among the operational techniques at *front* and army level will be increased Soviet reliance on more numerous operational maneuver groups both at levels employed earlier and further forward in the operation. The Soviets will probably use two such groups at *front* level and at least one group at army level in main attack sectors of the *front* and TVD.[6] Depending on the nature of the defense the Soviets will commit these groups to combat from the first up to the fifth day of operations. Against an unprepared defense, the Soviets can be expected to lead their offensive with multiple operational maneuver groups.

The Soviets will adjust the structure of these tank-heavy groups and provide tailored support to enable them to deal with the realities of modern combat and, thus, maneuver successfully on the changing battlefield. Tailored support would include greater quantities of mechanized infantry, increased artillery and engineer assets, dedicated helicopters and air support, and support packages tailored to the depth of their projected mission. The Soviets will experiment with a variety of force structures to determine which is best suited to perform successfully the function of sustained operational maneuver.

At the tactical level and, to an increasing extent at the operational level as well, the Soviets will rely on forward detachments and other functional groups to pave the way for the successful conduct of operational maneuver. These forward detachments, also tailored to meet the requirements of the situation, will perform tactical maneuver functions at army, division, and even regimental level. In some instances they will initiate the offensive in order to pre-empt defenses which are unmanned or in the process of being manned. Against prepared defenses they will initiate the operational exploitation after completion of a short and violent penetration of tactical defenses by main force motorized rifle and tank divisions. If a planned penetration phase is required against a heavy defense, the Soviets will rely on massed firepower and task-organized tank and motorized rifle forces to effect penetrations in numerous narrow sectors of the defense, after which forward detachments will initiate the operational exploitation. Forward detachments, while conducting tactical maneuver during penetration of tactical defenses, can also initiate operational maneuver by paving the way for operations by operational maneuver groups. Forward detachments lead the OMGs through the fragmented tactical defense and into the operational depths of the enemy defense.

Soviet theorists now suggest that tactical missions call for securing objectives along multiple axes throughout the depth of the enemy's defense, whose seizure fragments the defense and renders it untenable. At the tactical level, specifically designated and tailored maneuver forces (usually forward detachments) had earlier performed this function, while tailored operational maneuver forces did likewise at the operational level. Today, and in the future, all tactical units and subunits are likely to operate in this fashion.

This offensive posture may significantly alter traditional concepts of echelonment, not only by reducing the number of ground echelons, but also by supplementing the ground echelon with a vertical (air assault) echelon, which will add greater depth to battle. In essence what has emerged is a Soviet concept of land–air battle juxtaposed against the US concept of AirLand battle. This concept will likely involve the fielding, by the Soviets, of air assault forces within most levels of their force structure.

In the case of both the operational maneuver group and the task-organized forward detachment, the Soviets will continue to develop the vertical dimension of each in the form of air assault units designated to cooperate with the ground groups and detachments. The armor-heavy ground dimension and the infantry-heavy air dimension, when combined, will form a well balanced and potent force operating in the enemy's operational rear area. Thus, the use of air assault battalions in conjunction with army and division forward detachments will increase, as will similar use of larger air assault units to complement the operations of *front* and army level operational maneuver groups. It is likely the Soviets will use one air assault brigade to cooperate with each army OMG. At *front* level, use of multiple air assault brigades or an air assault corps is likely in conjunction with the operations of *front* OMGs.[7]

At *front*, army, and divisional level the Soviets will increase their deployment of conventional (as well as nuclear capable) fire support means, including antitank and antiaircraft artillery, antiaircraft missiles, conventional tube artillery and helicopter gunships. The same will apply to other combat support forces, such as engineer assets for obstacle clearance and the employment of tactical bridging. The Soviets consider added artillery and air firepower as the principal means for dealing with improved battlefield defenses and for unleashing the capability for performing both tactical and operational maneuver.[8]

As a further means for creating chaos in enemy defenses, the Soviets will use extensive radio-electronic combat measures to disrupt enemy command and control in conjunction with expanded operations by special operations forces against enemy rear areas in order to sow confusion and paralyze the enemy command and control and logistical structure. The Soviets consider disruption of the enemy rear area as a critical and essential adjunct to successful operations along the front.

Soviet recognition of the changing nature of the battlefield and the growing importance of operational and tactical maneuver has prompted them to emphasize the necessity for creating force entities whose structures are flexible enough to fight and survive on a fragmented battlefield where the forces of both sides are intermixed. This, in turn, provides a strong motive for Soviet force restructuring, which will probably result in the reemergence of the corps and brigade structure with which the Soviets have experienced so much success in the past.

The Soviets increasingly believe that rapid technological changes and the appearance of new high precision weapons have altered the traditional balance between the offense and defense, as well as the dynamics of transition between the offense and defense.[9] In the classic Clausewitzian sense, the defender was accorded advantage by his ability to chose the location and nature of the defense as he awaited the enemy's blow. The attacker had the advantage of choosing the time of the attack and the point of main effort. Today, armed with new weaponry, the defender can strike the enemy at long range, and at a time of his own choosing before the enemy deploys for the attack. Thus, the defender can initiate the engagement and undercut the attacker's time advantage. Through the use of long-range high precision weapons the defender can strike first, and materially alter the initial correlation of forces. These weapons also increase the importance of employing sophisticated selective mobilization in a prewar period. The entire relationship between offense, defense, and counterattack has blurred as weapons' engagement ranges and lethality have increased. That process has been described by the Soviets as "maneuver by fire."

In these circumstances the nature of close-in battle has changed. On the one hand, achieving close-in battle has become more difficult, and potentially costly, against a fully or partially-deployed defender because of his improved means of distant engagement. On the other hand, the ability of an attacker to close quickly with the enemy has become more important, because by closing rapidly the attacker can deprive the defender of his ability to employ high precision weapons to their fullest effect. This altered relationship has also placed greater premium on an attacker conducting rapid initial maneuver to intersperse his forces among those of the defender so as to insure that combat remains fragmented. Fragmented combat, characterized by forces striving to achieve point or area objectives rather than securing lines (linear battle), also hinders effective enemy employment of high precision and tactical nuclear weapons. This is, in essence, analogous to the Soviet anti-nuclear techniques of the 1970s, only now writ large. In this regard surprise provides additional dividends for the attacker.

For an offensive force other new techniques have increased in importance. Forces on the offensive must avoid creating large-scale concentrations in their rear areas. Thus, traditional second echelons must be replaced by smaller, more numerous, and more mobile forces. This follows the Soviet judgment in the 1970s that operational second echelons were potentially vulnerable to tactical nuclear strikes. At that time the Soviets responded by deemphasizing the role of operational second echelons and by arguing for increased reliance on operational maneuver forces and reserves. Now that judgment applies to the tactical level as well. This will also effect traditional physical concentration of artillery, while relying on maneuver by fire to achieve requisite striking power. Command and control centers, key logistical installations, and communications nodes will either have to be hardened, concealed, or become mobile enough to move frequently.

Operational and tactical maneuver will become even more critical, and forces conducting maneuver will have to employ more extensively basic raiding techniques. Specialized forces such as air assault, reconnaissance–diversionary, and enveloping groups and detachments will acquire new importance as well. In this sense, the enemy will be engaged and defeated not by classic penetration and envelopment operations conducted by deeply echeloned, patterned forces employed in a specific and limited number of main attack sectors, but rather by numerous operational and tactical cutting blows delivered along numerous axes, by vertical *desants*, and by strikes against the enemy rear area by ground and air-delivered forces.

Associated with these newly evolving combat techniques is the growing importance of cybernetic techniques, such as automated planning and command and control to speed decision-making prior to and during combat, and the advanced exploitation of a combination of intelligence and fires by use of such concepts as reconnaissance-strike (recce-strike).

As articulated by one writer, the chief characteristics of future battle will be:

1. transformation of traditional land operations into land-air operations;
2. broadening of the role of mobility in all troop operations;
3. development and dissemination of the practice of combat operations within enemy formations, especially raid operations;
4. the initiation of battle at increasingly greater distances;
5. the growth of the significance of the "information struggle," having as its goal the steering of the enemy in the direction of one's own plans and intentions.[10]

It is clear that the Soviets believe the pace of technological change has quickened, and will continue to quicken, with possible unforeseen consequences. A political corollary for dealing with this uncertainty is to display a defensive posture, in order to slow the pace of change and to gain time and resources to foster R&D necessary to deal with it. In this sense, a high-profile defensive stance would accord with the traditional Soviet understanding that in military art the defense is a temporary state which facilitates future resumption of the offensive. The litmus test of Soviet defensive sincerity is whether a similar defensive orientation appears at the operational and tactical levels.

Since January 1988, Soviet military publications have begun to include articles on defensive operational and tactical techniques. These articles appear to be in direct response to promulgation by the Soviet political and military leadership of a defensive military doctrine. In fact, many of these articles make direct reference to the new Soviet doctrine, as if deliberately illustrative of the new trend. While the total number of offensive articles has diminished somewhat, the tone of the articles has not changed.

This offensive scheme posits certain distinct requirements, among which are:

- the achievement of a degree of surprise to create necessary force superiorities and gain initial advantage. This involves deception regarding attack intentions, timing, location, and scale.
- avoidance of major attack indicators. This requires renunciation of large scale mobilization, extensive pre-war theater preparations, and use of selective mobilization techniques.
- reliance on shallow strategic, operational, and tactical echelonment to offset lack of mobilization, to reap maximum surprise, and to establish high initial offensive momentum.
- early commitment of tactical and operational maneuver forces to achieve rapid penetration, to enmesh forces quickly, to avoid enemy nuclear response, and to diminish the effectiveness of enemy high precision fires.
- development, and proliferation to the lowest command level (battalion), of advanced cybernetic techniques to speed planning and increase the efficiency of command and control during combat.

In addition to meeting these requirements, the Soviets now believe the presence of high precision weapons on the battlefield requires the careful tailoring of combat forces at all levels, in order for these forces to be able to sustain operations and survive as they seek to achieve their missions on a more fragmented battlefield. Consequently, the Soviets seem intent upon converting their entire force structure to the operational maneuver group and forward detachment model, on the presumption that what suits these maneuver forces probably suits other line forces as well. This portends Soviet adoption, in whole or in part, of a corps, brigade, and tailored combined arms battalion force structure.

Future developments will reveal to what degree the Soviets are wedded to these offensive concepts, and how sincere they are regarding the newly proclaimed "defensiveness" of their military doctrine. Given the growing ambiguity regarding distinctions between the offensive and the defense at the operational and tactical levels, the answer to the question of how sincere the Soviets are probably rests at the doctrinal level; that is, to what degree actual Soviet policies, and military force levels and structure reflect "defensiveness."

FORCE STRUCTURE

The Soviets will continue to alter their force structure in response to changing technology and altered requirements of the modern battlefield. Forces at all levels will continue to move away from the more austere, armor-heavy structure of the 1960s, which was keyed first and foremost to nuclear survivability, to a new structure more reminiscent of the mid-to-late 1950s. Specifically, the Soviets will tailor force TOEs to permit units to deal with the more heavily urbanized terrain of the 1980s and 1990s and the increased proliferation of more sophisticated battlefield weaponry. This process will involve an increase in the motorized rifle (or mechanized) component of armored forces at division, army, and *front* level.[11] Tank or mechanized armies, and new tank, mechanized, or combined arms corps will be better balanced vis-à-vis armor and armored infantry and will move to a square configuration (one to three tank and one to three motorized rifle or mechanized units) similar to the older mechanized armies and mechanized divisions of the mid-1950s. Within these forces, and other units as well, will be found greater amounts of artillery (antitank, antiaircraft and gun), increased sapper support, and a helicopter component as well. In a sense, future changes will parallel those undertaken in 1946, when the Soviets set about creating forces suited to conventional combat in a central European environment (the 1945 Soviet armored and mechanized force structure was the product primarily of operational experiences in southern Russia and Poland, where terrain was essentially flat, open, and rural).

Re-publication in 1985 of a 1946 speech by General P. A. Rotmistrov to GOFG (Group of Occupation Forces Germany) probably underscores Soviet belief that they face force structure problems similar to those they faced in 1946 — namely to replace the former armor-heavy force with a balanced combined arms force which can cope with warfare in an age of high technology weaponry, on an increasingly urbanized and forested battlefield in central Europe, as well as in other varied regions of the world. Rotmistrov, then chief of armored and mechanized forces in GOFG, analysed First Belorussian Front armored operations during the Berlin operation and concluded that the Soviet force structure was too tank-heavy and that it lacked the combined arms balance necessary to fight successfully in more heavily forested, urbanized, and hilly central Europe.[12] Re-publication of Rotmistrov's speech, in all likelihood, signifies that the process of force structure reform is well underway, if not nearly complete. This restructuring is likely to reach down to regimental and battalion level as the Soviets provide these units and subunits with a combined arms mix more suited for their increasingly independent role in operations.

Along with implementing basic structural changes, the Soviets have experimented with new types of forces modeled closely, in their combined arms mix, after the former mobile groups and forward detachments. Experience has shown the Soviets believe offensive success has depended, and will continue to depend, on effective conduct of maneuver through use of maneuver groups. To be effective these groups must possess combat qualities which distinguish them from the remainder of the force structure. In the past (prior to 1954) armored or mechanized forces played this role because their superior firepower and maneuverability accorded them marked advantage over foot or hoofbound forces. In earlier stages of mechanization and motorization (1955 to 1960), tracked units were used because of their firepower, superior cross-country mobility, and reduced vulnerability to nuclear effects. More recently (the 1970s) armor-heavy units have performed the role because of their strength and speed.

Today armor is integrated throughout the force structure, and most units are highly mechanized. In addition, proliferation of sophisticated anti-tank weaponry and other fire support means has forced the Soviets to look for other attributes which can provide necessary unique qualities to operational and tactical maneuver forces. They believe they have found the answer through development of sophisticated, integrated concepts for operational and tactical maneuver; careful tailoring of maneuver forces to improve their survivability and sustainability; development of command and control measures suited to such operations; employment of pre-combat formations which permit units to fight in other than linear formation; exploitation of the time factor in operations by the use of norms and operational and tactical calculations in both routine planning and planning during combat; and, finally, increased reliance on the vertical dimension of maneuver.

Current sophisticated Soviet maneuver concepts, involving concerted use of multiple tactical and operational maneuver groups, exploit the fact that quantity has a quality of its own. Multiple maneuver groups operate in tandem, employing techniques specifically designed to pre-empt, unhinge, and paralyze a defense. Their sheer number contributes to the likelihood of their success.

Extensive Soviet study of past operational and tactical maneuver indicates they must continue to pay close attention to the structure of operational and tactical maneuver groups. The necessity for concealing both their intent to employ maneuver and the manner in which they will conduct it, requires that they pay increased attention to combat deception. While it is virtually impossible for the Soviets to conceal their intent to employ maneuver, it is possible, through use of deception to conceal those forces which will conduct it. This the Soviets have done extensively and effectively in the past.

Deception will make it difficult for Westerners to ascertain the exact Soviet force structure, to detect accurately alterations in that structure, and to identify which units will perform precise missions. It is likely the Soviet peacetime force structure does not actually mirror wartime structure (at least in terms of unit designations), and peacetime order of battle almost certainly does not reflect wartime order of battle.[13]

What has been written thus far reflects military reality as the Soviets see it. The changes which have occurred accord with that reality. To these purely military considerations of force structuring now must be added new political and economic considerations. Since early 1987 the Soviets have enunciated a "defensive" military doctrine based on what they call "reasonable sufficiency" in terms of force levels and force composition. Both "defensiveness" and "reasonable sufficiency" are principally political aspects of Soviet military doctrine reflecting a new Soviet military stance suited to new global and domestic political and economic realities. The principal political realities are the slow erosion in the political dominance of the United States in the West and the growth of new power centers in Western Europe, the Far East, and in the Third World. This changing world political order may make diplomacy and appeals to public opinion as potent political tools as the looming presence of stark military force, and much less dangerous for contending parties. Economic crises in both the United States and the Soviet Union also make military force a far less appealing tool of international diplomacy. In a more practical sense the Soviets require that economic assets be shifted from the military to the economic sphere to shore up or rebuild the Soviet economy and fulfill the promises of *perestroika*.

The new political and economic realities also impel the Soviets to stress efficiency in the military and to emphasize quality over quantity in the future. In this sense the military, political, and economic motives are converging to produce a new Soviet military force structure and military posture. Which motives remain the strongest and what consequences will ensue only time and Soviet actions will reveal.

Several tentative judgments can be made concerning the future Soviet force structure. All are based on the premise that both tactical and operational maneuver [mobile] forces will continue to exist in peacetime and will be used, when required, in wartime. Currently, the Soviet wartime force structure appears to consist of *fronts* containing three–four combined arms and one–two tank armies. Armies consist of a combination of tank and motorized rifle divisions and separate specialized units (see table 113). Tank armies perform the function of operational maneuver at *front* level, either singly or in pairs. Within the combined arms army, the tank division performs the same function. Separate tank regiments of combined arms armies (the size of former tank corps) and separate tank battalions of motorized rifle divisions (the size of former tank brigades) perform the tactical maneuver function. Designated operational and tactical maneuver forces today probably already secretly carry the designation they have had in the past, that of corps and brigade.[14]

TABLE 113

CURRENT SOVIET GROUND FORCE STRUCTURE

UNIT	FUNCTION
Front	
3-4 combined arms armies	
1-2 tank armies	operational maneuver
Combined Arms Army	
2-4 motorized rifle divisions	
1-2 tank divisions	operational maneuver
1 separate tank regiment	tactical maneuver
Tank Army	
2-4 tank divisions	
1-2 motorized rifle divisions	
1 separate tank regiment	tactical maneuver
Motorized Rifle Division	
3 motorized rifle regiments	
1 tank regiment	
1 separate tank battalion	tactical maneuver
Tank Division	operational maneuver
3 tank regiment	
1 motorized rifle regiment	

The Soviets may overtly convert *front* operational maneuver groups into corps configuration (see table 114). In this case tank armies would consist of a combination of tank and mechanized corps, with tank corps tank-heavy and mechanized corps balanced combined arms entities. The corps will include a separate tank or motorized rifle brigade to serve as corps forward detachment, together with carefully tailored support.

Within combined arms armies, tank or mechanized corps will conduct operational maneuver and employ their own tactical maneuver force in the process. Separate tank corps or brigades will serve as army forward detachments. Motorized rifle divisions will employ separate tank or motorized rifle brigades as their forward detachments. The Soviets will continue to employ air assault forces in cooperation with operational and tactical maneuver forces. In some instances, air assault units will perform the maneuver function in their own right.[15] While multiple air assault brigades or a full air assault corps will cooperate with a *front* or an army OMG, air assault

TABLE 114
FUTURE SOVIET FORCE STRUCTURE: MIXED DIVISION AND CORPS
STRUCTURE

OPTION 1

UNIT	FUNCTION
Front	
2-4 combined arms armies	
1-2 tank armies	operational maneuver
Combined Arms Army	
3-4 motorized rifle divisions	
1 tank on mechanized corps	operational maneuver
1 separate tank brigade	tactical maneuver
Tank Army	operational maneuver
2 tank corps	
1-2 mechanized corps	
1 separate tank brigade	tactical maneuver
Motorized Rifle Division	
3 motorized rifle regiments	
1 tank regiment	
1 separate tank brigage	tactical maneuver
Tank Corps	operational maneuver
3-4 tank brigades	
1 motorized rifle brigade	
Mechanized Corps	operational maneuver
3-4 mechanized brigades	
1-2 tank brigades	

brigades will operate in tandem with either army OMGs or the army forward detachment, and an air assault battalion (heliborne) will cooperate with either the army forward detachments or similar divisional entities. The motorized rifle division will employ an air assault company or battalion to support division forward detachment operations.[16]

The Soviets can conceal operational and tactical maneuver elements within their force structure, and satisfy political and economic purposes as well, by converting the entire force structure to corps configuration (see table 115). In this case both combined arms armies and new mechanized [tank] armies would consist of a varied mix of tank, mechanized, and motorized rifle corps (former divisions), each of which would consist of a differing mixture of brigades. In addition, the Soviets may re-create formations which they formerly called fortified regions (*ukreplennyi raion*). In the

TABLE 115

FUTURE SOVIET FORCE STRUCTURE: CORPS AND BRIGADE STRUCTURE

OPTION 2

UNIT	FUNCTION
Front	
1-3 combined arms armies	
1-2 mechanized armies	operational maneuver
Combined Arms Army	operational maneuver
2-4 motorized rifle corps or	
fortified regions	
1 tank or mechanized corps	
Mechanized Army	
1-2 tank corps	
1 mechanized corps	
Tank Corps	
3 tank brigades	
1 mechanized brigade	
1 air assault brigade	
Mechanized Corps	
2 mechanized brigades	
2 tank brigades	
1 air assault brigade	
Motorized Rifle Corps	
3 motorized rifle brigades	
1 mechanized or tank brigade	
Fortified Region	
2-3 fortification brigades	
1-2 motorized rifle or	
mechanized brigades	

the past these ostensibly defensive entities operated as economy of force units both on the defense and during offensive operations. Soviet experience indicates that these formations could also be termed defensive regions. If so designated, their subordinate units would likely be called fortified regions. Specific types of these new corps and brigades would perform operational and tactical maneuver functions while the remaining units would fulfill a wide range of general combat tasks. Adoption of a corps structure would not only conceal the operational and tactical maneuver core of the Soviet armed forces, it would also blur distinctions and comparisons between NATO and Soviet forces and accord potential advantage to the Soviets in MBFR discussions. The tailoring involved in creating such a force could permit reduction in overall force strength and in the overall quantity of some weapons systems (most notably, tanks and tube artillery) and create perceptions in the West of a reduced threat, whether or not the threat actually diminishes.

Much of the impetus for the Soviet desire to recreate a corps and brigade structure arises from their belief that flexibility will be essential in future operations and that requisite flexibility can only be realized by means of careful tailoring of self-sufficient force entities at corps and brigade level. This relates also to the Soviets' recent judgment that such flexibility and independence will be necessary at battalion level as well.

At the tactical level the Soviets are already committed to tailoring forces to a greater extent than in the past. In 1986 Colonel General D.A. Dragunsky noted "the revived capabilities of the battalion, and the increased significance of the independent operations of subunits, naturally places great demands on the commander."[17] Dragunsky's work reflects a growing trend among Soviet theorists to argue for greater tailoring of forces at regimental and battalion level, so that these forces can operate more independently and better sustain operations.

The tailoring process is likely to involve reassignment to army level of those forces and weapons not of immediate use to battalions, regiments and divisions (or brigades and corps). Conversely, forces and weapons of immediate use to battalions and regiments, such as antitank, self-propelled artillery, anti-aircraft, tactical bridging, engineer assets, some helicopter lift, etc. will be assigned to those subunits and units in greater quantities. In essence, the Soviets will create battalion tactical groups formed around the nucleus of tank and motorized rifle battalions which will be similar to flexibly tailored groups at brigade and corps level.

The new Soviet combined arms army will consist of those type corps required to perform its mission. Normally, it will include a nucleus of motorized rifle corps and fortified regions to perform defensive missions and, on occasion, a tank or mechanized corps to cooperate with the motorized rifle corps in performing offensive missions. The mechanized army will consist of tank and mechanized corps. Armies will be tailored in their make-up to suit specific operating conditions. Soviet wartime *fronts* will consist of from three to five armies. The normal balance of forces will consist of one to three combined arms armies and one to two mechanized armies with tailored supporting arms.

There are other possible variations the Soviets could adopt in their force restructuring program. For example, they could reduce the number of type corps by creating only two types, such as tank and mechanized, tank and motorized rifle, or mechanized and motorized rifle corps. Likewise, they could create a second type motorized rifle corps with heavier weaponry in place of the fortified region. An even more radical restructuring could involve the abolition of the army level of command and the direct sub-ordination of multiple corps to *fronts*. In wartime however, the army level of command is likely to re-emerge.

The new Soviet force structure, characterized by force tailoring at all levels, will better match the current Soviet claim that "With the enemy using high precision weapons, the role of the first echelon has to grow. It must be capable of achieving a mission without the second echelon."[18] In light of the Gorbachev 7 December 1988 speech and subsequent pronouncements it appears that the Soviets may have chosen the second option, that is, conversion to a full corps and brigade structure, or another option even more defensive in its appearance.[19] It remains to be seen to what degree and at what speed these force changes will take place.

CONCLUSION

The Soviets will keep abreast of technological changes in weaponry and will study the impact of those changes at all levels of war in all environments. They have already recognized the significance of the cosmos in the strategic realm. They are no doubt improving their ABM capability and developing laser and particle beam technology in the antisatellite and missile defense field. They understand well the dilemma of modern antitank and tank warfare and are likely to progress with a program to develop laser battlefield weaponry (antitank and antiaircraft) and new passive defenses against such weaponry (such as small armored vehicles and new types of armor). As they develop these new weapons and defenses against them, they will adjust their force structure to accommodate new realities in weaponry after extensive experimentation and field testing.

Above all, the Soviets will develop and articulate doctrine, publicly and internally, to suit their own particular political goals, in consonance with economic and other realities. Fundamental changes in the thrust, and not just the semantics, of Soviet doctrine will become apparent only when Soviet military science and force-structure also change. Only those changes, as a part of a necessary unity within doctrine, will indicate the true meaning of current concepts of "defensiveness" and "reasonable sufficiency."

In the realms of military technique and force structuring, the Soviets will pursue the Clausewitzian dictum that, in the absence of real practice in war, one must study the past experiences of war. As convinced devotees of this view, the Soviets will tap their militarily rich past for general inspiration and precise guidance on the proper techniques for conducting war. To deal properly with the complex Soviet threat, one must be aware of that rich experience and the context in which the Soviets use it.

NOTES

CHAPTER ONE

1. "Istoriia" [History], *Sovetskaia istoricheskaia entsiklopediia* [Soviet historical encyclopedia] (Moskva: Izdatel'stvo "Sovetskaia Entsiklopediia," 1965), 6:578–590.
2. D. A. Volkagonov, S. A. Tiushkevich, "Voina" [War], *Sovetskaia voennaia entsiklopediia* [Soviet military encyclopedia] 8 vols. (Moskva: Voenizdat, 1976), 2:301. Hereafter cited as *SVE* with appropriate date, volume and page.
3. *Slovar' osnovnykh voennykh terminov* [Dictionary of basic military terms] (Moskva: Voenizdat, 1965), translated and published by U.S. Air Force, 1977, 37. Hereafter cited as *Slovar*; see also "Doktrina voennaia" [Military doctrine], *SVE* 1976, 3:225–229.
4. A. A. Grechko, "Voennaia nauka" [Military science], *SVE* 1976, 2:183–184.
5. V. E. Savkin, *Osnovnye printsipy operativnogo isskustva i taktika* [The basic principles of operational art and tactics] (Moskva: Voenizdat, 1972), 99–112.
6. S. A. Tiushkevich, "*Zakony i obychai voiny*" [Laws and customs of war], *SVE* 1977, 3:375–378.
7. S. P. Ivanov, A. I. Evseev, "Voennoe iskusstvo" [Military art], *SVE* 1976, 2:211.
8. "Voennoe iskusstvo" [Military art], *Voennyi entsiklopedicheskii slovar'* [Military encyclopedic dictionary] (Moskva: Voenizdat, 1983). Hereafter cited as *VES*.
9. A. A. Sidorenko, "Printsipy voennogo isskustva" [Principles of military art], *SVE* 1978, 6:542–543.
10. Ibid.
11. N. V. Ogarkov, "Voennaia strategiia" [Military strategy], *SVE* 1979, 7:555.
12. See bibliography.
13. V. G. Kulakov, "Operativnoe iskusstvo" [Operational art], *SVE* 1978, 6:53.
14. I. G. Borets, "Taktika" [Tactics], *SVE* 1979, 7:628–634.

CHAPTER TWO

1. V. G. Kulakov, "Operativnoe iskusstvo" [Operational art], *SVE* 1978, 6:53.
2. Ibid.
3. V. G. Reznichenko, *Taktika* [Tactics] (Moskva: Voenizdat, 1966).
4. Kulakov, 55.
5. Ibid., 54.
6. "Predislovie" [Preface], *Voprosy strategii i operativnogo iskusstva v sovetskikh voennykh trudakh (1917–1940 gg)* [Questions of strategy and operational art in Soviet military works (1917–1940] (Moskva: Voenizdat, 1965), 11 (hereafter cited as *Voprosy strategii*).
7. Ibid., 10.
8. S. S. Kamenev, "Ocherednye voennye zadachi" [Successive military objectives], *Voprosy strategii*, 149–152.
9. Zakharov, 12. For a view of how Tukhachevsky expanded this view into a broader concept of deep battle, see Tukhachevsky, "Voprosy sovremennoi strategii" [Questions of modern strategy], "Voina" [War] and "Novye voprosy voiny" [New

questions of war], *Voprosy strategii*, 90–144.

10. Ibid.

11. V. Matsulenko, "Razvitie operativnogo iskusstva v nastupatel'nykh operatsiiakh" [The development of operational art in offensive operations], *Voenno–Istoricheskii Zhurnal* [Military Historical Journal], No.10 (Oct. 1967) :39–40 (hereafter cited as *VIZh*).

12. Zakharov, 13.

13. M. N. Tukhachevsky, "Voina" [War], 1926, *Voprosy strategii*, 104–105.

14. A. A. Svechin, "Strategiia" [Strategy], 1927, *Voprosy strategii*, 220.

15. Zakharov, 12. For details see, V. K. Triandafillov, "Kharakter operatsii sovremennykh armii" [The characteristics of modern army operations], 1929, *Voprosy strategii*, 291–345.

16. V. Matsulenko, "Razvitie taktiki nastupatel'nogo boia" [The development of the tactics of offensive battle], *VIZh*, No. 2 (Feb. 1968): 28–29; M. Zakharov, "O teorii glubokoi operatsii" [Concerning the theory of deep operations], *VIZh*, No. 10 (Oct. 1970): 10–13.

17. V. Daines, "Razvitie taktiki obshchevoiskovogo nastupatel'nogo boia v 1929–1941 gg" [The development of the tactics of combined arms offensive battle in 1929–1941], *VIZh*, No. 10 (Oct. 1978): 96.

18. Zakharov, 22.

19. A. Konenenko, "Boi vo Flandrii" [Battle in Flanders], *VIZh* No. 3 (March 1941): 25.

20. Zakharov, 23.

21. Kulakov, 55.

22. Contents of Directive No. 3, Order No. 306 and Order No. 325, described in A. Radzievsky, "Proryv oborony v pervom periode voiny" [Penetration of a defense in the first period of war], *VIZh*, No. 3 (March 1972): 17–18; "Prikaz NKO No. 306 ot 8 oktiabria 1942 g" [Order of the People's Commissariat of Defense No. 306 of 8 Oct. 1942], *VIZh*, No. 9 (Sept. 1974): 62–66; and "Prikaz NKO No. 325 ot 16 oktiabria 1942" [Order of the People's Commissariat of Defense No. 325 of 16 Oct. 1942], *VIZh*, No. 10 (Oct. 1974): 68–73.

23. "Directive of the General Staff Concerning the Study and Application of War Experience, 9 November 1942 No. 1005216, Inclosure: Instructions Concerning the Study and Application of War Experience in Army Group (*Front*) and Army Staffs," translated by U.S. Army General Staff G–2, 277.

24. *Polevoi ustav Krasnoi Armii 1942* [Field Regulation of the Red Army 1942] (Moskva: Voenizdat, 1942), translated by the Office of the Assistant Chief of Staff, G–2, GSUSA.

25. *Polevoi ustav Krasnoi Armii 1944 (Pu–44)* [Field Regulation of the Red Army 1944) (Moskva: Voenizdat, 1944], translated by Office of the Assistant Chief of Staff, G–2, GSUSA.

26. *Nastavlenie po proryvu pozitsionnoi oborony (proekt)* [Instructions on the penetration of a positional defense (project)] (Moskva: Voenizdat, 1944), translated by the Directorate of Military Intelligence, Army Headquarters, Ottawa, Canada, 73.

27. "Changes in the articles of the Field Manual Project, pertaining to the military employment of cavalry", *Sbornik materialov po izucheniia opyta voiny, No. 2, sentiabr'-oktiabr'-1942 gg* [Collection of materials for the study of war experience, No. 2, September–October 1942] (Moskva: Voenizdat, 1942), translated by US Army General Staff, G–2, Eurasian branch.

28. M. Burshtynovich, "Bases of Offensive Battle of a Rifle Regiment and Battalion," *Voennyi Vestnik* Jan. 1947, as quoted in Raymond Gartoff, *Soviet Military Doctrine* (Glencoe, Illinois: The Free Press, 1953), 69.

29. N. P. Polev, *Nastupatel'nyi boi strelkovogo korpusa* [Offensive battle of the rifle corps], I.V. Frunze Military Academy of the Red Army – Lesson: translated by Office of the Assistant Chief of Staff, G–2, GSUSA, 24 May 1954, 2–3.

30. Ibid., 3.
31. Z. Zlobin, "Sovremennaia frontovaia operatsiia" [Contemporary *front* operations], *Voennaia Mysl'* [Military Thought] April–May 1945, translated by The Directorate of Military Intelligence, Army Headquarters, Ottawa, Canada, 3.
32. Yu Kostin, "Air Landings in Contemporary Operations," *Voennaia Mysl'* [Military Thought] Aug. 1946, translated by USA General Staff, G–2, Eurasian branch, 11–12.
33. I.V. Maryganov, *Peredovoi kharakter sovetskoi voennoi nauki* [The advanced character of Soviet military science] (Moskva: Voenizdat, 1953), 100–101.
34. V. A. Semenov, *Kratkii ocherk razvitiia sovetskogo operativnogo iskusstva* [A short sketch of the development of Soviet military art] (Moskva: Voenizdat, 1960), 114.
35. Ibid., 287–288.
36. Ibid., 289.
37. V. D. Sokolovsky, *Voennaia Strategiia* [Military Strategy] (Moskva: Voenizdat, 1968), translated by Foreign Technology Division (FTD), 192–193.
38. Ibid., 209.
39. Ibid.
40. A. A. Strokov, ed., *Istoriia voennogo iskusstva* [History of Military Art] (Moskva: Voenizdat, 1966), 612.
41. See the following works: P. A. Kurochkin, ed., *Obshchevoiskovaia armiia v nastuplenii* [The combined arms army in the offensive] (Moskva: Voenizdat, 1966); A.I. Radzievsky, ed., *Armeiskie operatsii* [Army operations] (Moskva: Voenizdat, 1977); I. E. Krupchenko, ed., *Sovetskie tankovye voiska 1941–1945* [Soviet tank forces 1942–1945] (Moskva: Voenizdat, 1973); P.A. Rotmistrov, *Vremia i tanki* [Time and Tanks] (Moskva: Voenizdat, 1972); A. I. Radzievsky, *Tankovyi Udar* [Tank blow] (Moskva: Voenizdat, 1977); A. I. Radzievsky, *Proryv* [Penetration] (Moskva: Voenizdat, 1979); O.A. Losik, ed., *Stroitel'stvo i boevoe primenenie sovetskikh tankovykh voisk v gody Velikoi Otechestvennoi voiny* [The formation and use of Soviet tank forces in the years of the Great Patriotic War] (Moskva: Voenizdat, 1979); I. I. Lisov, *Desantniki-vozdushnye desanty* [Airlanding troops – airlandings] (Moskva: Voenizdat, 1968); D. S. Sukhorukov, *Sovetskie vozdushno-desantnye* [Soviet airlanding forces] (Moskva: Voenizdat,1980); I. Kh Bagramian, ed., *Istoriia voin i voennogo iskusstva* [History of Wars and Military Art] (Moskva: Voenizdat, 1970); and V. E. Savkin, *Osnovnye printsipy operativnogo iskusstva i taktiki* [The basic principles of operational art and tactics] (Moskva: Voenizdat, 1972).
42. Kulakov, 57.
43. Sokolovsky, 209.
44. Ibid., 289.
45. Ibid., 300.
46. Kulakov, 56.
47. Ibid.
48. Ibid., 57.
49. Ibid., 57; F. Graivoronski, "Razvitie sovetskogo operativnogo iskusstva" [The development of Soviet operational art], *VIZh* No. 2 (Feb. 1978): 24–25.
50. V. G. Reznichenko, *Taktika* [Tactics] (Moskva: Voenizdat, 1987), 206.
51. M. Zakharov, "Teorii glubokoi operatsii" [Concerning the theory of deep operations], *VIZh* No. 10 (Oct. 1970): 20.

CHAPTER THREE

1. N. N. Kuznetsov, "Strategicheskaia tsel'" [Strategic aim], *SVE* 1979, 7:552; see also N. V. Ogarkov, *et al.*, ed, *VES*, 710.
2. "Teatr voiny" [The theater of war], *SVE* 1980, 8:9.; M. M. Kozlov, "Teatr voennykh deistvii" [The theater of military operations], *SVE* 1980, 8:9; *VES*, 732.

3. "Strategicheskoe napravlenie" [The strategic direction], *SVE* 1979, 7:555; *VES*, 711.
4. "Strategicheskaia zadacha" [The strategic mission], *SVE* 1979, 7:550; *VES*, 710.
5. "Operatsionnoe napravlenie" [The operational direction], *SVE* 1978, 6:64 (Moskva: Voenizdat, 1978), 6:64; *VES*, 516.
6. "Operativnaia zadacha" [The operational mission], *SVE* 1978, 6:50; *VES*, 514.
7. *VES*, 516; M. M. Kir'ian, "Operatsiia" [The operation], *SVE* 1978, 6:64–67. The Soviets also recognize the term campaign (*kampaniia*) as "a series of strategic operations and other forms of military actions in a continental or ocean theater of military operations united by an overall concept and directed at the achievement of important military-political aims." The campaign represents a separate stage of war usually designated by calendar limits (year, season) and the name of a country or region which the theater of military operations encompasses. The campaign, lacking a unifying plan, is a more general term than operation. The Soviets have deemphasized its use as an analytical category in the post-war years. See M. I. Cherednichenko, "Kampaniia" [The campaign], *SVE*, 1977, 9:55–56.
8. *VES*, 516.
9. M. I. Cherednichenko, "Strategicheskaia operatsiia" [The strategic operation], *SVE* 1979, 7:551–552; *VES*, 710.
10. *VES*, 710. This qualification does not appear in the Soviet Military Encyclopedia definition of 1979.
11. Ibid., 787; M. M. Kozlov, "Frontovaia nastupatel'naia operatsiia" [The *front* offensive operation], *SVE*, 1980, 8:336.
12. *VES*, 787.
13. Ibid., 788; M. M. Kozlov, "Frontovaia oboronitel'naia operatsiia" [The *front* defensive operation], *SVE* 1980, 8:339.
14. M. M. Kir'ian, "Armeiskaia nastupatel'naia operatsiia" [The army offensive operation], *SVE* 1976, 1:239; *VES*, 43; K.L. Kushch-Zharko, "Armeiskaia oboronitel'naia operatsiia" [The army defensive operation], *SVE* 1976, 1:245.
15. *VES*, 505; "Ob'edinenie" [The large unit, union], *SVE* 1978, 5:679–680.
16. *VES*, 688; G.A. Parkhalin, " Soedinenie" [Formation, combination], *SVE* 1979, 7:426–427.

CHAPTER FOUR

1. "Lenin", *VES*, 397; N. N. Azovtsev, E.I. Rybkin, "Lenin", *SVE*, 1977, 4:599–611.
2. Ibid.
3. Ibid.
4. "Lenin", *VES*, 398.
5. N. V. Ogarkov, "Strategiia voennaia" [Military strategy], *SVE*, 1979, 7:560.
6. N. Kh. Bagramian, ed., *Istoriia voin i voennogo isskusstva* [A history of wars and military art] (Moskva: Voenizdat, 1970), 83. A.A. Strokov, ed., *Istoriia voennogo iskusstva* [A history of military art] (Moskva: Voenizdat, 1966) and M. M. Kozlov, "Frontovaia nastupatel'naia operatsiia" [The *front* offensive operation], *SVE*, 1980, 8:336–339 cite differing figures. Bagramian's figures include the long eastern front offensive in 1919–20.

	Strokov	Kozlov
offensive sector	300–500 km	400–600 km
offensive depth	200–300 km	200–300 km
duration of offensive	30–50 days	25–30 days
tempo of advance	6–10 km/day	6–10 km/day – rifle forces
		15–20 km/day – cavalry forces

7. For a thorough survey of Civil War military theory and practice and force organization see G.V. Kuz'min, *Grazhdanskaia voina i voennaia interventsiia v SSSR* [The Civil War and military intervention in the USSR] (Moskva: Voenizdat, 1958); *Direktivy komandovaniia frontov Krasnoi Armii 1917–1922 gg.* [Directives of the Red Army's *front* commands 1917–1922] (Moskva: Voenizdat, 1978), 4. Hereafter cited as *Directivy*.

8. Bagramian, 85. See also I. Krasnov, "Kharakternye cherty nastupatel'nykh operatsii Krasnoi Armii v grazhdanskoi voine" [The characteristic features of offensive operations of the Red Army in the Civil War], *VIZh* No.3 (March 1976): 96–102.

9. *Direktivy*.

10. Bagramian, 86–87. See also V. Kulikovsky, "Razvitie taktiki Krasnoi Armii v gody grazhdanskoi voiny" [The development of Red Army tactics in the Civil War], *VIZh* No. 12 (Dec. 1971): 69–75.

11. "Edinaia voennaia doktrina i Krasnaia Armiia" [The unified military doctrine and the Red Army], *SVE*, 1977, 3:300. See also R. H. Baker, "The Origins of Soviet Military Doctrine," *Journal of the Royal United Services Institute for Defense Studies*, No. 3 (March 1976): 38–43.

12. Baker, 39.

13. M. V. Frunze, "Front i tyl v voine budushchego" [The front and rear in future war], *Voprosy strategii i operativnogo iskusstva v sovetskikh voennykh trudakh 1917–1940 gg.* [Questions of strategy and operational art in Soviet military works – 1917–1940] (Moskva: Voenizdat, 1965), 64–65, hereafter cited as *Voprosy strategii*.

14. I. B. Berkhin, *Voennaia reforma v SSSR 1924–1925* [Military reform in the USSR – 1924–1925] (Moskva: Voenizdat, 1958). A rifle corps consisted of two to three rifle divisions, an artillery battalion and support units.

15. S. S. Kamenev, "Ocherednye voennye zadachi" [Successive military objectives], *Voprosy strategii*, 149–152.

16. M. Zakharaov, "Predislovie" [Preface], *Voprosy strategii*, 12.

17. V. K. Triandafillov, "Kharakter operatsii sovremennykh armii" [The character of operations of modern armies], *Voprosy strategii*, 291–345.

18. Bagramian, 103. For details on the nature of successive operations, see R. Savushkin, "K voprosu o zarozhdenii teorii posledovatel'nykh nastupatel'nykh operatsii – 1921–1929 gg." [Concerning the creation of the theory of successive offensive operations – 1921–1929], *VIZh* No.5 (May 1983): 77–83.

19. V. Matsulenko, "Razvitie operativnogo iskusstva v nastupatel'nykh operatisiiakh" [The development of operational art in offensive operations], *VIZh* No. 10 (Oct. 1967): 39–40.

20. A. A. Svechin, "Strategiia" [Strategy], *Voprosy istorii*, 238.

21. Bagramian, 103.

22. V. Matsulenko, "Razvitie taktiki nastupatel'nogo boia" [The development of the tactics of offensive battle], *VIZh* No. 2 (Feb. 1968): 28–29; M. Zakharov, "O teorii glubokoi operatsii" [Concerning the theory of deep operations], *VIZh* No. 10 (Oct. 1970): 10–13.

23. A. Riazansky, "The Creation and Development of Tank–Troop Tactics in the Pre–War Period," *Voennyi vestnik* [Military Herald] (Nov. 1966): 25–32, translated in *Selected Readings in Military History: Soviet Military History 1, The Red Army 1918–1945* (Combat Studies Institute, Ft Leavenworth, Kansas, 1984). Hereafter cited as *VV*.

24. Bagramian, 102; Strokov, 311.

25. Ogarkov, "Strategiia voennaia," 561.

26. N. V. Ogarkov, "Glubokaia operatsiia" [The deep operation] *SVE* 1976, 2:574; V. Daines, "Razvitie taktiki obshchevoiskovogo nastupatel'nogo boia v 1929–1941 gg" [The development of the tactics of combined arms offensive battle – 1929–1941], *VIZh*, No. 10 (Oct. 1978): 96.

27. I. Korotkov, "Voprosy obshchei taktiki v sovetskoi voennoi istoriografii – 1918–1941 gg" [Questions of general tactics in soviet military historiography – 1918–1941], *VIZh*, No. 12 (Dec. 1977): 89.
28. Daines, 96.
29. Kozlov, "Frontovaia ...," 337.
30. Bagramian, 106.
31. Ogarkov, "Glubokaia operatsiia", 576; Matsulenko, "Razvitie operativenogo iskusstva ....," 40, states that shock armies contained three–four rifle corps.
32. Strokov, 316.
33. Strokov, 317; Bagramian, 108.
34. Bagramian, 110; Daines, 96–101; Strokov, 318–321.
35. Strokov, 321. For details on Soviet employment of tank echelons see R. A. Savushkin, N. M. Ramanichev, "Razvitia taktiki obshchevoiskovogo boia v period mezhdu grazhdanskoi i Velikoi Otechestvennoi voinami" [The development of combined arms battle tactics in the period between the Civil War and Great Patriotic War], *VIZh*, No. 11 (Nov. 1985), 21–28. Confirmed by Western reports among which is P. R. Faymonville, "The Use of Tanks in Combat Under the Provisions of the Field Service Regulations on 1936," Enclosure 1 to *Dispatch 857–350* (American Embassy, Office of the Military Attaché, USSR: 26 May 1937). Similar attaché reports from Riga (Latvia), Tallin (Estonia), and Warsaw (Poland) substantiate in detail Soviet armored force developments in the 1930s.
36. On 1 January 1938 Red Army strength was 1,518,400 men. K. F. Skorobogatkin, ed., *50 let vooruzhennykh sil SSSR* [50 years of the Soviet Armed Forces] (Moskva: Voenizdat, 1968), 198, hereafter cited as *50 let*.
37. The most detailed account of mechanized force development in the 1930s is in A. Ryzhakov, "K voprosy o stroitel'stve bronetankovykh voisk Krasnoi Armii v 30–e gody" [Concerning the formation of Red Army armored forces in the 1930s], *VIZh*, No. 8 (Aug. 1968): 105–111. Numerous Western reports (formerly classified) substantiate Soviet creation of this large mechanized–armored force structure. These include *Intelligence Summary for April 20, 1934* (Washington, D.C.: Military Intelligence Division (G–2), War Department General Staff, 1934), 14706–14714; *Intelligence Summary for May 4, 1934* (Washington, D.C.: Military Intelligence Division (G–2), War Department General Staff, 1934), 14730–14736; *Intelligence Summary for Dec. 24, 1937* (Washington, D.C.: Military Intelligence Division (G–2); War Department General Staff, 1937), no pagination; "Organization of Motor–Mechanized Units," *Soviet Russia G–2 Report* (Washington, D.C.: Military Intelligence Division, War Department 28 Nov 1933), 1–3; "Progress of Motorization and Mechanization in the Red Army," *Soviet Russia G-2 Report* (Washington, D.C.: Military Intelligence Division, War Department, July 1933); "Notes on the Organization of Mechanized Units," *Soviet Russia G–2 Report* (Washington, D.C.: Military Intelligence Division, War Department, 17 April 1933); "Organization and Strength of Motor-Mechanized Units," *USSR G–2 Report* (Washington, D.C.: Military Intelligence Division, War Department, 8 Oct. 1938). All reports are based on Military Attaché (M/A) reports.
38. Leonard Shapiro, "The Great Purge," *The Soviet Army* (London: Weidenfeld and Nicolson, 1956), 69.
39. "Pomnit' uroki istorii. Vcemerno ukrepliat' boevuiu gotovnost'" [Remember the lessons of history. Strengthen combat readiness in every possible way], *VIZh*, No. 6 (June 1988), 6.
40. Zakharov, "Predislovie," 22.
41. Strokov, 316; Bagramian, 106. For an excellent articulation of Soviet views on operational art and tactics in late 1940 and 1941 see *Zakliuchitel'naia rech' narodnogo komissara oborony soiuza SSSR 1940 geroia i marshala Sovetskogo Soiuza S.K. Timoshenko na voennom soveshchanii, 31 dekabria 1940g.* [Concluding speech of the People's Commissar of Defense of the Soviet Union, Hero and

Marshal of the Soviet Union S. K. Timoshenko at a military conference, 31
December 1940] (Moskva: Voenizdat, 1941). In it Timoshenko fully articulated
mobile concepts of 1936 stating: "The mobile group in *front* offensive operations is
called upon to perform the mission of creating conditions for developing tactical
success into operational, and sometimes into operational-strategic."
42. Bagramian, 111; Strokov, 319. For details on the Soviet debate concerning use of
tanks see *M. A. Moscow Report No. 1384*, 19 November 1938 which contains a
series of articles translated from *Krasnaia Zvezda* [Red Star] which provide
detailed analysis of combined arms operations in Spain and the difficulties
encountered there by tank units.
43. Bagramian, 112; Strokov, 321.
44. Ryzhakov, 109–111.
45. Zakharov, "Preduslovie," 23.
46. O. A. Losik, ed., *Stroitel'stvo i boevoe primenenie sovetskikh tankovykh voisk v
gody Velikoi Otechestvennoi voiny* [The formation and combat use of Soviet tank
forces in the years of the Great Patriotic War] (Moskva: Voenizdat, 1979), 44.
47. V. G. Kulakov, "Operativnoe iskusstvo" [Operational art], *SVE*, 1978, 6:55.
48. G. Isserson, "Razvitie teorii sovetskogo operativnogo iskusstva v 30–e gody" [The
development of Soviet operational art in the 1930s], *VIZh*, No. 3 (March 1965): 61.

CHAPTER FIVE

1. Strokov, 323–324.
2. *50 Let*, 269–271.
3. For this process, see *Directive of the General Staff Concerning the Study and
Application of War Experience, 9 November 1942, No. 1005216, Inclosure: Instructions Concerning the Study and Application of War Experience in Front and Army
Staffs*, translated by U.S. Army General Staff, G–2.
4. Strokov, 389; Bagramian, 185–186.
5. N. A. Sbytov, "Stavka verkhovnogo glavnokomandovaniia" [The Stavka of the
High Command], *SVE*, 1979, 7:511–512.
6. Strokov, 389–391; Bagramian, 187–189.
7. A. Radzievsky, "Proryv oborony v pervom periode voiny" [Penetration of a
defense in the first period of war], *VIZh*, No.3 (March 1972): 17–18.
8. Strokov, 391; Bagramian, 189–190. More detail found in S. Lototsky, "Iz opyta
vedeniia armeiskikh nastupatel'nykh operatsii v gody Velikoi Otechestvennoi
voiny" [From the experience of conducting army offensive operations in the years
of the Great Patriotic War], *VIZh*, No. 12 (Dec. 1965): 3–14.
9. "Prikaz NKO No. 325 ot 16 Oktiabria 1942 g" [Order of the People's Commissariat
of Defense No. 325 of 16 October 1942], *VIZh*, No. 10 (Oct. 1974): 68–73.
10. Bagramian, 192–193; Strokov, 391–392.
11. "Prikaz NKO No. 306 ot 8 Oktiabria 1942 g" [The Order of the Peoples' Commissariat of Defense No. 306 of 8 Oct. 1942], *VIZh*, No. 9 (Sept. 1974): 62–66.
12. Bagramian, 193–194; Lototsky, 4–8.
13. *50 let*, 333–337; A. Radzievsky, *Tankovyi udar* [Tank blow], (Moskva: Voenizdat,
1977).
14. Strokov, 425–426.
15. Bagramian, 243; Lototsky.
16. G. A. Kavraisky, "Artilleriiskoe nastuplenie" [The artillery offensive] *SVE*, 1976,
1:270–271; K. Kazakov, "Sovershenstvovanie artilleriiskogo nastupleniia"
[Perfection of the artillery offensive], *VIZh*, No. 10 (Oct. 1970): 33–39.
17. Bagramian, 245–246.
18. Ibid.
19. Matsulenko, "Razvitie taktiki ..."; Strokov, 427.

20. Strokov, 429.
21. *Polevoi ustav Krasnoi Armii 1944* (PU–44) [Field Regulation of the Red Army 1944] (Moskva: Voenizdat, 1944), translated by the Office of the Assistant Chief of Staff G-2, GSUSA.
22. I. V. Maryganov, *Peredovoi kharakter sovetskoi voennoi nauki* [The advanced nature of Soviet military science] (Moskva: Voenizdat, 1953).
23. Bagramian, 407–409; N. D. Saltykov, "Operatsiia gruppy frontov" [The operation of a group of *fronts*], *SVE*, 1978, 6:68.
24. Bagramian, 417; Strokov, 568.
25. Bagramian, 418; Lototsky, 7–8.
26. Bagramian, 420–422; Matsulenko, "Razvitie operativnogo ...," 48–50. For a good discussion of forward detachments, see I. Vorob'ev, "Forward Detachments in Offensive Operations and Battles," *Voennaia mysl'*, April 1965, translated in FDD 957, 6 April 1966. For details on the use of forward detachments in Manchuria, see D. Glantz, *August Storm: Soviet Operational and Tactical Combat in Manchuria, August 1945, Leavenworth Paper No. 8* (Ft. Leavenworth, KS. Combat Studies Institute, 1983). See also a forthcoming volume on the forward detachment and Soviet conduct of tactical maneuver.
27. Bagramian, 426–428; A. Radzievsky, *Tankovyi udar*, Losik. Among the many articles focusing on distinct aspects of tank operations are: P. Kurochkin, "Operations of Tank Armies in the Operational Depth," *Voennaia mysl'* (Nov. 1965): 97–166, translated by FDD; A. Maryshev, "Deistviia tankovykh voisk pri proryve oborony protivnika" [Operations of tank forces in penetrating an enemy defense], *VIZh*, No. 6 (June 1982); N. Kobrin, "Iz opyta vydvizheniia tankovykh armii iz raionov sosredotocheniia dlia vvoda v srazhenie" [From the experience of the movement of tank armies from assemby areas for introduction into battle], *VIZh*, No. 9 (Sept. 1976); A. Radzievsky, "Vvod tankovykh armii v proryv" [Introduction of a tank army into a penetration], *VIZh*, No. 2 (Feb. 1976); I. Garkusha, "Osobennosti boevykh deistvii bronetankovykh i mekhanizirovovannykh voisk" [The peculiarities of combat operations of armored and mechanized forces], *VIZh*, No. 9 (Sept. 1975); I. Taran and V. Kolesnik, "Organizatsiia sviazi v bronetankovykh i mekhanizirovannykh voiskakh destvuiushchikh na razobshchennykh napravleniiakh" [The organization of communications of armored and mechanized forces operating on separate directions], *VIZh*, No. 5 (May 1982); A. Tsynkalov, "Iz opyta povysheniia zhivuchesti tankov v nastupatel'nykh operatsiiakh" [From the experience of increasing the survivability of tanks in offensive operations], *VIZh*, No. 3 (March 1983).
28. Bagramian, 435.
29. Strokov, 573–575; A. I. Radzievsky, *Proryv* [Penetration] (Moskva: Voenizdat, 1979).
30. Bagramian, 450–451; N. Kireev, N. Dobenko, "Iz opyta boevogo primeneniia peredovykh otriadov tankovykh (mekhanizirovannykh) korpusov" [From the experience of the combat use of forward detachments of tank (mechanized) corps], *VIZh*, No. 9 (Sept. 1982): 20–27; N. Kireev, "Presledovanie protivnika soedineniiami i ob'edineniiami bronetankovykh i mekhanizirovannykh voisk" [Pursuit of the enemy by formations and large units of armored and mechanized forces], *VIZh*, No. 6 (June 1977): 82–90.
31. Bagramian, 454–455; Strokov, 581–585.

CHAPTER SIX

1. I. Korotkov, "O razvitii sovetskoi voennoi teorii v poslevoennye gody" [Concerning the development of Soviet military theory in the postwar years], *VIZh* No. 4 (April 1964): 40.

2. M. Cherednichenko, "Razvitie teorii strategicheskoi nastupatel'noi operatsii v 1945–1953 gg" [The development of the theory of the strategic offensive operation, 1945–1953], *VIZh* No. 8 (Aug. 1976): 39.
3. *50 Let*, 459, 474–479. There were 6 million in the "operating armies" in January 1945 and a total of 11,365,000 in the Soviet Army and Navy. Demobilization reduced this total to a strength of 2,874,000 in 1948.
4. M. Burshtunovich, "Bases of Offensive Battle of a Rifle Regiment and Battalion," *VV* (Jan. 1947) as quoted from R. Gartoff, *Soviet Military Doctrine*, Glencoe, Ill.: The Free Press, 1953, 69.
5. Cherednichenko, 41.
6. Ibid.
7. Ibid, 42. See also M. M. Kir'ian, ed., *Voenno-tekhnicheskii progress i vooruzhennye sily SSSR* [Military-technical progress and the armed forces](Moskva: Voenizdat, 1982), 239–242.
8. Cherednichenko, 42–43; Bagramian, 477; V. Miagkov, "Razvitie teorii boevogo primeneniia aviatsii v 1946–1953 gg" [The development of the theory of the combat use of aviation – 1946–1953], *VIZh*, No. 2 (Feb. 1976).
9. Z. Zlobin, "Sovremennaia frontovaia operatsiia" [Contemporary *front* operations], *Voennaia mysl'* (April–May 1945), translated by the Directorate of Military Intelligence, Army Headquarters, Ottawa, Canada, 3. Hereafter cited as *VM*.
10. Bagramian, 476; Cherednichenko, 42, 44.
11. Cherednichenko, 44.
12. Ibid, 42.
13. V. A. Semenov, *Kratkii ocherk razvitiia sovetskogo operativnogo iskusstva* [A short sketch of the development of Soviet military art] (Moskva: Voenizdat, 1960), 289.
14. For the nature of the revolution in military affairs, see the collection of articles published in *Problemy revolutsii v voennom dele* [The problems of the revolution in military affairs] (Moskva: Voenizdat, 1965).
15. V. D. Sokolovsky, *Voennaia strategiia* [Military strategy] (Moskva: Voenizdat, 1968), translated by Foreign Technology Division (FTD), 192–193.
16. Ibid, 209.
17. Ibid.
18. Strokov, 612.
19. N. Krylov, "Raketnye voiska strategicheskogo naznacheniia" [Strategic rocket forces], *VIZh*, No. 2 (July 1967): 15–23.
20. V. Sokolovsky, M. Cherednichenko, "Nekotorye voprosy sovetskogo voennogo stroitel'stva v poslevoennyi period" [Some questions of Soviet military construction in the postwar period], *VIZh*, No. 3 (March 1965): 9, 12; *50 let*, 500–501.
21. Semenov, 290–291.
22. Ibid.
23. Ibid.
24. Ibid.
25. Bagramian, 499.
26. Sokolovsky, 209.
27. Strokov, 616.
28. Bagramian, 501.
29. Ibid, 502; V. Margelov, "Razvitie teorii primeneniia vozdushno-desantnykh voisk v poslevoennyi period" [The development of the theory of the use of airborne forces in the postwar period], *VIZh*, No. 1 (Jan. 1977): 54.
30. Bagramian, 503; N. Kireev, "Primenenie tankovykh podrazdelenii i chastei pri proryve oborony protivnika" [The use of tank subunits and units in penetrating an enemy defense], *VIZh*, No. 2 (Feb. 1982): 37–38.
31. Bagramian, 504.
32. Ibid; V. G. Reznichenko, *Taktika* [Tactics] (Moskva: Voenizdat, 1966); K. Andrukhov, V. Bulatnikov, "The Growing Role of Airborne Troops in Modern

Military Operations", *VM*, No. 2 (July 1966). English translation, FPIE 0475/67, 17 May 1967, 175.

33. Bagramian, 505–508.
34. Ibid, 506–507.
35. Bagramian, 510–513; V. Reznichenko, "Osnovnye napravleniia razvitiia sovetskoi taktiki v poslevoennye gody" [The basic direction of the development of Soviet tactics in the postwar years], *VIZh*, No. 8 (Aug. 1971): 34–38.
36. P. Tsigankov, "Razvitie taktiki nastupatel'nogo boia strelkovykh (motostrel-kovykh) i tankovykh podrazdelenii v poslevoennye gody" [The development of the tactics of offensive battle of rifle (motorized rifle) and tank subunits in the postwar years], *VIZh*, No. 7 (July 1977): 41–45. Reznichenko, *Taktika*, 266–267 notes that tank battalions can attack on frontages of approximately 800 meters. See also D. F. Loza, G. I. Garbuz, I. F. Sazonov. *Motostrelkovyi batal'on v sovremennom boiu* [The motorized rifle battalion in modern combat] (Moskva: Voenizdat, 1965), translated by DTIC, 29. All provide only the width of battalion sectors. Other sector widths are derived from that of battalions and Soviet experience and inference.
37. An extensive analysis of tactical air assault (helicopter) landings is found in I. S. Liutov, P. T. Sagaidak, *Motostrelkovyi batal'on v takticheskom vozdushnom desante* [The motorized rifle battalion in tactical air landings] (Moskva: Voenizdat, 1969).
38. Reznichenko, *Taktika*, 336–337. Loza, 29–30.

CHAPTER SEVEN

1. Evidenced, for example, by publication of General P. A. Kurochkin's "Operations of Tank Armies in the Operational Depth," *VM*, No. 11 (Nov. 1965), 97–126 (translation).
2. A. A. Sidorenko, *Nastuplenie* [The offensive] (Moskva: Voenizdat, 1970); V. E. Savkin, *Osnovnye printsipy operativnogo iskusstva i taktiki* [The basic principles of operational art and tactics] (Moskva: Voenizdat, 1972); A. Kh. Babadzhanian (ed.), *Tanki i tankovye voiska* [Tanks and tank forces] (Moskva: Voenizdat, 1968); I. Kh. Bagramian (ed.), *Istoriia voin i voennogo iskusstva* [History of war and military art] (Moskva: Voenizdat, 1970).
3. Sokolovsky, 289.
4. *Ibid.*, 300.
5. I. Kh. Bagramian (ed.), *Voennaia istoriia* [Military history] (Moskva: Voenizdat, 1971), 345.
6. *Voprosy strategii i operativnogo iskusstva v sovetskikh voennykh trudakh (1917–1940 gg.)* [Questions of strategy and operational art in Soviet military works (1917–1940)] (Moskva: Voenizdat, 1965). Five years later Zakharov introduced a companion book, *Voprosy taktiki v sovetskikh voennykh trudakh (1917–1940 gg.)* [Questions of tactics in Soviet military works (1917–1940)] (Moskva: Voenizdat, 1970).
7. P. A. Kurochkin (ed.), *Obshchevoiskovaia armiia v nastuplenii* [The combined arms army in the offensive] (Moskva: Voenizdat, 1966).
8. A. I. Radzievsky (ed.), *Armeiskie operatsii* [Army operations] (Moskva: Voenizdat, 1977); I. E. Krupchenko (ed.), *Sovetskie tankovye voiska 1941–1945* [Soviet tank forces 1941–1945] (Moskva: Voenizdat, 1973); P. A. Rotmistrov, *Vremia i tanki* [Time and tanks] (Moskva: Voenizdat, 1972); O. A. Losik (ed.), *Stroitel'stvo i boevoe primenenie sovetskikh tankovykh voisk v gody Velikoi Otechestvennoi voiny* [The organization and combat use of Soviet tank forces in the Great Patriotic War] (Moskva: Voenizdat, 1979); I. I. Lisov, *Desantniki-vozdushnyi desanty* [Airlanding troops – airlandings] (Moskva: Voenizdat, 1968);

D. S. Sukhorukov, *Sovetskie vozdushno-desantnye* [Soviet airlanding forces] (Moskva: Voenizdat, 1980); S. K. Kurkotkin (ed.), *Tyl sovetskikh vooruzhennykh sil v Velikoi Otechestvenoi voine* [The rear of the Soviet armed forces in the Great Patriotic War] (Moskva: Voenizdat, 1977); A. I. Radzievsky (ed.), *Taktika v boevykh primerakh: vzvod, rota, polk, diviziia* [Tactics by combat example: platoon, company, regiment, division] (Moskva: Voenizdat, 1974–1976).

9. V. G. Kulikov, "Operativnoe iskusstvo" [Operational art], *SVE*, 6:53. Kulikov uses the terms *soedinenie* and *chast'* which mean formation and unit and which are equivalent respectively to division and regiment in English parlance. The Russian term *ob'edinenie* means large unit and corresponds to a Soviet *front* (army group) and army.

10. Among the many articles see F. Sverdlov, "K voprosy o manevr v boiu" [Concerning the question of maneuver in combat], *VV*, No. 8 (Aug. 1972), 31; V. Savkin, "Manevr v boiu" [Maneuver in battle], *VV*, No. 4 (April 1972), 23.

11. V. G. Reznichenko, *Taktika* [Tactics] (Moskva: Voenizdat, 1987), 72.

12. For example see I. Vorob'ev, "Novoe orushie i printsipy taktiki" [New weapons and tactical principles], *Sovetskoi voennoe obozpenie* [Soviet military review], No. 2 (Feb. 1987), 18.

13. Extensive Soviet analysis of this theme of initial war has produced many studies, including S. P. Ivanov, *Nachal'nyi period voiny* [The initial period of war] (Moskva: Voenizdat, 1974); M. Cherednichenko, "O nachal'nom periode Velikoi Otechestvennoi voiny" [Concerning the initial period of the Great Patriotic War], *VIZh*, No. 4 (April 1961), 28–35; P. Korkodinov, "Facti i mysli o nachal'nom periode Velikoi Otechestvennoi voiny" [Facts and ideas about the initial period of the Great Patriotic War], *VIZh*, No. 10 (Oct. 1965), 26–34; V. Baskakov, "Ob osobennostiakh nachal'nogo periode voiny" [Concerning the peculiarities of the initial period of war], *VIZh*, No. 2 (Feb. 1966), 29–34; A. Grechko, "25 let tomu nazad" [25 years ago], *VIZh*, No. 6 (June 1966), 3–15; I. Bagramian, "Kharakter i osobennosti nachal'nogo perioda voiny" [The nature and peculiarities of the initial period of war], *VIZh*, No. 10 (Oct. 1981), 20–27; V. Matsulenko, "Nekotorye vyvody iz opyta nachal'nogo perioda Velikoi Otechestvennoi voiny" [Some conclusions from the experience of the initial period of the Great Patriotic War], *VIZh*, No. 3 (March 1984), 35–42; A. I. Evseev, "O nekotorykh tendentsiiakh v izmenenii soderzhaniia i kharaktera nachal'nogo perioda voiny" [Concerning some tendencies in the changing form and nature of the initial period of war], *VIZh*, No. 11 (Nov. 1985), 11–20.

14. Iu. Molostov, A. Novikov, "High precision weapons against tanks," *Soviet Military Review*, No. 1 (Jan. 1988), 13.

15. Reznichenko, 200.

16. Ibid.

17. David M. Glantz, *Soviet Conduct of Tactical Maneuver: The Role of the Forward Detachment* (Ft Leavenworth, KS: Soviet Army Studies Office, 1988).

18. Reznichenko, 206.

19. M. Zakharov, "O teorii glubokoi operatsii" [Concerning the theory of deep operations], *VIZh*, No. 10 (Oct. 1970), 20.

20. These force structure tables include "validated" threat data and also postulate the existence of a specialized unit within the division designated to conduct tactical maneuver missions (the separate tank battalion). This reinforced battalion corresponds in structure and mission to the separate tank brigades which performed similar missions for Soviet divisions in World War II. The Russian term *otdel'nyi* means "separate" (i.e. distinct from line units but still under division control). The term "independent" (*samostoiatel'nyi*) implies the unit is not under division control.

The tables also note the existence of experimental mobile corps similar in structure to former tank or mechanized corps and probably designated to perform specialized operational maneuver tasks, singularly for armies or in groups for *fronts*. These corps have a better balance of tank and motorized rifle units than either tank or motorized rifle divisions.

21. The late 1950s was the last period the Soviets emphasized the importance of combined arms conventional combat before the late 1960s, when the Soviets moved away from the single nuclear option back to renewed emphasis on combined arms conventional combat. From 1981 to 1986 Soviet ground force strength rose from 1,825,000 to 1,992,000. See U.S. Department of Defense, *Soviet Military Power 1987* (Washington, D. C.: Government Printing Office, 1987), 71, and Defense Intelligence Agency, *Force Structure Summary – USSR, Eastern Europe, Mongolia, and Afghanistan*, Oct. 1986, 39.

22. V. E. Savkin, *Osnovnye printsipy operativnogo iskusstva i taktiki* [Basic Principles of Operational Art and Tactics] (Moskva: Voenizdat, 1972), 228. Translated by U.S. Air Force.

23. Headquarters, Department of the Army, *FM 100-2-3*, "Soviet Army Troops Organization and Equipment." July 1984, 4–48; Defense Intelligence Agency, *Soviet Armed Forces Motorized Rifle Division*, Feb. 1968 (declassified 1982), 4.

24. "Soviet Army Troops", 4–160 – 4–162; Headquarters, Department of the Army, *FM 30-40*, "Handbook on Soviet Armed Forces," 30 June 1975, 4–8. Soviet writings since the mid-1970s stress that forward detachments have utility at the operational as well as the tactical level of war – that is, to lead the advance of armies as well as divisions. In the latter stages of World War II, Soviet army commanders used tank corps, mechanized corps, or reinforced tank brigades for such a purpose. The post-war mechanized and combined arms armies used heavy tank and self-propelled gun regiments both to support the assault and to spearhead the pursuit. The re-equipping of these regiments with tanks in the early 1970s better suited them to act as forward detachments whose use, and perhaps loss, would not adversely affect the structure of their parent unit. Recent extensive study by the Soviets of the combat requirements of forward detachments has led them to experiment with new task-organized structures suited to the mission. This experimentation applies to both the operational maneuver group at *front* and army levels and the forward detachment at army level. The experimental corps (variously called New Army Corps [NAC], Unified Army Corps, tank, or mechanized corps) are part of this experimentation.

25. *Soviet Military Power 1987*, 89; "Soviet Army Troops," 4–172, 4–176, 4–180, 4–181.

26. Kulikov, 57.

27. N. Kireev, "Primenenie tankovykh podrazdelenii i chastei pri proryve oborony protivnika" [The use of tank subunits and units in penetrating an enemy defense], *VIZh*, No. 2 (Feb. 1982), 38–40.

28. M. A. Gareev, *M. V. Frunze – Voennyi teoretik* [M. V. Frunze – Military theoretician] (Moskva: Voenizdat, 1984), 236–246.

29. S. G. Gorshkov, *Morskaia moshch' gosudarstva* [Seapower of the state] (Moskva: Voenizdat, 1976); S. G. Gorshkov, *Morskaia moshch' gosudarstva* [Seapower of the state] (Moskva: Voenizdat, 1979).

30. Among the many references to the new military doctrine see S. Akhromeev, "The Doctrine of Averting War and Defending Peace and Socialism," *World Marxist Review*, XXX No. 12 (Dec. 1987), 40–41; D. T. Iazov, *Na strazhe sotsializma i mira* [On guard for Socialism and Peace] (Moskva: Voenizdat, 1987), 23; D. T. Iazov, "Perestroika v rabote voennykh kadrov" [Perestroika in the work of military cadres] *VIZh*, No. 7 (July 1987), 4.

31. Ogarkov, "Strategiia voennaia," 564.

32. The observation is based on the informed judgments of the authors and a reading of extensive Soviet works on experience with deep, mobile operations. Publication of these works has increased geometrically since the late 1960s. For the sake of analysis, the Soviets subdivide their Great Patriotic War (1941–1945) into three distinct periods, each characterized by basic unifying conditions. The first period

lasted from June 1941 to November 1942; the second period from November 1942 through December 1943; and the third period from January 1944 through May 1945.

33. The Soviets are also prepared to conduct a protracted war, but only reluctantly, for they understand what that would involve. They also understand the difficulties and risks associated with an attack after only limited preparations. In this circumstance, the chances for achieving surprise through *maskirovka* are greater and could outweigh the risks.

Writings on the initial period of war reach the following conclusions:

- the tendency for the massive use of new means of armed struggle to have increasing importance in the initial period of war;
- the tendency for the results of the initial period to have increasing influence over the subsequent course of hostilities;
- the tendency for the scale of military operations to increase;
- the tendency of both sides to use surprise as the most important factor;
- the tendency for the initial period to shorten as a result of improved weaponry;
- the tendency for the role of maneuver to increase in importance.

34. The Soviets repeatedly have renounced the intention of "gnawing through" (*progryzanie*) a deeply arrayed defense. For example see A. A. Strokov, *Voennaia istoriia* [Military history] (Moskva: Voenizdat, 1966), 616. In some offensive situations, for example, against a prepared defense organized in depth, the Soviets accept the necessity for deeper echelonment. The echelonment, however, would not be so deep as to deprive the Soviets of the ability to commit forces in sufficient quantities to penetrate enemy defenses and sustain the offensive into the operational depths. In general, deeper, more resilient enemy defenses increase Soviet force requirements, force the Soviets to echelon their forces more deeply, increase necessary preparation time, reduce the possibility of achieving surprise, and provide more lucrative potential nuclear targets. Consequently, the enemy has more time to make political-military decisions, which might include use of nuclear weapons. For all of these reasons and the likelihood that a more protracted military operation could result, the Soviets tend to dismiss this option.

In their study of past operational experiences the Soviets have, in recent years, concentrated on those operations in which massive Soviet initial blows produced significant strategic gains (e.g. Belorussia − June 1944, Iassy-Kishinev − August 1944, Vistula–Oder − January 1945, and Manchuria − August 1945). In all of these operations multiple Soviet *fronts* attacked in a single echelon and each *front* concentrated the bulk of its forces in first echelon. The results seemed to justify the practice.

35. M. M. Kir'ian (ed.), *Vnezapnost' v nastupatel'nykh operatsiiakh Velikoi Otechestvennoi voiny* [Surprise in offensive operations of the Great Patriotic War] (Moskva: "Nauka," 1986).

36. For example see Soviet analysis of the operational and tactical techniques of U.S. and NATO armies in N. K. Glazunov and N. S. Nikitin, *Operatsiia i boi* [The operation and battle] (Moskva: Voenizdat, 1983); S. V. Grishin and N. N. Tsapenko, *Soedineniia i chasti v boiu* [Formations and units in battle] (Moskva: Voenizdat, 1985).

37. This is the author's judgment based on extensive inferences made in Soviet sources.

38. Cherednichenko, "Strategicheskaia operatsiia," 552.

In Russian, *Teatr voennykh deistvii (TVD)* means "theater of military operations." This is synonymous with the current DOD acronym − TSMA − (Theater of Strategic Military Action). TVDs or TSMAs exist with a theater of war (*Teatr voiny − TV*.

39. N. V. Ogarkov, *Vsegda v gotovnosti k zashchite otechestva* [Always in readiness to

280   SOVIET MILITARY OPERATIONAL ART

defend the homeland] (Moskva: Voenizdat, 1982), 35.
40. Ogarkov, "Strategiia voennaia," 564.
41. Kulikov, 56.
42. A. K. Zaporozhchenko, "Strategicheskii eshelon" [Strategic echelon], *SVE* 1979,
7:554; V. I. Beliakov, N. I. Reum, "Strategicheskie reservy" [Strategic reserves],
SVE 1979, 7:553.
43. The Soviets have experimented with TVD commands in the past. During 1941 and
1942 the *STAVKA* controlled operations in key strategic sectors using strategic
directions (*strategicheskie napravleniia*) such as the Northeastern, Western, and
Southwestern Directions, with a commander and headquarters for each. Only the
Western Direction echeloned its *fronts* in depth while the other directions
employed their *fronts* in a single echelon. This command structure proved
unwieldy, and after mid-1942 the *STAVKA* controlled strategic operations by
groups of *fronts* by using a *STAVKA* representative. From 1942 on, the Soviets
employed virtually all *fronts* in a single echelon, except during the Kursk defense,
when one *front* (Steppe) was held in the rear, in *STAVKA* reserve, to conduct the
counteroffensive.
   In late July 1945 the *STAVKA* formed a TVD headquarters to control air,
ground, and naval operations in the Far East. This headquarters, its staff, and
functions became a model for recent Soviet development of a TVD structure.
44. Kir'ian, "Armeiskaia nastupatel'naia operatsiia," 243.
45. Ibid.
46. P. Simchenko, "Manevr – kliuch k pobede" [Maneuver – key to victory], *VV*, No. 4
(April 1977), 70. Other articles include G. Lobachev, "Vysokii temp nastupleniia –
nepremennoe uslovie pobedy" [High offensive tempo – an indispensable condition
for victory], *VV*, No. 2 (Feb. 1977).
47. Kireev, "Primenenie tankovykh podrazdelenii i chastei," 39.
48. Molostov, Novikov, 13.
49. Ibid.
50. Kir'ian, *Vnezapnost'*.
51. D. A. Dragunsky, *Motostrelkovyi (tankovyi) batal'on v boiu* [The motorized rifle
(tank) battalion in battle] (Moskva: Voenizdat, 1986), 9.
52. Kozlov, "Frontovaia nastupatel'naia operatsiia", 339.
53. M. M. Kir'ian, "Operativnoe postroenie" [Operational formation], *SVE* 1978,
6:58. A mobile obstacle detachment (POZ) (*podvizhnyi otriad zagrazhdenii*) is a
temporary engineer formation responsible for obstacle (mine) laying and removal
and battlefield demolition to both impede the enemy advance (principally armor)
and protect a unit's flanks. It operates within units at all levels and cooperates with
anti-tank reserves and other combat units.
   This definition of a *front* operational formation has endured since the 1936 *Field
Service Regulation* with only slight modification. Echelonment of armies within
fronts has varied according to conditions. From 1941 to mid-1943, Soviet *front*
commanders generally employed a single echelon of armies to project maximum
firepower forward against the shallow German defenses. However, Soviet armies,
with relatively light firepower, had difficulty sustaining these offensives, in particular, as German defenses matured. In both the Moscow and Stalingrad operations, the Soviets used a single echelon of armies within *fronts*. After mid-1943,
Soviet *front* commanders, on occasion, began employing second echelon armies
(Orel, Belgorod-Khar'kov, Smolensk, Chernigov-Pripiat). But, as mobile forces
matured and increased armor and artillery assets were added to armies, Soviet *front*
commanders again employed their armies in single echelon. Such was the case in the
Ukrainian operations (January – April 1944), Belorussia, Lublin-Brest, Hungary,
and in the Baltic States. Where second echelon armies were employed, they were
few in number (L'vov–Sandomierz, one of seven armies; Iassy–Kishinev, one of six
armies). *Front* second echelons in the massive strategic operations of 1945 were

insignificant. In the Vistula–Oder operations, the 1st Belorussian Front had one of eight combined arms armies in second echelon, and it played virtually no role in the operation. The 1st Ukrainian Front had two of eight armies in second echelon (for geographical reasons only) and committed the armies to combat on days two and four of the operation, respectively. In the Berlin operation, the 1st Belorussian Front had one of nine armies in second echelon and the 1st Ukrainian Front one of eight. In Manchuria, the three Soviet *fronts* had one army out of a total of eleven armies in *front* second echelon.

These were real operational formations set against the backdrop of regulations which mandated use of one, two, or even three echelons but which said two were normal.

Theoretical writings after the war maintained the traditional verbiage describing the number of required echelons. In the 1960s, however, the prospect for war on a nuclear battlefield seems to require *front* use of at least two echelons for greater dispersion of forces and, hence, safety from nuclear attack. In the seventies, the Soviet return to conventional concerns has been accompanied by renewed study of pre-1960 echeloning practices and a resurgent interest in shallower echelonment to produce greater concentration of forces, more rapid advances, and better-sustained offensive momentum on the battlefield. Although the traditional Soviet definition of echelonment has endured, more frequently the Soviets qualify the term second echelon by associating it with a reserve, i.e. second echelon (reserve).

54. *Ibid.* No mention is made of the operational maneuver group. However, in "Armiia" [Army], *SVE* 1976, 2:255, the statement is made that during World War II "the tank army became the most important means of developing a penetration and conducting *operational maneuver*." S. F. Begunov and A. V. Postovalov in "Manevr" [Maneuver], *SVE* 1978, 5:114, state, "Operational maneuver is conducted according to the decisions of the large unit [*front*, army] commanders in the interest of fulfilling combat missions in operations. It is carried out by large units and formations [corps or divisions], units [regiments, brigades] of all types of forces and specialized forces ..." Y. Novikov and F. Sverdlov in *Maneuver in Modern Land Warfare* (Moscow: Progress Publishers, 1972), a translation of a work originally published in 1967, state on p.29, "Operational maneuver is undertaken to achieve success in an operation in keeping with the concept and under the guidance of the commander of an operational unit... Operational maneuver is aimed at changing the situation in the course of an operation to facilitate the fulfillment of intermediate assignments or even bring the whole operation to a successful conclusion. It may take the form of maneuver with nuclear strikes delivered by operational or tactical missiles or army air force, or maneuver by *operational groups* from one sector to another to exploit the success or outflank an enemy group on the defensive, etc."

55. Such as in a "short warning" attack on NATO. The Soviets would expect to face an unprepared defense if they attacked with 48 hours of preparation and a partially prepared defense if they attacked with 96 hours of preparation. Longer preparation time would force the Soviets to attack a prepared defense. This is an author's judgment based on extensive study on Soviet perspectives regarding NATO defenses.

56. Kir'ian, "Armeiskaia nastupatel'naia operatsiia," 239–244.

57. Traditionally the Soviets have used the terms *army, division*, and *regiment* to describe multi-purpose line units expected to perform a variety of routine combat functions (such as offense, defense, retrograde operations). They have used the terms *corps* and *brigade* to describe experimental units or units organized and tailored to perform a specific combat function. TOE rifle, motorized-rifle, tank, mechanized, and airborne divisions and regiments fall into the former category. Units such as airborne, tank, mechanized and air assault units, specifically designated to perform operational or tactical maneuver functions or other

specialized duties, have carried the designation corps and brigade (for example the air assault and divisionary brigades).

Some confusion results when one compares the relative size of functional corps and brigades with line divisions, regiments and battalions. Former Soviet tank and mechanized corps were of division strength with from 168 to 230 tanks and SP guns each. Former tank brigades were either of regimental strength (90–150 tanks) or of reinforced battalion strength (45–70). Thus, the current separate tank regiments of Soviet armies, with about 150 tanks each, are as strong as small tank corps or large tank brigades. If used as forward detachments, the Soviets could use either designation. Current separate tank battalions of motorized rifle divisions are similar in size and structure to the former tank brigades, which were used as forward detachments for a wide range of Soviet formations. The recent experimental mechanized or unified army corps are smaller than former tank armies but larger than former tank or mechanized corps. In essence, they were test-beds from which future corps of varying composition would evolve. Various derivations of the original test corps were probably designed to perform the function of operational maneuver singly, as operational maneuver groups serving armies, or in combination (2 or 3) within a tank or mechanized army, as the operational maneuver group within *fronts*. In light of new political and military realities, the new types of corps will now evolve to satisfy a variety of both defensive and offensive combat functions, including that of operational maneuver. It is likely that some formations in the current Soviet force structure have already been reconfigured as corps and brigades and these are probably the nucleus of the Soviet's operational maneuver force. This reconfiguration process will continue and will likely include some corps configured to perform a distinctly defensive function as well. The following chart reviews Soviet formation and use of maneuver forces:

ORGANIZATION OF OPERATIONAL MANEUVER FORCES

PERIOD	FRONT	ARMY
1936–Jul 1941	1-2 Mechanized Corps or Cavalry Corps	1 Mechanized Corps
July 1941– March 1942	-	1 Cavalry Corps (+)
March 1942– June 1942	-	1-2 Tank Corps or Cavalry Corps (+)
June 1942– July 1943	2-4 Tank Corps or 1 temporary mobile group	1-2 Tank or mechanized corps, or cavalry corps (+)
July 1943– August 1945	1-3 Tank armies and/or 1 cavalry mechanized group	1 Tank or mechanized corps
1946–1958	1-2 Mechanized Armies	1-2 Tank or mechanized divisions
1958–1962	1 Tank army	1 Tank division
1968	No designated force	No designated force

| Present | 1-2 Tank armies | 1 Tank division (unified or mechanized corps) |
| Future | 1-2 Tank or mechanized armies | 1 Mechanized (unified corps) |

58. Kireev, 38–40; P. Tsigankov, "Razvitie taktiki nastupatel'nogo boia strelkovykh (motostrelkovykh) i tankovykh podrazdelenii v poslevoennoie gody" [The development of the tactics of offensive battle of rifle (motorized rifle) and tank subunits in the postwar years], *VIZh*, No. 7 (July 1977), 43–45.

59. Reznichenko, 206, in his 1987 edition of *Taktika*, differentiates between ground and air echelons, stating:

> While analysing the future development of offensive combat tactics, one can propose that, under the influence of modern weapons and the greater saturation of ground forces with aviation means, the combat formation of forces on the offensive is destined to consist of two echelons – a ground echelon, whose mission will be to fulfill the penetration of the enemy defense and develop the success into the depths, and an air echelon created to envelop defending forces from the air and strike blows against his rear area.

60. Kozlov, "Frontovaia oboronitel'naia operatsiia," 341–342.
61. Kir'ian, "Operativnoe postroenie," 60.
62. *Ibid.*, 58.
63. K. L. Kushch-Zharko, "Armeiskaia oboronitel'naia operatsiia" [The army defensive operation], *SVE* 1976, 1:244–248.
64. I. G. Pavlovsky, "Taktika" [Tactics], *SVE* 1979, 7:631.
65. "Boevoi poriadok" [Combat formation], *SVE* 1976, 1:532–534. The size of offensive sectors depends on the nature of the combat, echelonment, and enemy strength. Thus, sectors can range from 8–20 kilometers for division, 3–8 kilometers for regiment and 1–2 kilometers for battalion.
66. For the most current view on the use of tactical level forward detachments see, F. D. Sverdlov, *Peredovye otriady v boiu* [Forward detachments in battle] (Moskva: Voenizdat, 1986).
67. Kir'ian, "Armeiskaia nastupatel'naia operatsiia," 243–244; Kireev, 39.
68. Kireev, 39; for composition of the forward detachment, see "Peredovoi otriad" [The forward detachment], *VV*, No. 2 (Feb. 1983), 36; "Modern Battle: Questions and Answers", *Soviet Military Review* (May 1981), 29–31.

Forward detachments, as distinct from advanced guards, have been a feature of Soviet tactical combat since the 1930s. Their task was to perform the function of tactical maneuver, that is, maneuver designed to facilitate achievement of tactical missions. While all tactical forces can maneuver, over time specific units evolved to specialize in tactical maneuver for the benefit of and in coordination with other tactical forces. The forward detachment, employed primarily from division to army level, performed this specialized task. Initially, these forward detachments, normally in the strength of a reinforced rifle regiment or tank brigade, led the advance to a meeting engagement or initiated pursuit operations. By 1943, rifle armies and corps routinely used forward detachments. More importantly, after 1942 forward detachments led the operations of mobile groups (tank corps, mechanized corps, and tank armies) in virtually every offensive operation. By 1945, these forward detachments had proliferated in number and size, and they often initiated offensive operations by mobile forces. By war's end, rifle divisions, rifle corps, combined arms armies, and all mobile forces employed forward detachments on the offensive. Use of these units contributed to the increased sustained depth of operations. In fact, their impact became operational as well as tactical.

Forward detachments maintained their currency throughout the 1950s and 1960s, although in the nuclear years their role changed. Since the early 1970s, the Soviets have studied forward detachment operations extensively and have renewed faith in their utility on the conventional battlefield. Soviet theorists consider forward detachments, along with operational maneuver groups (mobile groups), to be the most important ground force units in the context of *front* and army operations.

Standard Soviet texts such as Reznichenko's *Tactics* feature forward detachments, as have numerous articles and monographs including the following:

I. Vorob'ev, "Peredovye otriady v nastupatel'noi operatsii i boiu" [Forward detachments in offensive operations and battle], *VV*, No. 5 (April 1968), 37–45; N. Kireev, "Presledovanie protivnika soedineniiami i ob'edineniiami bronetankovykh i mekhanizirovannykh voisk" [Pursuit of the enemy by formations and large units of armored and mechanized forces], *VIZh* No. 6 (June 1977), 82–90; O. Losik, "Sposoby vedeniia vysokomanevrennykh beovykh deistvii bronetankovymi i mekhanizirovannymi voiskami po opytu Belorusskoi i Vislo–Oderskoi operatsii" [The means of conducting highly maneuverable combat operations by armored and mechanized forces based on the experience of the Belorussian and Vistula–Oder operations], *VIZh*, No. 9 (Sept. 1980): 18–25; N. Kireev, "Primenenie tankovykh podrazdelenii i chastei pri proryve oborony protivnika" [The use of tank subunits and units in the penetration of the enemy defense], *VIZh*, No. 2 (Feb. 1982): 33–40; N. Kireev and N. Dovbenko, "Iz opyta boevogo primeneniia peredovykh otriadov tankovykh (mekhanizirovannykh) korpusov" [From the experience of the combat use of forward detachments of tank (mechanized) corps], *VIZh*, No. 9 (Sept. 1982): 20–27; "Peredovoi otriad" [The forward detachment], *Voennyi Vestnik* [Military Herald] No. 2 (Feb. 1983): 36; M. Loginov, "Forcing a River on the Move," *Soviet Military Review* No. 1 (Jan. 1983): 19–21; V. Perelygin, "Sviaz' v peredovom otriade" [Communications in a forward detachment], *Voennyi Vestnik* No. 5 (April 1986): 77–81; F. D. Sverdlov, *Peredovye otriady v boiu* [Forward detachments in battle] (Moskva: Voenizdat, 1986).

69. Kireev, "Primenenie," 39.
70. N. Miroshichenko, "Razvitie taktiki oboronitel'nogo boia strelkovykh (motostrelkovykh) podrazdelenii v poslevoennye gody" [The development of the tactics of defensive combat of rifle (motorized rifle) subunits in the postwar years], *VIZh*, No. 4 (April 1971): 30–37; L. Korzun, "Razvitie taktiki oboronitel'nogo boia motostrelkovykh i tankovykh podrazdelenii v poslevoennye gody" [The development of the tactics of defensive combat of motorized rifle and tank subunits in the postwar years], *VIZh*, No. 10 (Oct. 1980): 34–41. A regiment will defend in a 10–15 kilometers sector and a battalion in a sector of 3–5 kilometers.

CHAPTER EIGHT

1. N. V. Ogarkov, *Vsegda v gotovnosti k zashchite otechestva* [Always in readiness to defend the homeland] (Moskva: Voenizdat, 1982), 44.
2. The Soviets have extensively employed deception (*maskirovka*) prior to conducting offensive (and defensive) operations in the past. A major facet of deception has been the creation of false groupings of forces, the masking of actual force composition, and the concealed regrouping of strategic reserves and other forces. Organizational changes within GSFG, and its predecessor GOFG, the imbalance of different type divisions indicate the possibility of a peacetime structure which

masks actual wartime structure. For example, divisions formerly in 3d Guards Mechanized Army and 4th Guards Mechanized Army (old 3d and 4th Guards Tank Armies) are now found in 3d Shock Army, 20th Guards Army and the Northern Group of Forces. GOFG originally consisted of the "Berlin" armies (those which liberated Berlin). These were 1st, 2d, 3d and 4th Guards Tank Armies, 3d and 5th Shock Armies, and 8th Guards Army. In 1947 5th Shock Army was demobilized and 3d and 4th Guards Mechanized (Tank) Armies became cadre armies of four divisions each. After 1949 3d and 4th Guards Mechanized Armies were brought to full strength only to be renamed 20th and 18th Guards Armies after 1958. Neither of these two guards armies earned its honorific during the war. 18th Guards Army disappeared from the order of battle in the early 1960s, with 3d Shock Army picking up its remnants.

3d Shock Army emerged an unbalanced force of four tank divisions and one motorized rifle division, whereas it (and other shock armies) had been combined arms armies in the past. It is possible that 3d Shock Army, 20th Guards Army and the two tank divisions of NGF (which were originally in 4th Guards Mechanized. Army) form the nucleus of wartime 3d Shock and 3d and 4th Guards Tank Armies. This would provide GSFG with the capability of generating two *fronts* in wartime, each consisting of one Soviet combined arms army and two Soviet tank armies. Each of these could be augmented by selective reinforcements and one East German Army.

Based on extensive past Soviet offensive experiences, it is inconceivable the Soviets would not employ 3d and 4th Guards Tank Armies in wartime on a principal strategic axis. It is equally inconceivable the Soviets would not resort to *maskirovka* prior to hostilities.

The Soviets maintain extensive stockpiles of equipment of all types in the forward areas which could be used to equip new units rapidly deployed forward. This equipment would figure significantly in any Soviet deception plan. See *Soviet Military Power–1987*, 95, 101.

3. Cherednichenko, "Strategicheskaia operatsia," 552.

4. The Soviet *Military-Historical Journal* [*VIZh*] in 1986 has begun an extensive debate in the form of published papers and critiques concerning the nature and form of strategic operations.

5. The Soviets have stressed these themes in their military journals since the mid-1970s.

6. This judgment and others concerning operational maneuver groups are based upon extensive Soviet analysis of operational maneuver in the past and reflection on how changing conditions have affected its conduct. Since publication of Kurochkin's 1984 article on tank armies, the Soviets have argued for the increased use of operational maneuver forces similar to the mobile groups used in the past. Kurochkin's, Radzievsky's and Losik's works stress the utility of multiple operational maneuver forces. In many of the operations selected for analysis, *front* commanders had multiple tank armies or cavalry-mechanized groups at their disposal, i.e., Vistula–Oder operation (1st Belorussian and 1st Ukrainian Fronts), Berlin operation (1st Belorussian and 1st Ukrainian Front), Proskurov–Chernovtsy operation (1st Ukrainian Front), Zhitomir–Berdichev operation (1st Ukrainian Front) and Belorussian operation (3d Belorussian Front). The use of two such groups provided for more flexible and better sustained operational maneuver to greater depths.

7. The Soviets have written about the vertical dimension of operational maneuver since the early 1930s. Only since the late 1960s have they developed forces to implement these theoretical concepts. That development has been slow but steady and currently involves use of heliborne assault battalions at army level and an air assault brigade at *front*. The logical extension of these theoretical writings could be the continued expansion of the vertical dimension to include use of an air assault

corps (division size) or multiple air assault brigades at *front* level, an air assault brigade or multiple heliborne assault battalions at army level, and a heliborne assault battalion or company at division level (also evidenced perhaps by the appearance of a helicopter unit at division level).

8. While continuing to emphasize the value of tactical and operational maneuver, within the past several years the Soviets have also focused on conducting defensive operations within the context of successful deep operations. This probably reflects increased Soviet concern for repelling counterattacks which they see as one of the manifestations of the U. S. doctrine of Airland Battle.

9. For example see Longin Mucha, "Defensive Military Doctrine – The Essence of Changes", *Zolnierz Wolnosci* [Soldier of Freedom], 13 July 1982, 3 (hereafter cited as *ZW*); Zdzislaw Galewski, "Another Way of Looking at Defense", *ZW*, 15 January 1988, 3; Tadeusz Urbanczyk, "The Dialectic of the Defense and Offense", *ZW*, 11 February 1988, 5; Zbigniew Scibiorek, "Several Notes on Defense", *ZW*, 13 May 1988, 3; Michal Huzarski, "Notes on the Modern Tactical Defense", *ZW* 31 May 1988, 3. All translations done by Harold Orenstein, Soviet Army Studies Office, Ft Leavenworth, KS. Since 1980, the Soviets have steadily increased the number of articles they have published on defensive matters. Initially, these articles focused on defense within the framework of offensive operations. More recently, these articles have focused on the defense in its own right.

10. Stanislaw Koziej, "Anticipated Directions for Change in Tactics of Ground Forces" *Przeglad Wojak Labowych* [Ground Forces Review] No. 9 (September 1986), 9. Translated by Harold Orenstein in *Selected Translations From the Polish Military Press*, Vol 1 (Ft Leavenworth, KS: Soviet Army Studies Office, 1988), 7.

11. The terminology tank, merchanized, and motorized rifle represents a progression based on the relative number of armored units in the force vis-à-vis motorized rifle units. The following chart summarizes the differences:

COMPOSITION OF MOBILE FORCES

1942 Tank Corps	9 tank battalions 6 motorized battalions
1944 Tank Corps	9 tank battalions 6 motorized rifle battalions
1945 Tank Corps	11 tank battalions 4 motorized rifle battalions
1942 Mechanized Corps	9 mechanized battalions 6 tank battalions
1944 Mechanized Corps	9 mechanized battalions 6 tank battalions
1945 Mechanized Corps	10 motorized rifle battalions 6 tank battalions (plus 3 SP gun regiments [battalion size]
1945 Tank Army (3 corps version)	28 tank battalions 18 motorized rifle battalions
1945 Tank Army (2 corps version)	25 tank battalions 9 motorized rifle battalions
1946 Tank Division	11 tank battalions (plus 4 SP gun battalions) 7 motorized rifle battalions

1968 Tank Division	9 tank battalions 3 motorized rifle battalions
1946 Mechanized Division	11 motorized rifle battalions 7 tank battalions (plus 3 SP gun battalions)
1956 Mechanized Division	9 motorized rifle battalions 8 tank/SP gun battalions (plus 1 SP gun battalion)
1946 Mechanized Army	36 motorized rifle battalions 36 tank battalions (plus 14 SP gun battalions)
1958 Motorized Rifle Division	9 motorized rifle battalions 6 tank battalions
1986 Motorized Rifle Division	9 motorized rifle battalions 6 tank battalions (plus one separate reinforced tank battalion)

As indicated, tank units contain from 60–75 percent tank battalions vis-à-vis motorized rifle battalions. Mechanized units have a balanced mix of tank and motorized rifle battalions, while motorized rifle units have a preponderance of motorized rifle battalions. Recent Soviet writings stress the necessity to create a balanced mix of combined arms units in all forces. This would involve addition of motorized rifle and support forces to tank armies and divisions, the beefing up of support within motorized rifle divisions and the tailoring of operational maneuver forces at *front* and army level, both to provide a better mix of tank and motorized rifle units and to increase supporting units necessary for these groups to conduct sustained operations in more urbanized terrain. Hence, the Soviets may return to the mechanized nomenclature for operational maneuver groups at *front* and army levels. In any case, it is likely the Soviets will experiment with a variety of unit mixes before settling on new sets of TOEs. The term, "New Army Corps," formerly used by the intelligence community to describe new experimental Soviet units is a contradiction in terms: the Soviets have never possessed army corps. It is more likely the Soviets will name these formations either unified, mechanized, tank, or combined arms corps, in consonance with tradition and depending on their ultimate composition.

12. "Iz doklada komandyiushchego bronetankovymi i mekhanizirovannymi voiskami Gruppy sovetskikh voisk v Germanii marshala bronetankovykh voisk P. A. Rotmistrova na voenno-nauchnoi konferentsii po izucheniiu Berlinskoi operatsii" [From the report of the commander of armored and mechanized forces of the Group of Soviet Forces in Germany, Marshal of Armored Forces, P. A. Rotmistrov, at a military-scientific conference of the study of the Berlin operation], *VIZh*, No. 9 (Sept. 1985), 43–50. Support units added to Soviet armies and divisions have had the same effect as those added to Soviet units in 1946–47. They have improved the combined arms balance of the entire force. In addition to republishing Rotmistrov's report, the Soviets have published an increased number of articles dealing with operations in difficult terrain. While some of these reflect Soviet concern with warfare in Afghanistan, they also clearly pertain to operations in central Europe. These articles include six on the subject since May 1980 in *Voenno-istoricheskii zhurnal* [Military historical journal] and many in lower level journals.

13. The Soviets have been masters at concealing actual combat organization of their forces, both during wartime and before the outbreak of war. They did this well against the Germans in June 1941 (although almost for naught) and again in August 1945 against the Japanese. During wartime, although German intelligence

maintained a fairly complete Order of Battle for Soviet forces, they were repeatedly deceived regarding specific locations of major units and the organization of forces facing them in critical sectors. See David M. Glantz, *Soviet Military Deception in the Second World War* [London: Frank Cass, 1989]. For example, given the irrational composition of Soviet armies in GSFG, the disfunctional location of subordinate units, and Soviet past practice, it is virtually certain that wartime organization will differ from peacetime organization.

14. The appearance of new corps-type entities is consistent with the manner in which the Soviets have experimented with and formed new units in the past; in particular the way the Soviets developed operational maneuver forces during the war years. The appearance of brigade-type structures within motorized rifle divisions in forces deployed within the NATO Forward Area suggests Soviet experimentation with, and perhaps fielding of, tactical maneuver brigades designated to operate within divisions. These brigades also have direct antecedents during the war years.

15. Recent Soviet articles talk of air assault units performing as forward detachments in their own right. See, R. Salikhov, "V peredovom otriad" [In a forward detachment], *VV*, No. 3 (March 1987), 33–36.

16. See, J. F. Holcomb, Jr.; G. H. Turbiville, Jr., "Exploiting the Vertical Dimension: Continuing Development of the Soviet *Desant* Force Structure" (Ft Leavenworth, KS: Soviet Army Studies Office, 1987), 22–27.

17. D. A. Dragunsky, *Motostrelkovyi (tankovyi) batal'on y boiu* [The motorized rifle (tank) battalion in battle] (Moskva: Voenizdat, 1986), 9.

18. Iu. Molostov, A. Novikov, "High-precision weapons against tanks", *Soviet Military Review*, No. 1 (Jan. 1988), 13.

19. It is possible that the Soviets may choose a third option, that is, to decrease significantly the size and offensive capabilities of their forces by drastically restructuring the ground forces to match proposals made in the 7 December 1988 Gorbachev speech and subsequent pronouncements. Throughout the entire force structure the most offensive elements of the force (armor, air assault and assault bridging) would be severely truncated or abolished while all forces would have an expanded antitank, antiaircraft and engineer capability. This new structure could, but would not necessarily, involve the replacement of regiments and divisions with brigades and corps. It would probably involve creation of three basic types of units at each command level: fortification, motorized rifle, and mechanized or tank. Such a structure could consist of the following:

Battalions

Machine Gun/Heavy Weapons	Motorized Rifle	Tank (Mechanized)
3-5 heavy weapons companies	3-4 motorized rifle companies 1 tank company (10 tanks)	2-3 tank companies (10 tanks each) 1-2 motorized rifle company
Strength: no tanks	Strength: 10 tanks	Strength: 20-30 tanks

Regiments/Brigades

Machine Gun/ Artillery	Motorized Rifle	Tank (Mechanized)
2-3 MG/HW battalions 2-3 artillery battalions 1 tank company (10 tanks)	4 motorized rifle battalions (10 tanks each)	3 tank battalions (20-30 tanks each) 1 motorized rifle battalion (10 tanks)
Strength: 10 tanks	Strength: 40 tanks	Strength: 70-100 tanks

Divisions/Corps

Fortifications (Defensive)	Motorized Rifle	Tank (Mechanized)
4 MG/artillery regiments (Bdes) (10 tanks each)	4 motorized rifle regiments (Bdes) (40 tanks each)	2-3 tank regiments (Bdes) (70-100 tanks each) 1-2 motorized rifle regiments (Bdes) (40 tanks each)
Strength: 40 tanks	Strength: 160 tanks	Strength: 250-280 tanks

Armies

Combined Arms	Mechanized
3-4 motorized rifle divisions (corps) or fortification (defensive) divisions (corps)	1-2 motorized rifle divisions (corps) 2-3 tank (mechanized) divisions (corps)

Fronts

2-3 combined arms armies
1-2 mechanized armies

INDEX

Actions 42–6
Afghanistan 217, 287 n12
Africa 217
Air forces 26, 33, 34, 38, 61, 67, 77, 79,
  87, 169, 177, 196–7, 210, 254; assault
  units 86, 96–7, 214, 231, 232, 236,
  238, 239, 253, 262–3; defense units
  87, 198; offensives 12, 129, 148, 228–
  9; strategic operations 151, 168, 197–
  8; tactical operations 119, 172, 239
Air landing operations 31, 196–7
AirLand Battle 210, 253, 286 n8
American Civil War 17
Angola 217
Anti-aircraft weapons 169, 197, 214,
  229, 265
Anti-ballistic missiles 265
Anti-nuclear maneuver 208–9
Anti-tank defenses 87, 110–11, 115,
  116, 130, 136, 197, 242–3, 251, 265
Anti-tank guided missiles 182, 214
Arab–Israeli War 213, 218
Armaments industry 84
Armed conflict 5–6, *see also* War
Armed forces: elements 46–8; increase
  84–5; technical reconstruction 74–88
Armies 10, 20, 27, 28, 32, 33, 41, 214,
  251, 261, 281 n57; Civil War 57–8;
  combined arms *see* Combined arms
  forces; deep operations 81–2;
  defensive operations 110, 151–2, 234–
  6; 1920s 70; offensive operations 113,
  128; operational formation 170–1,
  231; operational maneuver groups
  252, 262–4; operations 45, 224–36;
Armored forces 153, 257, 259;
  operational role 113–14; tactics 73–4
Armored personnel carriers 181
Armored vehicles 61, 214
Arms limitations 219
Arms reductions 218
Army Group Center, German 139, 146
Army Group Don, German 122
Army Group South, German 122
Army groups 20, 46, *see also Fronts*
Artillery 24, 26, 33, 34, 70, 81, 87, 91,

102, 118, 133, 140, 153, 178, 214, 238,
  239, 253, 258; infantry support 84,
  115, 118, 133, 154; offensives 12,
  129, 148; operations 168, 172, 241
Atomic weapons *see* Nuclear weapons
Austria 139
Austro-Prussian War 17

Babadzhanian, A.Kh. 35, 206
Bagramian, I.Kh. 9, 36, 92, 206–7
Balaton, Lake 152
Balkans 146
Baltic Sea 139, 146
Barvenkovo–Lozovaia operation 115
Battlefields, changing nature 251
Battles 10, 16; close-in 255; future 256;
  large 30–1; set–piece 220; single
  climactic 20–1, 69
Belgorod–Khar'kov operation 280 n53
Belorussian Military District 78, 82
Belorussian operation 147, 149, 153,
  158, 168, 210, 280 n53
Berlin operation 140, 162, 280 n53
Blitzkrieg 99
BMPs 241
Brezhnev Doctrine 217, 248
Briansk 101
Brigades 281 n57
Budapest 139

Campaign, defined 270 n7
Capitalism 246
Cavalry 24, 29, 61, 66, 70, 79, 140–1,
  167
Chasti 46, 47, 48
Chernigov–Pripiat operation 280 n53
China 218
Civil War 10, 19, 21, 53–63, 68, 72, 78
Clausewitz, Karl von 17
Collectivization 51, 76
Colonial empires, breakdown 180
Combat equipment, forward storage
  249–50
Combat formations 48; infantry 72–3
Combat performance, Red Army 120
Combat support forces 141, 154–5,

253–4
Combined arms forces 14, 28, 35, 45,
72, 74, 80, 109–10, 127, 128, 162,
170–1, 174, 181, 185, 188, 196, 210,
215, 220, 231, 257, 258, 261, 262, 286
n11
Communication 199
Communist Party 2, 4, 11, 54
Conventional weapons 177, 183, 208,
211, 219, 238; high-technology 244;
technological revolution 53
Corps 281 n57; force structure 262
Cosmos 43, 247–8, 265
Council of Labor and Defense 78
Counteroffensives 56, 77, 109, 127, 167
Crimea 101
Cuba 180

Deception 114–15, 127–8, 139, 150, 158,
284 n2, 287 n13; strategic deployment
249
Decision-making, cybernetic techniques
256
Deep battle 12, 24, 25, 27, 29, 30, 32,
68, 71, 78–9, 83, 100, 210
Deep operations 24–7, 32, 33, 35–8,
77, 78–84, 98, 100, 141, 151, 194,
207, 210
Defenses 28; Great Patriotic War 135–
6; NATO 221; overcoming 218;
prepared 230–1, 240–1; Soviet Union
129–30, 192; tactical 83, 202, 242–3;
unprepared or partly prepared 227–
30, 238–41, 281 n55
Defensive operations 77, 82, 174, 198,
234–6; armies 45; Civil War 56, 57–9;
fronts 45; Great Patriotic War 151–2,
155–6
Defensiveness, military doctrine 217–
18, 219, 246, 256, 257, 260, 266
Denikin, Gen. A.I. 20
Divisions 46, 47–8, 211, 225, 238, 281
n57
Dnepr exercise 213
Dnepr River 122
Don River 122
Donbas 122
Dragunsky, D.A. 264
Dvina exercise 213

East Pomeranian operation 146
East Prussian operation 139, 146, 168
Echelonment 59, 61, 62, 92, 109, 116,
129–30, 132, 135, 150, 169, 170, 173,

200–2, 210, 220, 223, 224, 233, 234–6,
238, 241–2, 279 n34, 280 n53, 283 n59
Economy, Soviet 246, 260
Egorov, A.I. 28, 78
Engels, F. 54
Engineer support 115, 116, 119, 133,
140, 152, 258
Eremenko, A.I. 92
Ethiopia 217

Falklands War 213
Far East 140, 260
Fascism 50, 88
Field Regulations of the Red Army 1929
24, 71, 72, 78
Field Regulations of the Red Army 1936
24–5, 29, 79, 83, 141, 167, 280 n53
Field Regulations of the Red Army 1941
91
Field Regulations of the Red Army 1942
28, 29, 123, 131
Field Regulations of the Red Army 1943
28
Field Regulations of the Red Army 1944
29, 141, 162, 167
Finland 138, 146
First World War 18, 19–20, 53, 55, 56,
60, 72, 78
Five Year Plans 51, 75, 76
Fleets 46
Force structure 252, 254; future 258–65,
288 n19; Great Patriotic War 52, 101–
4, 120, 123–6, 136, 140–1; 1920s 66–8;
1930s 84–8; recent and contemporary
211–15; Stalinist 162; Zhukov
reorganization 32, 177–8, 180–3
Forces: regrouping 129, 150; strategic
deployment 48, 77, 248, 249
Fortified regions 263–4
Forward detachments 150, 158, 208,
209, 210, 231–3, 238, 239, 240, 241,
252–3, 257, 262, 278 n24, 283
n68
Fourth Panzer Army, German 121
France, German attack on 26
Franco-Prussian War 17–18
French Army 96
French Revolution 16
Fronts 10, 20, 24, 27, 28, 29, 31, 32, 33,
41, 46–7, 69, 77, 91, 146, 165, 214,
250, 251, 260; aviation 198–9; Civil
War 56, 57; counteroffensives 127;
deep operations 79–80; defensive
operations 82, 108, 109, 110, 151–2,
234–5; 1920s 70; offensive operations